A philosophy
of
music education

A philosophy
of
music education

second edition

BENNETT REIMER
Northwestern University

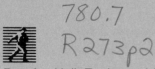

Prentice Hall, Englewood Cliffs, New Jersey 07632

LIBRARY OF CONGRESS
Library of Congress Cataloging-in-Publication Data

Reimer, Bennett.
  A philosophy of music education / Bennett Reimer.
    p.   cm.
  Includes index.
  ISBN 0-13-663881-3 : $20.00
  1. Music--Instruction and study. 2. Music--Philosophy and
aesthetics.   I. Title.
MT1.R435 1989
780'.7--dc19   88-21654
                                                       CIP
                                                        MN

Editorial/production supervision and
  interior design: Marina Harrison
Cover design: Baldino Design
Manufacturing buyer: Raymond Keating

©1989, 1970 by Prentice-Hall, Inc.
A Division of Simon & Schuster
Englewood Cliffs, New Jersey 07632

Printed in the United States of America
10 9 8 7 6 5 4 3 2 1

ISBN   0-13-663881-3   01

Prentice-Hall International (UK) Limited, *London*
Prentice-Hall of Australia Pty. Limited, *Sydney*
Prentice-Hall Canada Inc., *Toronto*
Prentice-Hall Hispanoamericana, S.A., *Mexico*
Prentice-Hall of India Private Limited, *New Delhi*
Prentice-Hall of Japan, Inc., *Tokyo*
Simon & Schuster Asia Pte. Ltd., *Singapore*
Editora Prentice-Hall do Brasil, Ltda., *Rio de Janeiro*

TO THE MEMORY OF MY FATHER

Contents

3   ART AND FEELING   39

4   CREATING ART   56

5   THE MEANING OF ART   75

6 EXPERIENCING ART 99

7 EXPERIENCING MUSIC 119

8 THE PHILOSOPHY IN ACTION: THE GENERAL MUSIC PROGRAM 148

9   THE PHILOSOPHY IN ACTION: THE PERFORMANCE PROGRAM   182

10   TOWARD THE TRANSFORMATION OF MUSIC EDUCATION   214

Preface

In the preface to the first edition of this book (1970) I commented that

> It is very difficult at present to come to an understanding of how music education can become "aesthetic education," because so little has been written directly on this subject. The philosophy offered in this book is an attempt to supply the background of understanding out of which effective action can be generated.

During the next decade or so the music education profession moved massively in the direction of what I and others had defined as aesthetic education. The underlying premises of this philosophical position became so deeply internalized and its characteristic words and phrases became so widely used in our common professional language that it almost seemed to have "always been that way." While many of the concepts of aesthetic education remain imperfectly understood and many of its implications for action remain imperfectly applied, the general view it proposes has become the bedrock upon which our self-concept as a profession rests.

PROBLEMS WITH THE TERM AESTHETIC EDUCATION

Although this philosophy has become pervasive in music education in both theory and practice, the term aesthetic education and some of the language associated with this concept have caused several problems. While many people are quite comfortable with the terminology, others find it confusing or even threatening. This occurs largely because the word "aesthetic" is borrowed from the field of professional philosophy, and although it is used occasionally in ordinary language it remains for the most part a technical term unfamiliar to those not trained in philosophy. As a result, the impression sometimes given was that aesthetic education is somehow different from music education or a variant of music education or a scholarly, pedantic approach to music education that involves teaching the concepts of that branch of philosophy called aesthetics.

Adding to the confusion was the rise in interest during the 1970s in attempts to forge cooperative arts programs. These were called by a variety of names, one of which was aesthetic education. So it was assumed by some that whenever the term was used, it involved, in some mysterious way, the teaching of all the arts. Since the concept of arts education is itself immensely complicated, the confusion surrounding the term aesthetic education was compounded.

Still another difficulty associated with the term is that it suggests to some people a focus on art for art's sake or music for music's sake, which seems to mean that art or music are then unrelated to the everyday lives that we as human beings actually live. Further, such an esoteric or elitist view could certainly not be relevant for the "common people," whose involvements with art are earthy and freewheeling. The term aesthetic education, suggesting Mozart string quartets and Couperin harpsichord pieces and other ornaments for the musically genteel, could not possibly pertain to the more rough and tumble world of music as it really exists for the majority in our culture.

All these misconceptions (for that is what they are) have to some degree impeded the growth of a shared philosophical view that could give our profession a more solid base on which to build. They have been "glitches in the system." But the underlying, essential thesis of aesthetic education, below any confusion the term might cause, is not any longer controversial for the vast majority of music educators. That thesis, simply put, is that while music has many important nonmusical or nonartistic functions, its musical or artistic nature is its unique and precious gift to all humans. Music education exists first and foremost to develop every person's natural responsiveness to the power of the art of music. If that goal is primary, others can be included whenever helpful. But when music itself, with its universal appeal to the human mind and heart, is bypassed or weakened in favor of nonmusical emphases that submerge it, we have betrayed the art we exist to share. It is that simple.

It is also that complex. What, precisely, is musical or artistic about music? What is not? How can we keep the two in fruitful balance? What does musical teaching do that nonmusical teaching does not? Is all music valid as music or only some music? What is good music? Why does music as an art matter so much to us, so that we claim it should be taught to all children?

On and on it goes. All these and many other questions need to be explored if music educators are to understand their subject and be effective in teaching it. The task of a philosophy is to deal with such questions so that actions can be based on understandings. This book will offer a base of theory on which effective practice can be grounded. In doing so, some of the language of aesthetics will have to be used. To avoid confusion whenever possible an attempt will be made to use terms related to music and art as we know it and practice it and teach it rather than terms more at home in professional philosophy. For example, the words "musical" and "artistic" and "intrinsic" will often be used to substitute for the word "aesthetic" because they usually mean the same thing but are more connected to our daily experience.

THE DURABILITY OF THIS PHILOSOPHY

As the years have passed since the publication of the first edition I have been asked with increasing frequency (and traces of anxiety) whether I have changed my position in any fundamental way. My answer has always been "No, I have not." At first the answer was given a bit apologetically because I expected that the philosophy I had offered would soon be joined by several other persuasive views that would inevitably influence my own position as I assimilated and adapted to their contending arguments. Nothing of the sort happened. No alternative philosophy has been proposed by anyone else (although there have been the usual disputes at the level of policy, discussed in Chapter One), and nothing I have come across in my own studies in aesthetics, philosophy, psychology, and related subjects has caused me to abandon the basic premises I had articulated. I have indeed changed in some of my understandings of these premises so I can now explain them with what I hope will be more accuracy and more power, and I have learned how to apply the ideas more effectively so that I can make what I hope will be more useful practical suggestions. But there has been no discovery that has led me to chart a new philosophical direction.

I have become more confident about this situation. It may well be that the philosophy articulated here, along with the additions, refinements, corrections, and alterations offered by those who work toward extending and improving it, does indeed capture the essential qualities of music and music education appropriately for our needs at this time in history. It is clearly the case that the human values served by music education as they are defined in this book are fundamental to present and emerging conceptions of the good life in a humane social order. In fact, as the literature on the need for new patterns of culture continues to grow, the relevance and essentiality of education in the arts become ever more apparent. Music educators can take heart, as I do, in the conviction that our contribution reaches to the core of our human valuing of meaning and self-knowledge and satisfaction—values becoming more widely recognized as central to individual and social health. We must continually reaffirm this conviction by probing its philosophical sources and bringing it to effective life in our professional actions. This book will assist in that process.

THE INCLUDE-EXCLUDE PROBLEM

I must confess a certain sense of frustration in offering this revision. It is that on almost every page of this book ideas are raised that practically beg for several more books to be written exploring their implications. The philosopher knows, better than most others, the layers that exist below anything he or she asserts. If one tried to deal with all those layers as one went along, one's writing would become so heavy that readers could only go into a trance trying to read it, and, also, one's book would soon become a multivolume epic. So one is forced to plunge ahead, ruthlessly leaving out all sorts of related material, trying desperately to keep things reasonably uncluttered yet sufficiently inclusive. Sometimes I feel this book has achieved some success at paring things down to manageable dimensions. Some readers, I am sure, will not agree. At other times I wish I had gone further into some matters. Some readers, I am just as sure, would have wished that also. To those who will feel that there is too much here I offer apologies. To those who will feel just as strongly that there is not enough I apologize as well. In a real sense both are correct. So beware, those of you who attempt to write philosophy for anyone else to read!

The author is grateful to *Design for Arts in Education*, the *Council for Research in Music Education*, and the *Journal of Aesthetic Education*, which published short sections of new material in this revision as parts of articles I wrote for them.

A philosophy
of
music education

Why have a philosophy of music education?

1

AN UNDERLYING PREMISE

This book is based on a single, fundamental premise that must be stated at the outset because everything that follows is designed to explain its meaning and its applicability. The premise is that the essential nature and value of music education are determined by the nature and value of the art of music. Other important determinants, such as the growth stages through which children pass, the functions of education in our society, and the many ways teachers teach and students learn, apply equally to all school subjects. The special character of music education is a function of the special character of the art of music itself. To the degree we can present a convincing explanation of the nature of the art of music and the value of music in the lives of people, to that degree we can present a convincing picture of the nature of music education and its value for human life.

The branch of philosophy concerned with questions of the nature and value of the arts is called "aesthetics." This book, therefore, will deal primarily with aesthetics (musical aesthetics in particular) but in a manner that applies concepts from aesthetics directly to the context of music education. This is certainly not the only possible approach to the formulation of a music education philosophy. Music and all the arts are multi-dimensional, and each dimension has implications for an understanding

1

of their nature and value. For example, psychologists are interested in the arts in a variety of ways—as a means to study perceptual mechanisms, as expressions of the unconscious, as a tool for therapy, and so on. Sociologists and anthropologists look to the arts for insights they offer about a variety of social system phenomena such as attitude formation, socioeconomic class differences in utilization of the arts, cultural beliefs as embodied in ceremonies using the arts, and so on. Historians have still another interest, viewing works of art as documents that give useful information about how people behaved in the past.

These and many other viewpoints about the arts are useful and necessary and illuminating. But none deals with the essential qualities of the arts in and of themselves—the very qualities that the branch of philosophy called aesthetics attempts to explain. Aesthetics is the study of that about art which is the essence of art and that about people which has throughout history caused them to need art as an essential part of their lives. So among all the disciplines of thought that are interested in the arts, aesthetics is the one devoted to an explanation of their intrinsic nature. That is why it is so important for music educators to understand some basic concepts in aesthetics, and how to apply them effectively in their teaching.

LIMITATIONS OF ANY PHILOSOPHY

It would be presumptuous in the extreme to imply that any philosophy, the present one included, can be taken to be a statement "for all time." Music education, as everything else, changes with time, so that a philosophy which is convincing at one time is likely to be regarded as primarily of historical interest at another. The record of change in philosophies must be gleaned from representative writings over the years: unfortunately there have been few if any books devoted entirely to systematic statements of music education philosophy. As one studies the changes in concepts about music education in history, it becomes impossible to entertain the notion that any single philosophy can be more than transient. This state of affairs keeps would-be philosophers humble (a most salutary condition), but it does not relieve them of the obligation to articulate the underlying beliefs of the time in which they live.

Above and beyond the effect of time and the changes time brings is the matter of the variability of beliefs at any one time in history. It is a truism that people differ in opinions about music education and that these differences always have and always will exist. But the fact that no philosophy will ever win total assent by all music educators does not remove the necessity for reasoned, careful, systematic statements which help make the field more understandable to all who are involved with it. A philosophy, then, must be conceived as being "of a time," and must also give recognition to the fact that it can only provide a point of departure for practitioners of that time.

And yet, having acknowledged the inherent limitations of any philosophy it must be maintained that some philosophy—some underlying set of beliefs about the nature and value of one's field—is required if one is to be effective as a professional and if one's profession is to be effective as a whole. Indeed, a continuing need of the profession is a statement of philosophy which captures the sense of where the profession stands and where it is going and which provides a common point of reference from which new and differing ideas can spring. And while the little word "A" in the title of this book indicates that the philosophy to be offered is a *particular* philosophy (it is not, to be very explicit, offered as *The* philosophy of music education), the writer believes that it does indeed capture the self-image of the profession as it has evolved at this point in history. Given the conditions of changing beliefs and differing beliefs, it still remains possible to characterize the general state of beliefs at particular times. There exists at present an extremely high level of agreement about the nature of music and music education among those who have given serious thought to this matter. What the profession seems to require at the moment is not persuasion about any particular philosophy, but continued refinement and careful application of the commonly held but imperfectly applied beliefs now current.

THE NEED FOR A PHILOSOPHY

The need for a philosophy exists at both the collective and individual levels. First, the profession as a whole needs a set of beliefs which can serve to guide the efforts of the group. The impact the profession can make on society depends in large degree on the quality of the profession's understanding of what it has to offer which might be of value to society. There is a continuing need for a better understanding of the value of music and of the teaching and learning of music. An uncomfortable amount of defensiveness, of self-doubt, of grasping at straws which seem to offer bits and pieces of self-justification, exists now in music education and has always seemed to exist. It would be difficult to find a field so active, so apparently healthy, so venerable in age and widespread in practice, which is at the same time so worried about its inherent value.

The tremendous expenditure of concern about how to justify itself—both to itself and to others—which has been traditional in this field, reflects a lack of philosophical "inner peace." What a shame this is. For, as will be made clear in this book, justification for teaching and learning music exists at the very deepest levels of human value. Until music education understands what it genuinely has to offer, until it is convinced of the fact that it is a necessary rather than a peripheral part of human culture, until it "feels in its bones" that its value is a fundamental one, it will not have attained the peace of mind which is the mark of maturity. And it also will not have reached a level of operational effectiveness which is an outgrowth of self-acceptance, of security, of purposes understood and efforts channeled.

While a philosophy can serve as a sort of "collective conscience" for music education as a whole, the strength of the field ultimately depends on the convictions of its members. As necessary as a philosophy might be for the overall effectiveness of a group, it is even more necessary that the individuals who comprise the group have come to an understanding of the nature and the value of their individual endeavors.

This is so for several reasons. Individuals who have a clear notion of what their aims are as professionals and are convinced of the importance of those aims are a strong link in the chain of people who collectively make a profession. Music education has been fortunate in having leaders who have held strong convictions, who have helped enormously to forge a sense of group identity. But too many convictions have been based on platitudes, on attractive but empty arguments, on vague intimations that music education is important with little in the way of solid reasoning to give backbone to beliefs. Many individuals have enormous dedication to this field but little more to base it on than fond hopes. This is why the profession gives the appearance—a very accurate appearance—of tremendous vitality and purposefulness and goodness of intentions while at the same time the nagging doubt exists as to whether it all makes much difference. In this situation, individuals who do have convincing justifications for music education, who exhibit in their own lives the inner sense of worth which comes from doing important work in the world, become some of the profession's most prized possessions. To the degree that individual music educators are helped to formulate a compelling philosophy, the profession will become more solid and secure.

Another reason for the importance of strengthening individual beliefs about music education is that the understanding people have about the value of their profession inevitably affects their understanding of the value of their personal lives. To a large extent people are what they do in life. If their occupation seems to them an important one, which they hold in respect and through which they can enrich both themselves and society, they cannot help but feel that a large part of their lives is important and respectable and enriching. If, on the other hand, people have the feeling that their work is of doubtful value, that it lacks the respect of others both inside and outside their field, that the contribution they make through their work is peripheral and inconsequential, they can only feel that much of their life is of equally dubious value.

It is crucial that people preparing to enter the profession of music education develop an understanding of the importance of their chosen field.

Perhaps at no other time in life is the need for self-justification as pressing as when people are preparing to take their place as contributing members of society. For such people there is an almost desperate need for a philosophy which provides a mission and a meaning for their professional lives. This is especially the case when, as in music education, the value of the field is not fully understood by its members, and is perhaps even less understood by professionals in related fields. Given the lack of convincing arguments about the importance of music education, the philosophical insecurity which manifests itself in superficial bases of self-justification, the general defensiveness of music educators toward their colleagues in other aspects of music and education, it is all too clear why so many music education undergraduates are more or less cynical, detached, insecure, defensive.

Two conditions are necessary if this situation is to be reversed. First, a philosophy is needed which does in fact offer a convincing basis for valuing music education. Second, systematic attention to the development of a professional philosophy should occur during undergraduate education. Seldom is an undergraduate course devoted to a consideration of the reasons underlying the practices of teaching and learning music. Whatever attention to philosophy exists, comes, if it comes at all, in bits and pieces at the beginnings of various other courses in which texts are used where part of chapter one is devoted to "the value of music education." Admirable as such statements might be they do not and cannot substitute for serious attention to the complex business of developing a consistent, penetrating philosophy. In fact, the perfunctory nature of attention to matters philosophical, both in college courses and by the texts used, which are intended to serve other purposes, reinforces the notion that there are few if any good reasons for music education to exist. The smatterings of rationales picked up here and there confuse more than they convince, weaken more than they strengthen, discourage more than they inspire.

Students deserve better than this. It is essential for the development of a sense of self-identity and self-respect that college students be given the opportunity to think seriously about their reasons for professional being. And they deserve to be introduced to a philosophy which is more than a protestation of good intentions. College students are far too sophisticated to be satisfied with superficial reasoning, and they are far too involved with life to be able to accept a philosophy which does not grasp their imagination and tap their zeal. The need to feel that life is significant, that actions do matter, that good causes can be served and good influences be felt, can be met more effectively and immediately by a sound philosophy than by any other aspect of their eduction. The return on the investment made in developing a professional philosophy is extremely high, not only in providing a basis for self-respect, but in channeling the dedication and commitment of people into a dedication and commitment to music education.

All that has been said about the purposes a philosophy serves for the music educator in training applies as well to the music educator in service. No matter how long one has been a professional, the need for self-understanding and self-esteem exists. In some ways these needs become more complex with time, as professional duties, responsibilities, problems, become more complex. For the veteran music educator (and some would argue that surviving the first year of teaching qualifies the music educator as "veteran"), a goal is needed which focuses efforts toward something more satisfying than another concert, more meaningful than another contest, more important than another class, broader than another lesson or meeting or budget or report. All these obligations and pleasures need to head somewhere. They need to be viewed as the necessary carrying out in practice of an end which transcends each of them—which adds to each of one's duties a purpose deep enough and large enough to make all of them worthwhile. It becomes progressively more difficult, very often, for the professional to see beyond the increasing number of trees to the forest which includes all of them. Without the larger view, without a sense of the inherent value of one's work, it is very easy to begin to operate at the level of daily problems with little regard for their larger context. Inevitably an erosion of confidence takes place, in which immediate concerns never seem to mean very much. Having lost a sense of purpose which was perhaps not very strong to begin with, teachers begin to doubt their value as professionals and as individuals.

The inspiring, rejuvenating, joyful nature of music itself is a strong barrier to loss of concern among those who deal with it professionally. This is one of the major benefits of being a music educator. But fortunate as this is, a set of beliefs which explains very clearly the reasons for the power of music remains necessary if the music educator is to function as more than a technician. Too often beliefs about music and arguments for its importance have been at the level of the obvious, with the secret hope that if one justified music education by appeals to easily understood, facile arguments, its "deeper" values would somehow prevail. Just what these deeper values are usually remains a mystery, but they are sensed. So one plugs along, using whatever arguments turn up to bolster oneself in one's own and others' eyes, trusting that all will turn out well in the end. But as time goes along, for the individual and for the profession as a whole, it becomes less and less possible to be sustained by hazy hopes. A time for candor presents itself, when the question can no longer be avoided: "Just what is it about my work that really matters?"

The function of a professional philosophy is to answer that question. A good answer should be developed while a person is preparing to enter the profession. If not, any time is better than no time. If the answer is a good one it will serve to pull together thoughts about the fundamental nature and value of one's professional efforts in a way which allows for these thoughts to grow and change with time and experience. It is not possible for a philosophy to serve such a purpose if the effort to accomplish the fundamental is based on the superficial. A strong philosophy must illuminate the deepest level of values in one's field. At this level one can find not only professional fulfillment, but the personal fulfillment which is an outgrowth of being a secure professional.

The final reason for the importance of a convincing professional philosophy is the fact that everything music educators do in their jobs carries out in practice their beliefs about their subject. Every time a choice is made a belief is applied. The music teacher, as every other professional, makes hundreds of small and large choices every day, each one based on a decision that one thing rather than another should be done. The quality of these decisions depends directly on the quality of the teacher's understanding of the nature of the subject. The deeper this understanding, the more consistent, the more focused, the more effective become the teacher's choices. Teachers who lack a clear understanding of their subject can only make choices by hunch and by hope, these being a reflection of the state of their beliefs. Music teachers who have forged a philosophy based on a probing analysis of the nature of music can act with confidence, knowing that whatever they choose to do will be in consonance with the values of the art they represent.

PHILOSOPHY AND ADVOCACY

A great deal of confusion exists as to the function of a philosophy in the realm of support seeking at the school-community-state-national levels; that is, at the level of policy or advocacy. The function of advocacy is to make the strongest possible case for the need for music education to school administrators or to school boards or to parents and other citizens who will be voting on school funding issues or to the great variety of other constituencies whose support or lack thereof will determine the health of music programs in American schools. Should a philosophy present the kind of arguments that would convince influential people to give music education the backing it would like to have?

A good answer would be "yes and no." At the "yes" level a philosophy should provide a profession with a sense of its most important purposes, so that any specific arguments it offers for community support can be based on a foundation that has been built with care and built to last. At the "no" level a philosophy devoted to providing a wide range of debating points that could be used in all the contexts in which the goal is to win the argument— that is, to gain whatever benefit is being sought from whatever person or group in whatever situation—could only be a philosophy so diverse and so superficial as to be useless philosophically.

This is because the task of philosophy is fundamentally different from the task of advocacy, however related the two must be. Philosophy strives to get below all the many reasons that might be given for the importance of a subject to that reason underlying them all—that essential, singular, unifying concept that identifies the subject as being both unique and necessary. To the extent a philosophy is able to explain convincingly how a subject offers values unattainable in any other subjects, to that extent it establishes that the subject must be available in education if those values are to be available. And to the extent a philosophy is able to establish that the values it uniquely offers are necessary for all people, to that extent it has demonstrated that the subject is essential in public education. Until those two arguments have been made—the argument for uniqueness and the argument for necessity—the philosophical endeavor is incomplete or faulty. In attempting to establish "first causes," a philosophy cannot be satisfied with the myriad secondary causes the subject might also serve because all such secondary reasons are either (1) not unique to the subject, or (2) not necessary for all people.

All unique, necessary subjects, music included, offer a great variety of secondary values. Some of these values, while not unique, are nevertheless desirable for all. For example, it is beneficial that performance groups offer an opportunity for students to involve themselves with others in a common cause, because doing so can be a very positive life experience. But such an experience can be gained in a great many other school subjects and activities: it is not necessary to have music for this. Hundreds of values of this sort have been claimed for music—values that are indeed desirable for all students but which can be just as well if not significantly better served by many other involvements. If such reasons are all music education has to offer, it can never be regarded as an essential subject in the schools because all these reasons establish clearly that music education has nothing to offer that is unique to music education.

On the other side of this issue, some values are claimed for music in education on the basis that they are unique to music but are not necessary for all people. These values have to do primarily with the development of musical talent. (Chapter Five will discuss the idea of talent as intelligence.) The argument is made that some students have very high levels of this special kind of ability and that for their sake, to allow them to become all they are capable of becoming as individuals, and for society's sake, which needs to have the contributions of excellent artists, the talents of these people must be discovered and carefully nurtured. Music educators are professionally equipped to identify students with unusual talent and can offer experiences to foster their growth.

This argument is unassailable. It is so clearly true and so compelling in importance that few if any people would dare dispute it. The problem with it, of course, is that it applies to very few people. Musical talent, like any other human ability, is randomly distributed: we can be confident that if we plotted it accurately it would form a normal curve. Only a tiny percentage of people at the very tail end of the curve have sufficient talent to become the professional performers, conductors, composers, teachers, scholars, that society needs and can provide for. We must have those people. But we do not need to have music programs in the public schools to get them.

Most nations in the world train their talented young people outside of the general education system, in special schools devoted to such purposes. That is the most cost-efficient way to do it. Debates about the improvement of American education have raised the issue of whether schools should be expected to do everything. Should not the schools devote themselves to those aspects of education necessary for all, those being considered the "basic" subjects, and let the special needs of small groups of students be handled in a variety of ways the community can provide outside the school setting? If schools continue to make those special offerings available, is it not reasonable to regard them as easily dispensable when times get tough and money becomes scarce? And is it not also reasonable to regard the special subjects, and the teachers of them, as frills rather than basics in education, so that support of them is contingent on generosity rather than necessity?

Music education in America has been very lucky that for historical and cultural reasons the answer generally given to these questions has been only "maybe" rather than "of course." But who would choose to live a professional life under the cloud of that "maybe," which can so easily become and has too often become "of course"? It is because we do live under that cloud that we are as insecure and defensive as we are. We deserve better. For, as it happens, music and the arts are unique in the values they offer, and these values are so fundamental to any notion of the good life as to be unquestionable in their necessity.

The business of a professional philosophy is to substantiate that claim. The business of policy or advocacy is to translate a philosophy into terms understandable to and convincing for a great variety of influential publics, each of which has a particular set of issues it is concerned about and a particular bias toward those issues reflecting the belief that those issues are the really important ones. School boards, for example, view the world through a particular set of lenses. PTA groups have a somewhat different set. State legislatures have still another, as do athletic program enthusiasts and "back to basics" champions and "save money at all costs" campaigners and "raise test scores" partisans and on and on and on in this culture made of countless special interest groups.

Arguments to such groups must be at least to some extent tailor made. It would be disastrous strategically to be so rigidly tied to the level of depth philosophy that arguments adapted to and relevant for the special interests of a particular group could not be presented. That would be to deify philosophy rather than to build on philosophy. Good policy advocates—that is, good politicians—are able to remain true to an underlying philosophy while at the same time addressing issues at a level of specificity and in a context of limited interests that must go beyond what a philosophy can or should deal with. The politicians we respect, and need, are the ones who can make broad-ranging arguments appropriate to a variety of special interests by choosing wisely among all the primary and secondary claims attaching to our subject. Such politicians never betray their subject by making claims so outrageously unrelated to the fundamental values of music as to embarrass the musicians and music educators they are supposed to serve. People who do so are politicians only in the worst sense of that word, and the effect they have is to weaken music education by dishonoring that which we most deeply believe. But that kind of political sham is not necessary. There are plenty of ways to wheel and deal in the world of school politics without demeaning one's integrity or the integrity of one's subject.

That is why the ongoing debate within music education as to whether we should make the case for our value on artistic bases or utilitarian bases is so fruitless and so self-defeating. It is never a case of one or the other. Philosophy as such, unadapted to political considerations, is seldom sufficient at the level of politics, while political arguments ungrounded in a philosophy or that do violence to a philosophy are dangerous. The question for effective advocacy is always how to balance philosophical honesty with practical efficacy, and this is never an easy question to answer. It requires people who understand the basic values of music education deeply yet are sensitive to the many other concerns held by various nonmusic constituencies. Recognizing this, we can end the tiresome, inappropriate pitting against each other of two dimensions that must be used to support each other. And we can get on with the work of building a philosophy that establishes the primary values of music education so that the secondary values have a leg to stand on.

THE PHILOSOPHICAL BASIS FOR PRACTICE

The same relationship that exists between philosophy and advocacy exists between philosophy and practice; that is, practice must be grounded in a secure philosophy but must go beyond it in countless specific ways. Teacher education programs consist largely of training in the practice of music education—methods courses, conducting courses, student teaching, and so on. All these are absolutely necessary, of course, but usually do not coalesce; they remain scattered in bits and pieces of skills and techniques and methodologies that continue to be scattered even when a student graduates and becomes a teacher. What is lacking in all this practical material is a center that holds everything together. A lack of a unifying core is felt deeply at the psychological level by many music educators who are able to function acceptably in specific practices but who have a sense of emptiness inside because the specifics do not add up to a meaningful whole. When the tremendous amount of energy it takes to be an effective music educator is not being fueled from a concentrated source of inner power, it begins to wane, feeding on itself and dissipating in endless but uncoordinated activity.

A philosophy provides the unifying power for the energies of music education at all levels of practice. As mentioned previously, each choice a teacher makes as a professional should carry out in practice a belief about the value of what is being taught. What are good objectives for a music program? What are good objectives for a particular rehearsal or class session? What should be said about a piece being listened to on a recording? How should one guide a student to finish a piece he or she is composing? How should one give evidence that learning is occurring? Which method should be used for a beginning instrumentalist? What should the choir sing for the next concert? How much time should be given to marching band activities? Which elementary textbooks should be adopted? On and on the decisions go, at every level from the most general to the most specific. Without a dependable source of beliefs about what is genuinely valuable in these and the thousands of other matters that must be decided, there is simply no way to make sense of teaching.

That source cannot be found among the secondary values of music or music education. It must be sought in a concept about what is of ultimate value about our art and the teaching of it. As it happens, such a concept has been formulated over a period of several decades and has been given added impetus in recent years by a variety of contributions from psychology and philosophy and educational theory. Put simply, it is that music and the other arts are a basic way that humans know themselves and their world; they are a basic mode of cognition. The older idea, prevalent since the Renaissance, that knowing consists only of conceptual reasoning, is giving way to the conviction that there are many ways humans conceive reality, each of them a genuine realm of cognition with its own validity and its unique characteristics. We know the world through the mode of conceptual rationality, indeed, but we also know it through the aesthetic mode and several other cognitive modes now being recognized, such as the interpersonal, the intuitive, the narrative/paradigmatic, the formal, the practical, and the spiritual, according to one recent attempt to map this newly explored terrain.[1]

Further, the older notion that human intelligence is unitary, being exclusively a manifestation of the level of ability to reason conceptually as measured by I.Q. tests, is also undergoing a profound revolution. The idea now gaining currency is that intelligence exists in several domains, such as the linguistic, the musical, the logical-mathematical, the spatial, the bodily kinesthetic, the interpersonal, and the intrapersonal, as proposed in one recent influential study.[2] The argument is being advanced that an education system focused exclusively or predominantly on one mode of cognition—the conceptual, and which recognizes only conceptual forms of intelligence as being valid, is a system so narrow in focus, so limited in scope, so unrealistic about what humans can know and the ways humans function intelligently, as to be injurious and even dehumanizing in its effects on the children and the larger society it is supposed to serve.[3]

These burgeoning ideas allow music education to affirm, with great courage, with great hope, with great relief, that it must be conceived as all the great disciplines of the human mind are conceived—as a basic subject with its unique characteristics of cognition and intelligence, that must be offered to all children if they are not to be deprived of its values. This affirmation has the power to strengthen the teaching and learning of music and the arts in the schools. At one stroke it establishes music and its sister arts as among the essential realms of education, prescribes the direction music education must take if it is to fulfill its unique educational mission, gives the profession a solid philosophical grounding, and provides the hope that the arts in education will play a far more important role for society in the future than they have in the past.

The philosophy offered in this book will explain the inner workings of music upon which these claims can be built. It will also attempt to bridge the gap between philosophy and practice by suggesting, at the level of general principles, how music education can be effective in bringing the unique, essential values of this art to all students. Chapter Two will explain the position to be taken as to the special cognitive status of music and the arts: that which humans know from art that is knowable only from art. Chapters Three through Seven will explore how this knowledge is produced and shared. Chapters Eight and Nine will offer guidelines for effective practice in the general music and performance aspects of the

---

[1]Elliot W. Eisner, ed., *Learning and Teaching the Ways of Knowing* (Chicago: National Society for the Study of Education, 84th Yearbook, Part II, 1985).

[2]Howard Gardner, *Frames of Mind: The Theory of Multiple Intelligences* (New York: Basic Books, 1983).

[3]For an excellent discussion of this point, see Elliot W. Eisner, *Cognition and Curriculum* (New York: Longman, 1982).

music program. Chapter Ten will raise the issue of a possible new future for music education as part of a larger arts education endeavor. Throughout, the methods of philosophical work will be employed—critical analysis of ideas, synthesis of ideas, speculative projection of ideas—and the purpose of philosophical work will be pursued—to create meanings by which we can live better lives.

Alternative views
about art
on which a philosophy
can be based

2

THE USES OF AESTHETICS

In the long, complex history of aesthetics thousands of views have been expressed about art. To one who examines these views with any degree of objectivity, it becomes evident that here, if no place else, is a perfect example of truth being relative. So strong is this impression, so overwhelming its effect, that one is tempted to throw up one's hands in despair, turn one's back on the entire field of aesthetics, and proclaim that in music education one might as well do whatever strikes one's fancy, since there probably exists plenty of justification for whatever this happens to be.

To yield to this temptation, however, is to give oneself up to ineffectuality. Of course there is no immutable truth in aesthetics. Of course there is no single or simple answer to every question. Of course there is no one guideline which will insure satisfactory results of action. The question is, can one accept this condition and at the same time develop a point of view which helps one's efforts to be as consistent, as effective, as useful for one's purposes as intelligence and modesty allow?

There is really no alternative but to answer "yes." Everything we do in this world is done in the face of imperfect and partial knowledge. But it is possible—in fact, it is necessary—to adopt some working premises and to use them (not be used *by* them) as guidelines to action, knowing full well that they may be altered or even dropped as conditions change. To refuse to work from a critically accepted position about the nature of one's subject is to avoid one of the central imperatives of human life, which is to carve out, from all existing possibilities, the most reasonable possibilities for one's purposes. Not to do so dooms one to intellectual and operational paralysis. To do so blindly and irrevocably ensures the same fate. Searching out a convincing, useful, coherent point of view, adopting it as a base of operations, examining it and sharpening it, tightening it while using it, opening it to new ideas and altering it as seems necessary, can help one to act with purpose, with impact, with some measure of meaningfulness.

The problem, of course, is to determine the best possible point of view. Several principles can help us do so. First, the field of aesthetics must be approached in a highly selective way. It would be beside the point (and quite impossible) to investigate indiscriminately the writings of every aesthetician in history, or every aesthetician of this century, or every aesthetician alive today, looking for leads to a philosophy of music education. Instead, the search must start with an acquaintance with the field of music education: its problems, its needs, its history, its present status. Aesthetics must be used by music educators to serve their own purposes. Otherwise they are likely to lose themselves in the history and problems of aesthetics, never to emerge with a workable philosophy. A philosophy should articulate a consistent and helpful statement about the nature and value of music and music education. Only those portions of aesthetics useful for this purpose need be used. Aesthetics must never be the master of music education—it must be its servant.

Second, the point of view adopted should be sufficiently broad to take into account all major aspects of music and music education but sufficiently focused to provide tangible guidelines for thought and action. No single aesthetician has supplied the breadth of conception needed for our purpose, although, as will be seen, some have been of unusual help. It will be necessary to identify an aesthetic position which includes major thinkers and which also has an identifiable structure of ideas which can be handled without being overwhelming in complexity.

Third, the point of view should be particularly pertinent to the art of music but at the same time capable of yielding equally valid insights into the nature of all the arts. Some aesthetic theories are heavily slanted toward the nonmusical arts, and while they offer insights into music, they do so only secondarily. An example would be the psychoanalytic theory of Carl G. Jung, which is immensely fruitful with ideas about literature, poetry, and the visual arts, but which has little to say about music (7).[*1] Obviously this situation should be reversed for our purposes, although a view confined to a single art, even music, would be unacceptable also.

Fourth, the view being sought must contain rich implications for education. It would be of little use to adopt a theory which offered few leads to teaching and learning music and the other arts no matter how strong the theory might be in other matters. Existentialist aesthetics, for example, has provided powerful insights into the nature of art and its role in human life (1).[2] But helpful as these insights are, they do not seem to lend themselves directly or abundantly to problems of mass education. It would be difficult, therefore, to depend on this particular view for a philosophy of music education.

Finally, any aesthetic position to be used as a basis for a philosophy must be relevant to the society in which we live and to the general conditions under which American education operates. Important as Marxism-Leninism has been in history, for example (1), it is quite peripheral to our concerns. The same can be said about Freudian aesthetics and Oriental aesthetics and Medieval aesthetics. All of these, and others, can be of use for particular purposes, but they cannot be the foundation on which our philosophy is to be built.

Of all existing aesthetic viewpoints,[3] one in particular fulfills the principles just outlined and does so with unusual power. This view is presented by Leonard B. Meyer (13) as one of three related aesthetic theories; Referentialism, Absolute Formalism, and Absolute Expressionism. An explanation of each of these theories will set the stage for the choice to be made as to which will best serve as the basis for a philosophy, and for our systematic examination of the implications of using this theory as a base of operations for music education.

REFERENTIALISM

The words "Absolutism" and "Referentialism" tell one where to go to find the meaning and value of a work of art. The Absolutist says that to find the meaning in a work of art, you must go to the work itself and attend to the internal qualities which make the work a created thing. In music, you would go to the sounds themselves—melody, rhythm, harmony, tone color, texture, dynamics, form—and attend to what those sounds do.

[*]References in parentheses refer to the Supplementary Readings at the ends of the chapters in this book.

[1]An excellent introduction to the monumental work of Jung is Carl G. Jung, ed., *Man and His Symbols* (Garden City, N.Y.: Doubleday, 1964).

[2]Also see Arturo B. Fallico, *Art and Existentialism* (Englewood Cliffs, N.J.: Prentice Hall, 1962).

[3]All the major "isms" in aesthetics are reviewed in Monroe C. Beardsley, *Aesthetics* (University: University of Alabama Press, 1977).

The Referentialist disagrees. According to this view, the meaning and value of a work of art exist outside of the work itself. To find that art work's meaning, you must go to the ideas, emotions, attitudes, events, which the work *refers* you to in the world outside the art work. The function of the art work is to remind you of, or tell you about, or help you understand, or make you experience, something which is extra-artistic, that is, something which is outside the created thing and the artistic qualities which make it a created thing. In music, the sounds should serve as a reminder of, or a clue to, or a sign of something extramusical; something separate from the sounds and what the sounds are doing. To the degree that the music is successful in referring you to a nonmusical experience, it is a successful piece of music. To the degree that the nonmusical experience is an important or valuable one the music is itself important or valuable.

Every work of art is influenced by a variety of circumstances impinging on the choices the artist made in creating it. Some of these stem from the artist—his or her personal and professional history, present life situation, characteristic interests, internalized influences from other artists, and so on. Other circumstances stem from the culture within which the artist works—the general belief system about the arts, important past and present political events, the existing social structure within which the artist plays a part, and so on. For the Referentialist, all these interacting artistic/cultural influences are significant as further clues leading outward to the nonartistic meanings and values of the art work. The internal qualities of the work (in music, melody, rhythm, and so on; in painting, color, line, shape, texture, and so on; in poetry, meter, rhyme, verbal imagery, and metaphor; and so on for all the arts) can either give the external meanings directly or through the intermediary of their surrounding artistic/cultural influences.

The referentialist view can be diagrammed as follows:

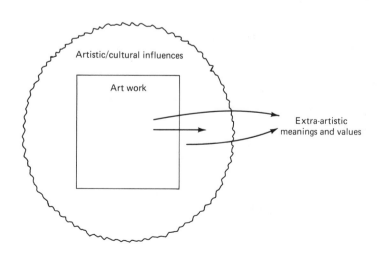

The most clear-cut example of Referentialism is the Communist theory of art, called "Socialist Realism." This view, which is the official aesthetic doctrine of Marxism-Leninism, regards art as a servant of social and political needs. The function of art is to further the cause of the state by influencing attitudes toward social problems and by illuminating the needs of the state and the proper actions to be taken to fulfill those needs. As stated in the Statute of the Union of Soviet Writers;

> Socialist Realism is the fundamental method of Soviet Literature and criticism [and of all art]: it demands of the artist a true, historically concrete representation of reality in its revolutionary development. Further, it ought to contribute to the ideological transformation and education of the workers in the spirit of socialism.[4]

According to Socialist Realism, and for any referential theory, the key factor of value in art is the nonartistic goodness of the art work's "message." If a particular art work has no identifiable, nonartistic message (a piece of pure instrumental music, for example), it must be regarded as merely a titillation of the senses with no value beyond that of sheer decoration. Of course any message in the art work must be presented attractively, but the artistic attractiveness only serves to make the message more vivid, more powerfully felt. To the extent that artistic interest becomes the central value of the work and nonartistic aspects are diminished in importance, the work is decadent and useless.

The message in an art work, according to Referentialism, need not be an intellectual or practical one; it can also be an emotional one. If a work makes people feel a particular, desirable, useful emotion, it would fulfill the conditions for good art. The emotion must be identifiable, it must be unambiguous and concrete, and it must be the kind which serves some non-artistic end, such as closer identification with fellow workers, or higher regard for the community, or deeper sympathy for those less fortunate, and so on. If the emotion in a work is not of this specific, nonartistically directed kind; if it is, instead, an integral and inseparable part of the artistic qualities in the work and is therefore experienced as an ineffable sense of feeling, the work is to that extent, again, decadent and useless.

The notion that art works arouse nonartistic emotions and that one must choose carefully which of these emotions *should* be aroused is as old as Plato, who felt that the kinds of music used by the general public should be severely limited so that their moral fiber would not be weakened through the effects of hearing voluptuous tunes. The strongest statement of this position in modern times is that of Leo Tolstoy. It will repay us to take a brief look at Tolstoy's views to make very explicit the consequences of taking a thoroughgoing referentialist viewpoint.

[4]Ibid., p. 360.

For Tolstoy the function of art is to transmit specific emotions from the artist to the recipient in the most direct and most powerful way the artist can devise. If the artist can transmit an emotion which is individual, that is, which is a particular, precise, concrete emotion, if the emotion is transmitted clearly and unambiguously, so there is no question about what the recipient should feel, and if the artist sincerely feels the emotion himself and has the need to express it, the work of art is likely to be a good one (10). All these principles illustrate the emotional dimension of Referentialism.

But in addition to transmitting a specific emotion and doing it well, the quality of the art work also depends on the desirability of the particular emotion transmitted. If it is a "bad" emotion the art work will be pernicious in its effects. If it is a "good" emotion the art work will be beneficent in its effects. So, inevitably, for Tolstoy and for any Referentialist, one must judge a work of art on the basis of its nonartistic subject matter—its content of reference to the world which is outside the work and which is separate from the work's artistic qualities. One can specify good and bad emotions according to one's view of what is good and what is bad in life. According to Tolstoy good emotions are those which lead toward Christian brotherhood. Unfortunately, very few art works fulfill his criteria of goodness. "In modern painting, strange to say, works of this kind, directly transmitting the Christian feeling of love of God and of one's neighbor are hardly to be found, especially among the works of the celebrated painters."[5]

Tolstoy finds very few art works in any medium that satisfy his demands for good art although occasionally a few crop up— *Uncle Tom's Cabin,* Millet's "The Man with the Hoe," china dolls, and other ornaments which are easily comprehensible to everyone. In music his position is illustrated most strikingly. The best examples of music are marches and dances, which approach the condition of having a distinct, easily understood message. The popular songs of the various nations are also great art, but in "learned" music there are precious few examples from which to choose—the Violin Aria by Bach; the E-flat Major Nocturne of Chopin; some scattered selections from Haydn, Mozart, Schubert. Beethoven is perhaps the poorest of composers and the weakest of his compositions is the Ninth Symphony. This is so because

> not only do I not see how the feelings transmitted by this work could unite people not specially trained to submit themselves to its complex hypnotism, but I am unable to imagine to myself a crowd of normal people who could understand anything of this long, confused, and artificial production, except short snatches which are lost in a sea of what is incomprehensible. And therefore, whether I like it or not, I am compelled to conclude that this work belongs to the rank of bad art.[6]

[5]Leo N. Tolstoy, *What Is Art?* trans. Aylmer Maude (Indianapolis: The Liberal Arts Press, 1960), p. 152. Reprinted by permission of The Liberal Arts Press Division of The Bobbs-Merrill Company.

[6]Ibid., p. 158.

But Beethoven is in good company, for in the same classification (along with paintings which display "all that odious female nudity")[7]

> belongs almost all the chamber and opera music of our times, beginning especially from Beethoven (Schumann, Berlioz, Liszt, Wagner), by its subject matter devoted to the expression of feelings accessible only to people who have developed in themselves an unhealthy, nervous irritation evoked by this exclusive, artificial, and complex music.[8]

The reason for dwelling a bit on Tolstoy's aesthetic views is that they present the most thorough statement of Referentialism available and can serve as a foil against which the other views to be presented can be compared. Another very obvious example of Referentialism should be noted, this one in musical aesthetics, because it also will help keep straight the three viewpoints to be explained here. This is the view of the English aesthetician Deryck Cooke (9).

Cooke is in agreement with Tolstoy that music is by nature a language and that, as with any good language, the meaning of the terms used in the language can be specified. This notion will be explored in several places throughout this book, so no explanation will be made at this point. It need only be noted that the conception of art as "language" (by which is meant a system of symbols having conventional referents) is a purely referential one and leads inevitably to a search for the proper "meanings" of the language's terms. While Cooke recognizes the difficulty of stipulating precise referents for musical "language terms," the difficulty, according to him, can be overcome by intellectual effort. As a step in this direction he analyzes the tones of the major, minor, and chromatic scales and several basic melodic patterns to find the emotional referent of each. To the extent that he succeeds in doing so, according to his theory, he succeeds in revealing the meanings hidden in the musical sounds. The task, obviously, is one of translation, of "breaking the code" so to speak (9, p. 34).

After long analyses of the use of various intervals and tone patterns, Cooke offers his conclusions as to their referents. A selection of these follows:

> Minor Second: . . . spiritless anguish, context of finality.
> Minor Third: . . . stoic acceptance, tragedy.
> Major Third: . . . joy.
> Sharp Fourth: . . . devilish and inimical forces.
> Major Seventh: . . . violent longing, aspiration in a context of finality.
> Ascending 1-(2)-3-(4)-5 (major): . . . an outgoing, active, assertive emotion of joy.

---

[7]Ibid., p. 153.
[8]Ibid., p. 157.

Ascending 1-(2)-3-(4)-5 (minor): . . . an outgoing feeling of pain—an assertion of sorrow, a complaint, a protest against misfortune.
Descending 5-(4)-3-(2)-1 (minor): . . . an "incoming" painful emotion, in a context of finality: acceptance of, or yielding to grief: discouragement and depression; passive suffering; and the despair connected with death.[9]

The use of these translations by the knowledgeable listener should allow for full participation in music's meaning. Is this oversimplifying the case? Not according to Cooke, for

Actually, the process of musical communication is fundamentally a very simple one, which only appears complicated because of its complicated apparatus. There is nothing more involved about it than there is in any form of emotional expression—say, a physical movement or a vocal utterance.[10]

Beethoven's music, for example, would not be needed if Beethoven could personally communicate his inner joy by jumping or shouting in the presence of an audience. To convert his emotion into permanent form he used sounds, so that many people, even after his death, could experience with him the joy that he felt (9, p. 209). Music, then, is essentially a giving vent to emotions through sounds.

REFERENTIALISM IN MUSIC EDUCATION

While the examples of Referentialism given here are obviously extreme ones, many opinions about and practices in music education share some of the same assumptions even if not as consistently or strongly. For example, the idea that when nonartistic subject matter exists in a work of art (fruit in a painting, political theories in a novel, a program in music), the art work is "about" that subject matter, is a referentialist assumption. If one isolates the subject matter, say, the story of *Til Eulenspiegel*, and teaches about it as if the story was what the music is about, one is acting as a Referentialist. If one adds a story or message to an art work which contains none, say, Mozart's *Eine kleine Nachtmusik*, one is, again, acting as a Referentialist. The same applies to "emotional" content. Teaching about love and its meaning as the content of the *Liebestod*, or identifying the content of Beethoven's Funeral March as "sadness," and teaching about sadness and its roots and implications, are practices compatible with Referentialism.

Music educators and others concerned with the arts in the schools will recognize that Referentialist assumptions are in operation in much that is done in the teaching of art. The isolating of and teaching about the

---

[9]Deryck Cooke, *The Language of Music* (London: Oxford University Press, 1959), pp. 90, 115, 122, 133. Quotations reprinted by permission of Oxford University Press.

[10]Ibid., p. 209.

meaning of the words in vocal music; the same process in program music; the searching out of a "message" in absolute music; the attempt to add a story or picture to music, either verbally or visually; the search for the right emotion-words with which to characterize music; the comparing of musical works with works in other art forms according to similarities in subject matter; these and many other practices attest to the presence of Referentialism in music education.

What are the values of art according to the Referentialist point of view? Obviously the values of art and of being involved with art are non-artistic values. Art works serve many purposes, all of them extra-artistic. If one can share these values one becomes a better citizen, a better worker, a better human being, to the extent that art influences one in nonartistic ways and these influences are assumed to be beneficial. Of course there is the danger that harmful works of art will have harmful effects, so care must be taken in the choice of art works. That is why societies which operate under a Referentialist aesthetic must exercise a high degree of control over the artistic diet of their citizens. Teachers, if they are Referentialists, are in the position of having to make decisions as to which art works are proper for their students and which improper, these judgments being based on the nonartistic effects of the art works' subject matter.

As with teaching practices based on Referentialism music educators will have no difficulty recognizing the Referentialist basis for many of the value claims made for music education. Studying music makes one a better person in many ways: it improves learning skills, it imparts moral uplift, it fulfills a wide variety of social needs, it provides a healthy outlet for repressed emotions, it encourages self-discipline, it provides a challenge to focus efforts upon, it gives a basis for worthy use of leisure time, it improves health in countless ways; it is assumed to be, in short, a most effective way to make people better—nonmusically.

FORMALISM

Let us return now to the aesthetic point of view called Absolutism. It will be recalled that this view asserts that the meaning and value of a work of art are to be found in the internal qualities which make the work a created thing—the very qualities which the Referentialist insists are only the bearers of meanings *outside* themselves. In music, according to Absolutism, the sounds and what they do are inherently meaningful, and if one is to share their meaning one must attend to the sounds and not only to what the sounds might remind one of in the extraartistic realm outside the music.

At the opposite end of the aesthetic spectrum from the Referentialist is the Absolutist who is also a Formalist. The Absolute Formalist asserts that the meaning of an art work is like no other meaning in all of human experience. Artistic events, such as sounds in music, mean *only themselves:* the meaning is completely and essentially different from anything in the world which is nonmusical:

> ... to appreciate a work of art we need bring with us nothing from life, no knowledge of its ideas and affairs, no familiarity with its emotions. Art transports us from the world of man's activity to a world of aesthetic exaltation. For a moment we are shut off from human interests; our anticipations and memories are arrested; we are lifted above the stream of life.[11]

The experience of art, for the Formalist, is primarily an intellectual one; it is the recognition and appreciation of form for its own sake. This recognition and appreciation, while intellectual in character, is called by Formalists an "emotion"—usually, the "aesthetic emotion." But this so-called "emotion" is a unique one—it has no counterpart in other emotional experiences:

> ... he who contemplates a work of art, inhabit(s) a world with an intense and peculiar significance of its own; that significance is unrelated to the significance of life. In this world the emotions of life find no place. It is a world with emotions of its own.[12]

Formalists do not deny that many art works contain references to the world outside the work. But they insist that all such references are *totally irrelevant* to the art work's meaning:

> ... no one who has a real understanding of the art of painting attaches any importance to what we call the subject of a picture—what is represented ... all depends on *how* it is presented, *nothing* on what. Rembrandt expressed his profoundest feelings just as well when he painted a carcass hanging up in a butcher's shop as when he painted the Crucifixion or his mistress.[13]

In music, since it is capable of being entirely untainted with nonartistic subject matter, the Formalist finds the clearest example of artistic meaning. In a complete reversal of Referentialism, the Formalist claims that "Definite feelings and emotions are unsusceptible of being embodied in music."[14] Instead, "The ideas which a composer expresses are mainly and primarily of a purely musical nature."[15] There is no correspondence

[11] Clive Bell, *Art* (New York: G. P. Putnam's Sons, 1914), p. 25. Quotations reprinted by permission of Putnam's, Professor Quentin Bell and Chatto & Windus Ltd., London.

[12] Ibid., pp. 26, 27.

[13] Roger Fry, *The Artist and Psycho-Analysis*, Hogarth Essays (London: Hogarth Press, 1924), p. 308. Reprinted by permission of Mrs. Pamela Diamand and the Hogarth Press.

[14] Eduard Hanslick, *The Beautiful in Music,* trans. Gustav Cohen (Indianapolis: The Liberal Arts Press, 1957), p. 21. Reprinted by permission of The Liberal Arts Press Division of The Bobbs-Merrill Company.

[15] Ibid., p. 23.

whatsoever between the beauty we find in the nonartistic world and the beauty we find in art, for the beauty in art is a separate kind. This is especially the case in music, in which the nature of the beautiful " . . . is specifically musical. By this we mean that the beautiful is not contingent upon nor in need of any subject introduced from without, but that it consists wholly of sounds artistically combined."[16]

Formalism concentrates so exclusively on the internal qualities of an art work and their inherent excellence of proportion as to deny the existence of extra-artistic meaning and value or at least to deny that they contribute anything of significance to the art work and the experience of it. Perhaps the artistic/cultural influences surrounding the work can be recognized, but these too are insignificant or at least secondary. What matters is the internal exquisiteness of formal relations and the incomparable experience they can give.

A diagram of Formalism would be as follows:

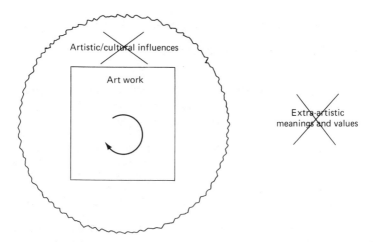

Unfortunately, it is given to few people to be able to enjoy the peculiar, special, esoteric kind of experience which the contemplation of formal relationships offers. According to the Formalist, most people, being inherently incapable of pure artistic enjoyment, satisfy themselves with nonartistic reactions to art works; that is, with reactions to the referents of the works. This completely misses the point of art, of course, but the Formalist assumes that this is to be expected. Given the special nature of the arts and the general insensitivity of most people, we should not be too concerned if the value of art is available on only a limited basis, and we should not have any illusions that most people will ever understand that the real value of art is quite different from what they think it is.

[16]Ibid., p. 47.

The further removed from the events and objects of life, the purer the appeal to the intellect which can apprehend fine distinctions in formal relations, the more exquisite the arrangement of artistic elements, the freer from ordinary emotions not directly dependent on form, the better is the art work and the more uncorrupted is the experience of it. In the rarified realm of pure form, untouched by the homeliness of ordinary life, Formalists find their satisfaction and their delight. They do not expect to find much company there.

FORMALISM IN MUSIC EDUCATION

Pure Formalism, as pure Referentialism, represents an extreme view of the nature and value of art. However, as some beliefs and practices in music education are based on assumptions of Referentialism, many are based on Formalist suppositions. The practice of isolating the formal elements of art works and studying them for their own sake is the counterpart of separating out the referential elements. The study of art as a "discipline," with primary attention given to the accumulation of information or the development of skills, is formalistic in flavor. That the major value of music education is intellectual; that the study of "the fundamentals" is, in and of itself, a beneficial thing; that musical experience consists primarily of using the mind to ferret out all possible tonal relationships; that music or art in general transports one from the real world into the ethereal world of the aesthetic; all these are assumptions compatible with Formalism.

Perhaps the most widespread application of Formalism to music education is the policy of teaching the talented and entertaining the remaining majority. Music education in recent history has focused major effort on developing the musical skills of children with talent, and in this it has achieved a high level of success. And why, after all, should one worry about the general population, which is never going to be musically educated anyhow? As with all special abilities real achievement in music is possible for a few, and these are the ones who can benefit from serious music education. As for music in general education, let it be pleasant, let it be attractive, let it be amusing, but don't expect authentic musical learning to take place. Teachers who care to devote themselves to music education for the masses, whether through missionary zeal or lack of musical ability, are certainly welcome to do so, but they should not expect to be regarded with the same respect as those who are engaged in serious music teaching. It is not surprising, given the pervasiveness of this formalistic view, however subliminal it might be, that music education has achieved so much in the performance program and so much less in the general music program. It is also not surprising that the entire profession has become alarmed over this situation and determined to improve upon it.

STRENGTHS AND WEAKNESSES OF REFERENTIALISM
AND FORMALISM

While Referentialism and Formalism are contradictory in the major aspects of their theories, both contain a measure of truth. One can agree with the Referentialist that art works are affected by their subject matter. One can also agree that art and feelings are intimately connected. Perhaps it is so that art can serve nonartistic ends. But how are these ideas reconciled with the equally convincing ideas that art works can be entirely devoid of subject matter and in any case always transcend subject matter; that reactions to art are not identical to ordinary emotions; that the value of art is inherently artistic rather than nonartistic?

When considering each of these two viewpoints separately it is difficult—perhaps impossible–to give full assent to either. There is no evidence to support the Referentialist's claim that artists or art lovers are better citizens, behave more morally, are more socially adjusted, are healthier, and so on. The use of art as propaganda—no matter whether for good or bad causes—perverts the nature of the artistic impulse. To translate the experience of art into nonartistic terms, whether conceptual or emotional, is to violate the meaningfulness of artistic experience. And to justify the arts in education on the basis of values least characteristic of art is to miss the point of what art really does have to offer.

At the same time it is not possible to regard art, with the Formalist, as an intellectual exercise. Surely art is intimately connected to life rather than totally distinct from it. The sense of significance we get from art is a sense applicable to the significance of human life, and the beauty or truth we find in art has some relation to the beauty or truth of life as lived and known. To assume that art is a fragile thing suitable for some people but irrelevant for most, and that education should reflect this exclusiveness, disregards the power and pervasiveness of art in human life and the obligation of education to share life's goods fully.

So while each view contains some truth, each also contains major falsehoods which prevent their use as a basis for a philosophy. Somehow their contributions to understanding must be preserved while their limitations are overcome.

ABSOLUTE EXPRESSIONISM

This brings us to a third aesthetic theory, Absolute Expressionism, which, it will be argued in this book, does in fact include the elements of truth found in both Referentialism and Formalism. But Expressionism is not in any sense a combination of the other two. It is a distinctive, coherent viewpoint, requiring systematic explanation if its major tenets are to be understood. These tenets, it is believed, will be found to be as widely acceptable by aestheticians, artists, and educators as any available in aesthetic theory. Further, the views of Absolute Expressionism seem to be most suitable to mass education in a democratic society; most true to the nature of art as art is conceived in our times; and most germinal of guidelines for teaching and learning music and the other arts in all aspects of educational programs.

In addition, and most important, this point of view provides a sound basis for the claim that the arts in education are both unique and essential for all children. Referentialism cannot argue for the uniqueness of the arts because its explanation of how art provides meaning applies to any system of signs and symbols that refer to meanings outside themselves, such as, most notably, language. And in Referentialism, the meanings for which works of art are signs or symbols are meanings not in any way peculiar to art: they are available in a great many other ways than only through art. Referentialists would claim that these extra-artistic meanings are essential for all children to share—a claim that is convincing. It is just that you do not need art (as Referentialists understand art) to share them.

Formalists claim that the experience of art is unique—so entirely that nothing else in life need even be connected to it. But in making this argument, and doing so very convincingly, it is forced to separate art from values considered essential for all people. Art becomes, in Formalism, a matter for the artistic elite, and it provides those few a special intellectual pleasure unlikely to be considered essential by any but that chosen few.

Absolute Expressionists disagree with Referentialists on two fundamental issues: (1) where you go to get what art gives and (2) what you get when you go there. While Referentialism insists that you must go outside the work, Absolute Expressionism insists that meaning and value are internal; they are functions of the artistic qualities themselves and how they are organized. But the artistic/cultural influences surrounding a work of art may indeed be strongly involved in the experience the work gives, because they become part of the internal experience for those aware of these influences. And the nonartistic references in a work of art, say, the words in a song, the story in program music, the crucifixion scene in a painting, the political conflicts in a play, and so on, are indeed powerfully influential in what the internal artistic experience can be. However, references are always transformed and transcended by the internal artistic form. The artistic meaning and value is always and essentially above and beyond whatever referents happen to exist in a work (if they happen to exist at all, as they do not in most instrumental music, abstract paintings and dances, and so on). That is why it is possible and quite common for works with trivial referents to be profound, timeless monuments of art—Robert Frost's "Stopping By Woods," Cezanne's paintings of fruit on rumpled table cloths, Beethoven's Pastoral Symphony, and so on. That is why it is also possible and quite common for works with important referents to be trivial or even demeaning as art—dime-store pictures of Jesus painted in day-glo colors on black velvet, love as depicted in "popular romance" novels, and so on. Reference, while influential, is never the point, according to Absolute Expressionism. References are only one part of a larger internal whole, and the experience of the work is always both larger than and different from any of its parts.

Absolute Expressionists agree with Absolute Formalists about where you go in art to get what it gives. Both insist you must go inside to the created qualities that make the work an *art* work. That is the "Absolute" part of both their names. But Expressionists include nonartistic influences and references as one part of the interior while Formalists exclude them.

As to the matter of what you get when you go inside, Expressionists do not agree with Formalists that the experience is an intellectual one— an experience only or primarily linked to the special emotion given by pure form. The "Expressionist" part of the position connects the experience of art with feeling—an idea it will take the remainder of this book to explain.

Here is a diagram of the Absolute Expressionist position:

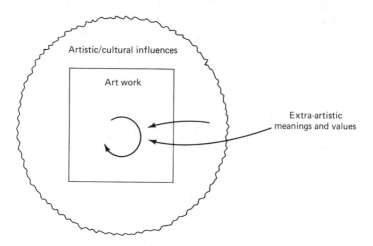

ABSOLUTE EXPRESSIONISM AND THE CLAIM FOR UNIQUENESS AND ESSENTIALITY

The implications of the Absolute Expressionist view will be explained and applied to music education in the remainder of this book. At this point it will be helpful to clarify the major claim this view makes—that the arts offer meaningful, cognitive experiences unavailable in any other way, and that such experiences are necessary for all people if their essential humanness is to be realized. This introductory explanation will provide a point of departure for the more detailed treatments in the following chapters, so that the details can be understood in relation to the larger issues they illuminate.

Let us look first at two activities so absolutely basic to any notion of education that it would be difficult for anyone to question their essentiality: reading and writing. If schools did nothing else, surely they would have to at least do this—to teach children to read and write sufficiently for functionality in the language of their culture. In some cultures in the world the expectation is that most people will achieve little more than "basic literacy," which enables them to read and write at only primitive, undeveloped levels. Those who achieve only this basic literacy are seldom if ever enabled to share fully in the world in which they live. Their capacity for leadership, personal and economic advancement, intellectual enhancement, and cultural enrichment tends to be severely limited by their limitations in these foundational behaviors of language literacy.

In cultures advanced in literacy, such as our own, basic literacy of that sort is so insufficient for any kind of successful quality of life that those instances in which schools must be satisfied with that level are correctly regarded as failures in our social and educational systems. We expect all our people to be able to share equally in the richness of our culture, and it is almost impossible for those to do so who are severely handicapped by only being able to function at the basic level of language literacy.

This is because there is a direct correlation between language and conceptual reasoning, language being the essential mode in which such reasoning takes place. In our society conceptual reasoning is so highly valued that it is usually equated with intelligence, as briefly mentioned in Chapter One. (Chapter Five will deal with this problematic idea in some detail.) So reading and writing, as the basic modes of language literacy, which equals conceptual reasoning ability, which equals level of intelligence, are absolutely fundamental to the entire educational enterprise as that enterprise is conceived in our culture.

How, exactly, do reading and writing improve the ability to reason, to be rational, to be logical, to be intelligent (as these words are commonly understood)? A close look at the inner workings of this process will lead us to the substantive claim to be made in this book about the value of the arts. The following material lays the groundwork for that claim.

* * * * * * * * * * *

Human beings constantly think. Thoughts flood our minds in a never-ending stream or torrent, overlapping, rushing ahead or slowing down, mixing together in countless blends, whirling around then shooting off in different directions. Internal thinking is not, in and of itself, linear and logical in its organization; it is more like a whirlpool in its dynamic disorder.

If we want to "think something through," or "get our thoughts straight," or "get our ideas sorted out" (all these phrases indicate a process of bringing some ordered arrangement into the natural dynamism of inner thinking), we can sit down in a quiet place and "get our head together." So we start to formulate logical, linear, ordered ideas. Unfortunately, as we do, the torrent of thinking continues, with all sorts of related and unrelated ideas flooding in and drowning those we're trying to separate out or interfering with them because they take us away from the particular ideas into a great many other streams of thought going in different directions. And our thoughts tend to evaporate—to disappear into thin air—as soon as we have them and focus on them. The fluid nature of inner thought simply cannot be entirely controlled by the very act of thinking inwardly.

What we need, to go beyond the dynamic flux of inner thinking, is some device to hold on to a thought so it cannot wash away, a means to give it permanent embodiment. We need to objectify it, that is, make it into an object so that it stays as it is. So what can we do? You guessed it: we can write it down.

Now we have done a quite remarkable, even astonishing thing, which, as far as we know, no other living organism on earth is remotely capable of doing. We have transformed an entirely inner process into an outer symbolic system that so closely corresponds to the form and shape and dynamic interrelations that previously existed only inwardly as to seem to us to be identical with what transpired within us. This capacity for symbolic transformation may be the most important distinguishing characteristic of the creature we call human.[17]

The incredible power and utility for conceptual thinking of writing a thought down is not just that we have been enabled, by doing so, to separate it out of the ongoing stream so that it now has been made "objectual" (material, substantive, embodied). We are now enabled, in addition, *to think reflectively about the thought itself.* We can examine the object that captures the thought—the sentence—and decide whether it presents the thought acceptably or poorly. And further, we can, by examining the sentence, *improve the thought itself by improving the sentence.* The act of improving the objectification of the thought—the sentence—actively improves the thought we now have. The outer embodiment and the inner process become inseparable. As we work on the quality of the object, we are also working directly and substantively on the quality of the inner process it objectifies. As our sentence improves, our thinking improves.

---

[17]An early and extremely influential explanation of the process of symbolic transformation is given by Susanne K. Langer, *Philosophy in a New Key* (New York: Mentor Books, 1942).

What constitutes "improvement"? As we ponder a sentence we have written, we may notice that a particular word seems to be weak. It does not quite express the shading of meaning we are seeking. So we try to think of a better word—one that is closer to what we want to capture but have not yet quite succeeded in capturing. We consult our memory and our dictionary or thesaurus for that better word. When we think of it or see it, it leaps out as the discovery we've been searching for. "Ah," we say, "that's better. That's more like it. That says it right." So we change the word. What we have done is to *clarify* the sentence's meaning and thereby clarify the thought we're trying to capture. A thought that is clearer is a thought that has been improved. It is better than the thought in its unclear, muddled state.

Notice that when we write down our thought in a sentence we then *read* the sentence to receive its meaning and to ponder whether that meaning is coming through clearly or whether it needs to be clarified. So writing is also reading: we are constantly and continually reading and rereading each word and sentence we have written. The reading part gives us back the meaning we have written, and we can then, in receiving it, judge whether it is given well. And, of course, we can read and share the thoughts *someone else* has captured who has gone through this identical process. Reading the clarified thought another has written gives us clarified meaning to share.

As we continue to ponder our sentence, we may realize that it is weak in form. It dawns on us that if we were to reorganize it by starting it in a different place and finishing it differently, the meaning would be strengthened. Or perhaps it is a group of sentences that needs to be shifted around. So we make the shifts—we *organize* the sentence or sentences differently and it works (if things are going well for us that day!) The thought or thoughts now have been strengthened. We have given better organization to the sentences bearing the thoughts, and the thoughts themselves are now better organized. Better organized thoughts are improved over those less well organized. And, of course, when we read a complex set of thoughts organized by someone else, we are able to share them as organized thinking.

The act of writing, and improving the writing, and reading the writing of someone else who has done so, *broadens* our thinking. One thought suggests another we could not have thought of until the first was captured. We are often amazed at where our thoughts lead us because we sense that we are discovering new thoughts that previous ones enable us to think of. Thinking that is broader is improved over thinking that is narrow and limited. We are taken by such thinking beyond where we were in our thinking before, whether we have or someone else has written those thoughts.

Writing and reading *deepen* our thinking. We are able to probe beneath the surface of our thoughts by the act of thinking about them more penetratingly, as writing allows us to do. We can stay with a thought, turning it over, examining its implications, getting further into its implied meanings, and finally restating it in a way that captures its depth rather than its surface. And we are taken deeply into thoughts when we read those another writer has succeeded in capturing more deeply.

The same processes allow thoughts to be more *concentrated*—to be rid of extraneous ideas that weaken rather than strengthen the unfolding concepts. Reading and writing *refine* reasoning and *sensitize* reasoning in the same ways.

They also *discipline* thinking. They require the thinker, whether he or she is writing and reading his or her own thoughts or reading those of another, to conform to the veracity of those unfolding thoughts, doing what the words and sentences require to have done as they both create meanings and yield up their meanings. The writer (or reader) cannot just do anything, capriciously, with those thoughts as they develop. They require respect and honesty, and the person dealing with them must be persistent and self-controlled and resolute in guiding their expression or in being guided by another's disciplined expression. And this purposeful, diligent involvement with the ideas *internalizes* them. They become part of the thought structure now characterizing that person's mind.

Here is a summary of the foregoing points, illustrating that writing and reading clarify reasoning, organize reasoning, broaden reasoning, and so on:

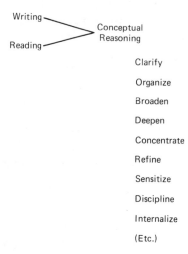

All these qualities of improved conceptual reasoning, and many more that could be mentioned, stem from this process of writing and reading. The higher quality of reasoning is a direct result of a process that enables thoughts to be precise, accurate, detailed, meticulous, subtle, lucid, complex, discriminating, powerful, meaningful. *In this profound sense, writing and reading educate reasoning.*

* * * * * * * * * * * *

With that explanation of reasoning as a background the claim about the value of the arts can now be offered:

Creating art, and experiencing art, do precisely and exactly for feeling what writing and reading do for reasoning.

This claim is made with the full intent that every sentence between the asterisked lines is to apply with as much validity to feeling as it does to reasoning. That section was written precisely to encompass the claim about the relation of art to feeling. Please reread that section, substituting the word feeling (or feels, feelings, subjectivity, affect, and so on) each time a word such as thinks, thoughts, ideas, reasoning, appears. And for terms such as symbol, sentence, word, write, substitute terms such as sounds, colors, melody, dance, painting, poem, and create.

Do this the first time through from the point of view of the composer or painter or poet or choreographer. Do so a second time from the point of view of the performer—musician, dancer, actor. Please do these exercises carefully and thoroughly, because the impact of the argument will then be understood fully.[18]

The summary diagram can now be completed as follows:

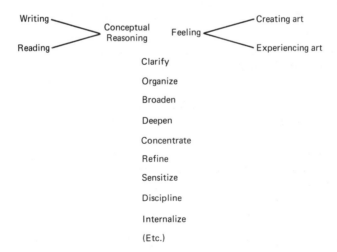

And the last sentence of that section now reads as follows: *In this profound sense, creating art and experiencing art educate feeling.*

The idea that the arts have a special relation to feeling—the Absolute Expressionist position—is pervasive in all cultures. That idea needs to be explained in some detail. The idea that education in the arts is the education of feeling has been pervasive in music education and to some extent

---

[18]My own realization of this exercise is given at the end of this chapter. Compare yours, because different ways of stating the same ideas add to one's understanding of the ideas.

in the other art education fields for several decades. That idea also needs detailed explanation. The argument presented here extends that idea beyond where it has been taken before in the literalness, specificity, and exactitude of its claim. It sounds perfectly reasonable to argue that reasoning can be educated in quality and depth and breadth and that we have the means to do so in education by using the forms of cognition appropriate to conceptual thinking—languages and other symbolic systems. The parallel claim being made here, that subjectivity can be educated in quality and depth and breadth, and that we have the means to do so in education by using the forms of cognition appropriate to the affective realm—the arts, sounds remarkable or even radical. To explain it and apply it with the full power of its potential, we will need to explore each of its major components.

The better we understand the concept of feeling, which is widely misunderstood, the better we will be able to organized our professional efforts to educate it (Chapter Three). We need a clear understanding of how creating art involves and educates feeling (Chapter Four), how feeling can be construed as meaning (Chapter Five), how we experience feelings as properties of objects and events (Chapter Six), the special nature of musical experience (Chapter Seven), and how all these foundational ideas can be brought to fruition in general music programs (Chapter Eight), performance programs (Chapter Nine), and arts programs (Chapter Ten), in ways that enable them to be artistically educative of feeling. For whatever other valuable contributions music and arts education might make to peoples' lives in extra-artistic ways, their unique and essential contribution is to educate feeling as only art, as art, is capable of doing.

This is an application to feeling of the material on pp. 29 to 32 dealing with conceptual reasoning. It is written from the point of view of nonperforming artists - composers, painters, poets and so on. After reading this and comparing it with your own solution, go through it again, changing the appropriate terms to reflect the point of view of performing artists— musicians, dancers, actors.

* * * * * * * * * * *

Human beings constantly feel. Feelings flood our minds and beings in a never-ending stream or torrent, overlapping, rushing ahead or slowing down, mixing together in countless blends, whirling around then shooting off in different directions. Internal feeling—subjectivity or affect—is not, in and of itself, linear and logical in its organization; it is more like a whirlpool in its dynamic structure.

If we want to "feel something through," or "get our feelings straight," or "get our feelings sorted out" (all these phrases indicate a process of bringing some ordered arrangement into the natural dynamism of inner affect), we can sit down in a quiet place and "get ourselves together." So we start to formulate logical, linear, ordered feelings. Unfortunately, as we do, the torrent of feeling continues, with all sorts of related and unrelated feelings flooding in and drowning those we're trying to separate out or interfering with them because they take us away from the particular feelings into a great many other streams of feeling going in different directions. And our feelings tend to evaporate—to disappear into thin air—as soon as we have them and focus on them. The fluid nature of inner feelings simply cannot be entirely controlled by the very act of feeling inwardly.

What we need, to go beyond the dynamic flux of inner subjectivity, is some device to hold on to a feeling so it cannot wash away; a means to give it permanent embodiment. We need to objectify it, that is, make it into an object so that it stays as it is. So what can we do? You guessed it: we can capture it in artistic materials—sounds, colors, gestures of the body, poetic metaphors, shapes, volumes, masses, acted conflicts, and so on.

Now we have done a quite remarkable, even astonishing thing, which, as far as we know, no other living organism on earth is remotely capable of doing. We have transformed an entirely inner process into an outer artistic/symbolic system that so closely corresponds to the form and shape and dynamic interrelations that previously existed only inwardly as to seem to us to be identical with what transpired within us. This capacity for symbolic transformation may be the most important distinguishing characteristic of the creature we call human.

The incredible power and utility for human subjectivity of giving a feeling artistic embodiment, that is, capturing the dynamic flow of feeling in the dynamic flow of a melody, or in the energies in a set of relations among colors, or in the intensities reverberating in a series of poetic images, or in the vitality of a sequence of body movements, and so on, is not just that we have been enabled, by doing so, to separate it out of the ongoing stream so that it has now been made "objectual" (material, substantive, embodied). We are now enabled, in addition, to *feel reflectively about the feeling itself.* We can examine the object that captures the feeling—the melody, the colors, the images, the dance movements—and decide whether it presents the feeling acceptably or poorly. And further, we can, by examining the melody (etc.), *improve the feeling itself by improving the melody.* The act of improving the objectification of the feeling—the melody—actively improves the feeling we now have. The outer embodiment and the inner process become inseparable. As we work on the quality of the object (the artistic materials), we are also working directly and substantively on the quality of the inner process it objectifies. As our melody improves our feeling improves.

What constitutes "improvement"? As we ponder a melody we have composed, we may notice that a particular tone or phrase seems to be weak. It does not quite express the shading of feeling we are seeking. So we try to think of a better tone or arrangement of tones—one that is closer to what we want to capture but have not yet quite succeeded in capturing. We consult our creative imagination and our storehouse of previous experiences with melodies for that better phrase. When we hear it, it leaps out as the discovery we've been searching for. "Ah," we say, "that's better. That's more like it. That sounds right." So we change the tones. What we have done is to *clarify* the melody's dynamic form and thereby clarify the feeling we're trying to capture. A feeling that is clearer is a feeling that has been improved. It is better than the feeling in its unclear, muddled state.

Notice that when we compose our feelings into a set of tones as in a melodic phrase we then *hear* the phrase to receive its affect and to ponder whether that affect is coming through clearly or whether it needs to be clarified. So composing is also experiencing through hearing: we are constantly and continually hearing and rehearing each tone and phrase we have composed. The hearing or experiencing or responding part gives us back the feeling we have composed, and we can then, in feeling it, judge whether it is given well. And, of course, we can experience and share the feelings *someone else* has captured who has gone through this identical process. Experiencing the clarified feelings another has composed gives us clarified subjectivity to share.

As we continue to ponder—to reexperience reflectively—our phrase or melody, we may realize that it is weak in form. It dawns on us that if we were to reorganize it by starting it in a different place and finishing it differently the affect would be strengthened. Or perhaps it is a group of phrases or melodies that needs to be shifted around. So we make the shifts—we *organize* the phrases or melodies differently and it works. The dynamic interplay of feeling has now been strengthened. We have given better organization to the phrases or melodies bearing the dynamics of feeling and the interplay of feelings themselves are now better organized. Better organized feelings are improved over those less well organized. And, of course, when we experience a complex set of structured feelings organized by someone else we are able to share them as an organized, composed feelingful experience.

The act of creating with artistic materials and improving what is being created, and experiencing the creation of someone else who has done so, *broadens* our feelingful experience. One creative act—one aesthetic decision—suggests another we could not have envisioned until the first was captured. We are often amazed at where our creative acts lead us because we sense that we are discovering totally new ways of feeling that previous ones enable us to experience. Feelingful experience that is broader is improved over such experience that is narrow and limited. We are taken, by such experiences, beyond where we were in our subjective possibilities before, whether we have or someone else has created those expanded expressive forms.

Creating art and experiencing art *deepen* our subjectivity. We are able to probe beneath the surface of our feelings by the act of experiencing them more penetratingly, as artistic creation allows us to do. We can stay with a feeling, turning it over, examining its implications, getting further into its implied affects, and finally reforming it in a way that captures its depth rather than its surface. And we are taken deeply into feelings when we experience those another artist has succeeded in capturing more deeply.

The same processes allow affective experiences to be more *concentrated*—to be rid of extraneous impulses that weaken rather than strengthen the unfolding expressive form. Experiencing art and creating art *refine* feeling and *sensitize* feeling in the same ways.

They also *discipline* our subjectivities. They require the one who is experiencing art, whether he or she is creating and experiencing his or her own developing feelings or sharing the created artistic form of another, to conform to the veracity of those unfolding dynamic structures, doing what the artistic materials require to have done as they both create the conditions of feeling and yield up their embodied feelings. The artist (or perceiver of art) cannot just do anything, capriciously, with those affective events as they develop. They require respect and honesty, and the person dealing with them must be persistent and self-controlled and resolute in guiding their expression or in being guided by another's disciplined artistic expression. And this purposeful, diligent involvement of the self with the feelings *internalizes* them. They become part of the inner subjective structure now characterizing that person's selfhood.

All these qualities of improved subjectivity, and many more that could be mentioned, stem from this process of creating and experiencing art. The higher quality of affective experience is a direct result of a process that enables feelings to be precise, accurate, detailed, meticulous, subtle, lucid, complex, discriminating, powerful, meaningful. In this profound sense, creating art and experiencing art educate feeling.

* * * * * * * * * * *

SUPPLEMENTARY READINGS

General writings on aesthetics. Each gives an overview of topics and ideas.

1. Beardsley, Monroe C. *Aesthetics.* University: University of Alabama Press, 1977.

2. Dickie, George. *Aesthetics: An Introduction.* Indianapolis: Pegasus, 1971.

3. Hofstadter, Albert and Kuhns, Richard, eds. *Philosophies of Art and Beauty: Selected Readings in Aesthetics from Plato to Heidegger.* Chicago: University of Chicago Press, 1976.

4. Kennick, W.E., ed. *Art and Philosophy: Readings in Aesthetics*. Second Edition. New York: St. Martin, 1979.

5. Margolis, Joseph. *Philosophy Looks at the Arts: Contemporary Readings in Aesthetics*. Philadelphia: Temple University Press, 1987.

6. Philipson, Morris and Gudel, Paul, eds. *Aesthetics Today: Selected Readings*. Magnolia, MA: Peter Smith, 1986.

7. Rader, Melvin, ed. *A Modern Book of Esthetics*. Fifth Edition. New York: H. Holt, 1979.

8. Sparshott, Francis, *The Theory of the Arts*. Princeton: Princeton University Press, 1982.

The following books are classic examples of the three basic aesthetic positions.

Referentialism

9. Cooke, Deryck. *The Language of Music*. London: Oxford University Press, 1959.

10. Tolstoy, Leo N. *What Is Art?* trans. Aylmer Maude. Indianapolis: The Liberal Arts Press, 1960.

Formalism

11. Bell, Clive. *Art*. New York: G. P. Putnam's Sons, 1914.

12. Hanslick, Eduard. *The Beautiful in Music*, trans. Gustav Cohen. Indianapolis: The Liberal Arts Press, 1957.

Expressionism

13. Meyer, Leonard B. *Emotion and Meaning in Music*. Chicago: University of Chicago Press, 1956, pp. 1–6. The first section of Meyer's book presents the three views and his intentions in exploring them.

Supplementary readings on Expressionism will be given for the next five chapters.

Art
and feeling

3

Throughout history the appeal of art has ben recognized to be wider than purely intellectual. The "emotions," the "feelings," the "affections," the "passions" have all been assumed to be a necessary part of art and sometimes are assumed to be the most important part of art. But what do these words signify? Is all art "emotional"? At one extreme some works seem to be very emotional—even violently so—but at the opposite extreme are many works that are cool and calculated, and in between there seems to be an infinite gradation of levels of emotionality. Can all art works on that broad continuum be related to feeling? Questions such as these are among the most perplexing in the entire realm of aesthetics and many people both inside and outside the arts professions will confess their confusion about them. For arts educators, it is essential that some clear answers be developed so that instruction can enhance peoples' affective experiences of art in ways that are germane to the nature of art.

REFERENTIALISM AND FORMALISM ON EMOTION IN ART

The positions taken by Referentialists and Formalists as to the relation of art to emotion are clear even though contradictory. For the Referentialist the emotions of art are the same as the emotions of life. The artist captures his or her emotion in the art work. The art work transmits the captured emotion to the perceiver. To the extent that an artist's emotion is a positive one and to the extent that he or she can infect other people with it through the intermediary of his or her art work, the artist is good, the art work is good, and the effect on the perceiver is good.

If one were a teacher of art, one would select good art works, that is, art works which transmit good emotions, and do everything one could to ensure that one's students felt the particular emotion the art work contained. If the teacher is effective in smoothing the way from the artist to the art work to the student, so that a minimum of emotional ambiguity creeps in, the teacher is successful in his job, or at least in this important aspect of his job.

What would the teacher actually have to do to be successful? First, he would have to decide which emotion is being presented. Clues could come from the circumstances of the artist's life at the time he created the work, from the title of the work if the artist or someone else was considerate enough to attach a helpful title to it, and from the references to emotion contained in the work. If none of these sources prove helpful, the teacher must make an "interpretation"—an educated guess, so to speak. He then helps his students go through the same process, by discussing the artist's life and what he may have felt when he made the work, what the title signifies, what the subject matter in the work suggests as to a likely emotion, and, finally, by encouraging interpretations if, as is unfortunately often the case, the emotion proves elusive. Once identifying the emotion in question or at the very least the *possible* emotion in question, the teacher can then focus the students' attention on the emotion to clarify its meaning and value in life.

Absolutists disagree with all of this, and Formalists would probably disagree violently. In fact, Formalism was primarily a reaction against the excesses of a late nineteenth century romanticism which indulged in fanciful, emotionalized interpretations of art works. To counter what they considered an unconscionable overemphasis on art's referential content, Formalists insisted on the purely artistic nature of art, even to the point of denying the possibility of any connection between art and emotion. It is not surprising that excesses on the side of "purity" occurred to balance out the excesses of referential "impurity." It is also not surprising that when one looks closely at the writings of most Formalists, one finds that a recognition of art's connection with feeling does in fact exist, but with feeling as an artistic component rather than a nonartistic component of art works (5).

There is no particular problem in understanding these extreme positions about art and emotion that art deals with emotion nonartistically or that art deals with emotion not at all. And the educational implications of each are clear. One either teaches referentially, as described, or one dismisses any concern with feelingful reactions to art, concentrating one's teaching on the purely formal components of art in as intellectually rigorous a fashion as one can devise. But neither position is convincing, artistically or educationally. The experiences most people have with art testify to the existence of feeling but feeling as somehow different from the emotions outside art. And to teach either by externalizing emotion from the artistic context in which it arises, or by ignoring the existence of feeling, seems to miss the point of art's peculiar emotional appeal. How can the existence of feeling in art be explained without recourse to the extremes of Referentialism or of Formalism, and how can instruction take advantage of the particular kind of affective involvement art provides?

IS MUSIC A LANGUAGE OF THE EMOTIONS?

A look at several common notions about art and emotion will help us answer these questions. The first and perhaps most widely believed is the idea that art—music specifically—is a "language of the emotions." This idea, of course, guides Deryck Cooke's discussion and also Tolstoy's. Every Referentialist view includes a language—like conception of how music functions. According to such a view the essential element of anything which can be called a language is present in music. This essential element is a *vocabulary*. A vocabulary is a collection of symbols, each one of which has an agreed upon reference, and which can be combined in various ways to produce more complex references. Words as used in conventional ways are symbols. Numbers, sounds such as the dots and dashes of Morse code, movements or positions such as semaphore code, graphs of various kinds used in scientific reports, picturizations such as hieroglyphics, systems of lines and dots such as musical notation—all these and many more are symbol systems, or symbolisms, made of vocabularies, constituting languages.

According to the Referentialist, musical sounds are conventional symbols in that they have meanings which can be agreed upon and which can be translated into other symbols such as words. The meaning of musical sounds, then, can be stated in words. (Of course musical sounds can also be translated into notation, but no one, Referentialists included, considers the notation the meaning of the sounds.) The question is, can musical sounds be considered to have the same kind of meanings which any language has, that is, meanings which can be specified in a dictionary and translated into equivalent symbols? Can Cooke's translations—a minor second designates "spiritless anguish," a major seventh designates "violent longing,"—be taken as a dictionary which contains the meanings of music?

The answer given by Absolutism, whether of the Formalist or Expressionist type, is "No." It is precisely in its "untranslatability"—its difference from language—that the unique value of music or any art exists:

> If all meanings could be adequately expressed by words, the arts of painting and music would not exist. There are values and meanings that can be expressed only by immediately visible and audible qualities, and to ask what they mean in the sense of something that can be put into words is to deny their distinctive existence.[1]

Conventional symbols certainly do exist in the arts. Bird calls in music, flowers or fruit in painting, political opinions in literature, bodies in sculpture, all are symbols in the conventional sense of having designated references. The Referentialist contends that *everything* in art is of this symbolic, language-like nature. The Formalist denies that the existence of symbols has anything whatever to do with the artistic meaning of an art work. The Expressionist recognizes that a symbol in an art work contributes to the art work's expressiveness, *but only in so far as the symbol becomes immersed in the artistic qualities of the work.* To the extent that a symbol remains a symbol in the conventional sense (in which sense a symbol is also a "sign" or a "signal") its meaning is meaning in the usual sense. Such meaning, however, is not in and of itself artistic.

These ideas can now be clarified in regard to emotion. If a piece of music designates a particular emotion, say, grief, as portrayed in a Baroque melodic formula or in a silent movie piano accompaniment to a particularly heart-rending event, the Referentialist would maintain that grief is the emotional meaning of the music. He would also maintain that *all* good music has such emotional designation; that is, all good music is a language of emotion. A major criterion of goodness, for the Referentialist, is the music's degree of effectiveness as a language for emotions—as a symbol system or sign system of emotion.

The Formalist would say that the melodic grief formula, either in the Baroque work or the "pit piano" piece, may indeed be a symbol of grief, but that this symbol contributes nothing to the musical emotion the work arouses. If the formal properties of the music are excellently constructed and presented the piece will be good whether or not an emotion symbol happens to be present.

The Expressionist assumes that so long as the grief formula is distinct from the musical qualities of the piece which contains it and is regarded as a distinct entity—as a bit of language—it is not yet musical in expressiveness. If, however, the formula, along with its designation, becomes an integral part of the sounds which are expressive *as sounds*, so that it loses its identity as a symbol while at the same time it contributes to the total affect of the piece, then the formula becomes part of the artistic content of the music. As salt adds flavor to a stew, losing its character as grains of salt but adding a particular flavor to the stew, the symbol must

---

[1]John Dewey, *Art as Experience* (New York: Capricorn Books, 1958), p. 74. Reprinted by permission of Capricorn Books.

be dissolved in the musical sounds, losing its character as a symbol but adding its symbol flavor to the total piece.

If a piece of music happens to contain an emotion symbol (most pieces do not), the music is good to the extent that the symbol becomes dissolved in expressive sounds which are *themselves* good.[2] So long as music remains at the level of language it is nonmusical. So long as responses to music are responses to emotional designations, the responses are nonmusical. So long as teaching gives the impression that emotion symbols, when they are present, are the emotional meanings of music, or that music devoid of symbols (as most music is) can be translated into emotion words, the teaching is nonmusical.

Music, then, is not in any sense a language. It is not a nonverbal language such as numbers or musical notation or "body language" or Morse code or many other examples of true nonverbal languages. It is also not an "indefinite language." That idea implies that music tries to be language but is only able to succeed minimally while "real" languages succeed fully. So music becomes a kind of failed language, like words used so poorly that their meanings are vague. The fact is, music and all the arts are not vague or indefinite at all. They are exquisitely precise in doing what they do, which is to capture and display the dynamics of feeling in meticulous, specific, exacting detail. They can do this because they operate in a realm of objectification and cognition not at all dependent on the two needs of language: (1) designative symbols, (2) arranged in logical, discursive order.[3] As we shall see in Chapter Five, the fact that the arts deal in a non-language mode of mentality is the basis for their power to do what language is incapable of doing. (The arts that use language as a primary medium—poetry, fiction, theater—always go beyond language in the ordinary sense, so they, too, are examples of how art functions rather than how language functions.[4])

IS MUSIC A MEANS OF SELF-EXPRESSION?

Another common idea about the relation of music and emotion is that music is an "expression of emotion." According to this idea, the composer uses sounds as a symptom of her emotional condition at the time she is composing. The sounds are a "working off" of her emotions, serving a purpose

[2]Chapter Seven discusses the means by which sounds become musically expressive.

[3]For a more detailed discussion of the differences between language systems and works of art, see the author's "Language or Non-Language Models of Aesthetic Stimuli," *Journal of Aesthetic Education*, 11, no. 3 (July 1977).

[4]An excellent explanation of how poetry uses language as a medium to achieve artistic ends beyond language is found in John Ciardi and Miller Williams, *How Does a Poem Mean* (Boston: Houghton Mifflin, 1959).

similar to slamming doors or pounding her pillow or slapping her forehead. To the degree that the composed sounds embody the emotion the composer is feeling, they are successful as music.

To be really effective as an expression of emotion, or as "self expression," one's behavior must be physical, overt, intimately connected to the emotion one is having at the moment. Jumping for joy, wringing one's hands in sorrow, shaking with fear, screaming in terror, sobbing with grief, beaming with happiness, all are effective expressions of emotion. They constitute, in fact, as exact a "language of emotions" as we are likely to ever have. Each physical act is a symbol of an emotion, and together they form an emotional vocabulary. None of them, it should be noted, requires any sort of artistic form. They are spontaneous, unselfconscious, uncontrolled in form. If a person's behavior seems rehearsed, self-conscious, controlled in its form, we suspect very strongly that the expression of emotion is not genuine—that the person is just "going through the motions."

If an artist were really expressing the way he felt at the moment of creation, his work could hardly be artistic. It would lack the organization of artistic qualities, expressive *in themselves,* which must be present if an art work is to be distinguishable from an emotional symptom. The better a particular behavior is as an expression of emotion, the less likely it is to contain formed artistic qualities which are themselves expressive. The creation of expressive qualities requires, in addition to intense involvement, a "working out" process which comes from controlled thought, and such thought is foreign to emotional discharge:

> . . . an inner agitation that is discharged at once in a laugh or cry, passes away with its utterance. To discharge is to get rid of, to dismiss; to express is to stay by, to carry forward in development, to work out to completion. A gush of tears may bring relief, a spasm of destruction may give outlet to inward rage. But where there is no administration of objective conditions, no shaping of materials in the interest of embodying the excitement, there is no expression. What is sometimes called an act of self-expression might better be termed one of self-exposure; it discloses character—or lack of character—to others. In itself, it is only a spewing forth.[5]

Whether a creative musician is a composer or a performer, the more his music is "self-expression," the less it can be musically expressive. Consider, for example, jazz, much of which contains as high a level of immediate involvement as any style of music. When the jazz performer's personal involvement is transformed into musical materials which are expressive *as music*, the effect can be very powerful artistically. As soon as musical quality disappears, so that the trumpet's shrieks are shrieks pure and simple, adding nothing to the musical expressiveness of the piece, the performance has become nonmusical. It may be moving, or perhaps embarrassing, depending on one's reaction to witnessing another person

[5]Dewey, *Art as Experience*, pp. 61, 62.

giving vent to her emotions, but it is not musically expressive. The performer in the concert hall whose interpretation approaches self-expression is particularly painful to regard, for we do not go to a concert to be onlookers of emotional self-expression, either of a composer or of a performer:

> Now, I believe the expression of feeling in a work of art—the function that makes the work an expressive form—is not symptomatic at all. An artist working on a tragedy need not be in personal despair or violent upheaval; nobody, indeed, could work in such a state of mind. His mind would be occupied with the causes of his emotional upset. Self-expression does not require composition and lucidity; a screaming baby gives his feeling far more release than any musician, but we don't go into a concert hall to hear a baby scream; in fact, if that baby is brought in we are likely to go out. We don't want self-expression.[6]

If music consisted of self-expression understood as giving vent to what one is feeling at a particular moment, education in music would be quite irrelevant. Why would one have to learn scales, for example, or how to distinguish a dotted rhythm pattern from a triplet, or what a modulation is, or how to correct the pitch of a sharp tone, or what sonata-allegro form is, or the appropriate accompaniment instruments for a folk song, or anything else for that matter, none of these things having anything whatsoever to do with the natural, instinctive capacity all humans are born with to express their emotions? And this is not just to belabor the obvious, because the widespread idea that music and the arts are merely means for emotional expression has a negative effect on how the arts are regarded in education. After all, if the arts are ways to express emotion, which anyone can do automatically at any time anyway, why should we care much about their presence and why should we think that they are a subject requiring serious, ongoing, structured study as do those subjects which educate our intelligence? To a large extent the devalued condition of the arts in education stems from the misconception that they deal with emotional expression and therefore have no genuine cognitive status. When arts educators contribute to that misconception, they undermine the very foundation they exist to strengthen. It is precisely because the arts can do what emotional expression cannot do that they are to be treasured and fostered in every person's education.

FEELING AS EVERYTHING THAT CAN BE FELT

Having dismissed the conceptions of music as a language of emotion and as an expression of emotion, the next logical and necessary step can be taken toward an understanding of music's expressive power, that is, to dis-

---

[6]Reprinted with the permission of Charles Scribner's Sons from *Problems of Art*, p. 25, by Susanne K. Langer. Copyright © 1957 Susanne K. Langer.

miss the conception of music as dealing with emotion at all. This is not in any sense to adopt the Formalist view of music as an intellectual exercise; rather it is to use words very carefully to help us distinguish subtle but important differences between expressiveness which is artistic and that which is not.

All of human experience is permeated with subjective responsiveness. Far from being little computers on legs, humans are creatures whose every act and every thought, from birth to death, is suffused with feeling. Feeling is part of human life as air is part of human bodies; it is as difficult to conceive human life without feeling as without air. (In science fiction stories and movies, humanlike creatures are always betrayed as being nonhumans by their lack of the essential human quality—feeling. And when creatures who look unhuman turn out to have feelings, we are always able to establish an empathetic relationship with them.) Much of what we know about our world—of what our world seems to us to be like—we know about by feeling about it. Our feelings are not just added on to our human existence as a separate element overlaying our physical or intellectual being; feeling saturates everything we are and do and is inseparable from everything we are and do. The nature of the human condition is very largely a nature of organisms that have the capacity to feel and are aware that they are feeling.

Let us call the feelingful aspect of human life "subjectivity"—the element in human reality of affective responsiveness. Human subjectivity is endlessly varied and infinitely complex. Its possibilities are inexhaustible, both in breadth and in depth. And subjectivity is part of all human experience: there is nothing that is real for human experience without the involvement of subjectivity.

In the vast realm of human subjectivity there is a section in which a few guideposts exist, marking off large areas of feeling which are somewhat related to one another or which share a particular, subtle shading. These guideposts, which are little more than occasional buoys in an ocean of subjective responses, have been given names. One of them, for example, is called "love." Love is a category word, and what it categorizes is an infinite number of possible ways to feel, these ways being somewhat related to one another. The breadth and depth of feeling which falls under the category love is so large and complex, so subtle and varied, that the word used as a category for it can only indicate its most general character. Even if one qualifies the word by adding others—parental love, romantic love, puppy love, platonic love—one is only adding a few more buoys to the ocean, each one of which is surrounded by a huge expanse of water. Parental love is another category word for another limitless domain of possible feelings. In fact, trying to narrow down feeling by using more descriptive category words has the opposite effect: each new category calls attention to a whole new realm of possibilities of feeling.

Another factor makes the realm of human subjectivity infinite in complexity and scope. This is the compound nature of human feeling. Think of the possibilities of feeling categorized by the word hate. Surely, as the history of humankind shows, these must be infinite. Now think of the possibilities of fear. Again, an infinite realm of feeling. But are these two categories really separate? Is there not a great deal of fear in hate? Could we not add a few more category-words to flavor the pot? How about envy and suspicion? Each word categorizes a huge realm of possibilities of feeling, and each overlaps and fuses with the others. Our affective experiences are seldom if ever discrete; instead, our feelings mingle and blend in countless, inseparable mixtures which the words of language cannot begin to describe because they are inherently not designed to do so.

Still another characteristic of subjectivity makes it unable to be captured by words—its fluidity. We do not feel in a static, unchanging way. At every moment our feelings are in motion, developing, changing, waxing and waning, gathering energy to a peak, then fading to quietude. As our feelings move continually, just as life itself moves on in continuous energy from moment to moment, they are constantly shifting in their mixtures, so that it is impossible to say at any single point, "Well, now I am feeling 62 percent happiness, 12 percent joy, and 26 percent anticipation." Our feelings are better envisioned as the surging waters underneath the buoys that have been given names, the waters mingling, moving, deep in some places (so deep we are not sure how far down our feelings might take us), shallow in others. Feelings are dynamic and organic, as are the forces of life itself.

For purposes of clarity let us agree to call all the possible category words (every buoy floating on the turbulent ocean) "emotions." And let us call what takes place in our actual subjective experience (the dynamic waters themselves) "feelings." Feelings themselves—experienced subjectivities—are incapable of being named, for every time we produce a name we are only producing a category, a buoy reminding us that underneath it lies a vast realm of possible ways to feel.

So the difference between emotion and feeling is a real one—it is the difference between words and experiences, the one being only a symbol (or sign) of certain possibilities in the other:

> Save nominally, there is no such thing as *the* emotion of fear, hate, love. The unique, unduplicated character of experienced events and situations impregnates the emotion that is evoked. Were it the function of speech to reproduce that to which it refers, we could never speak of fear, but only of fear-of-this-particular-oncoming-automobile, with all its specifications of time and place, or fear-under-specified-circumstances-of-drawing-a-wrong-conclusion from just-such-and-such-data. A lifetime would be too short to reproduce in words a single emotion [feeling].[7]

[7]Dewey, *Art as Experience*, p. 67.

Human experience is always accompanied by feeling, but our ability to stipulate what is being felt is bound by the extreme limitations of category words, which are incapable of pinpointing the immense complexity and fluidity of subjective responsiveness:

> We are given to thinking of emotions as things as simple and compact as are the words by which we name them. Joy, sorrow, hope, fear, anger, curiosity, are treated as if each in itself were a sort of entity that enters full-made upon the scene, an entity that may last a long time or a short time, but whose duration, whose growth and career, is irrelevant to its nature. In fact emotions are qualities, when they are significant, of a complex experience that moves and changes . . . . Experience is emotional [feelingful] but there are no separate things called emotions in it.[8]

Music can present a sense of human feeling because music is, in Dewey's words, "a complex experience that moves and changes." When attention is paid to the unchanging or constant aspect of music, a particular emotional shading can sometimes be identified which characterizes a piece. This particular identifiable emotional quality is usually called "mood":

> Because music flows through time, listeners and critics have generally been unable to pinpoint the particular musical process which evoked the affective response which they describe. They have been prone, therefore, to characterize a whole passage, section, or composition. In such cases the response must have been made to those elements of the musical organization which tend to be constant, e.g., tempo, general range, dynamic level, instrumentation, and texture. What these elements characterize are those aspects of mental life which are also relatively stable and persistent, namely, moods and associations, rather than the changing and developing affective responses [feelings] with which this study is concerned.[9]

There is no doubt that music can designate moods just as it can designate other things. But as with all designation in art the thing designated must enter into the artistic components of the work if it is to contribute to the artistic affect of the work. So long as mood remains the object of attention, isolated from the musical events in the work as a whole, the response has not yet become musical.

As we have seen, emotion words and mood words are merely reminders of general types of subjective experiences, the experiences themselves being complex, dynamic mixtures for which no words can exist. But the ocean of human feeling is far broader than that area of it in which the buoy categories called emotions or moods exist. One of the major misconceptions about the nature of feeling is to think that it is limited to the emo-

---

[8]Ibid., pp. 41–42.

[9]Leonard B. Meyer, *Emotion and Meaning in Music* (Chicago: University of Chicago Press, 1956), p. 7. Other typical statements about the distinction between emotion (or mood) and feeling are (8, p. 22), (9, p. 8), (4, p. 372).

tions, or even to the kaleidoscopic mixtures of emotions we have been discussing so far.

In fact our subjective lives are infinitely more vast than what the terms emotion and mood suggest. For we experience all of life as having a felt quality. As conscious beings, aware of ourselves in the world, we are always experiencing ourselves as involved with that world; that is, we are "sentient". Consciousness itself is affective: we know ourselves as live creatures because *we feel ourselves living.* Most of our self-knowing— our awareness of ourselves undergoing life—is not "emotional" at all. It is our mental sensation, our sensibility, our primal awareness of the vital, ongoing processes of life that we share as long as we are alive.

Because the word feeling has so often been assumed to be limited to the emotions, the use of the word feeling in connection with art has often been assumed to mean that all art must be emotional and that our experience of art can only be emotional. But that would be a very limited concept of the relation of art and feeling; it is not the concept being suggested here. It probably would be very helpful if a term other than feeling could be used to designate the enormous breadth of human subjectivity that includes but goes far beyond the emotions—"affect," perhaps, or "vital energy," or "sensibility." The word feeling will continue to be used in this book as the major term for human subjective experiencing, despite the propensity of people to conceive it far too narrowly, because its power and utility are too great to give up, at least until a clearly better alternative presents itself. So when the word feeling is used, please remember that it refers to the concept articulated in the following quote:

> The word "feeling" must be taken here in its broadest sense, meaning *everything that can be felt,* from physical sensation, pain and comfort, excitement and repose, to the most complex emotions, intellectual tensions, or the steady feeling-tones of a conscious human life.[10]

THE ARTS AND EVERYTHING THAT CAN BE FELT

If the only means available to humans to help them explore their subjective nature was ordinary language—whether words or some other type of designative system—a major part of human reality would be forever closed off to our conscious development. The subjective part of reality—the way life feels as it is lived—cannot be clarified or refined in our experience

---

[10]Susanne K. Langer, *Problems of Art* (New York: Charles Scribner's Sons, 1957), p. 15. Italics Langer's. This book is a veritable thesaurus of terms indicating the breadth of meaning of the word feeling. Langer's monumental attempt to explain the nature of human feeling as being the essential quality of human mentality is her three-volume work, *Mind: An Essay on Human Feeling* (Baltimore: Johns Hopkins University Press, 1967, 1972, 1982).

through the use of ordinary language. This is not because no one has taken the time to think up enough words to name all possible ways of feeling; it is because the nature of feeling is ineffable in essence.

Because ordinary language cannot be used to help us explore the complexities of feeling, it would seem at first thought that subjectivity is not capable of being educated, that it must remain in the dim, nether world between the conscious and unconscious. This is not the case, however. Humans *can* actively discover more about the nature of feeling; they *can* grow in their comprehension of the breadth and depth of human subjectivity. In so far as people succeed in doing so, the quality of their lives will be affected by the quality of their self-understanding. They will have deepened their ability to experience a major—perhaps *the* major—aspect of the human condition: subjective responsiveness.

The arts are the means by which humans can actively explore and experience the unbounded richness of human subjective possibilities.

How does art do this? Three components of the art process must be explained to show how art serves its special function of making the subjective comprehensible. These are (1) the creation of an art work, (2) the way an art work presents a sense of feeling, and (3) the experience of an art work. The next three chapters are devoted to these topics. For the present, the implications of the view of art as expressive of the life of feeling can be made explicit.

Art works do not tell us about feeling the way psychology does. That is, art works do not "conceptualize about" feeling. Instead, their intrinsic qualities present conditions which can arouse feeling. In the direct apprehension of these qualities we receive an "experience of" feeling rather than "information about" feeling. And this "experience of" is the particular, unique way that the arts provide insight into the nature of feeling. The arts are the most powerful tool we have for refining and deepening our experiences of feeling:

> Because the forms of human feeling are much more congruent with musical forms than with the forms of language, music can reveal the nature of feelings with a detail and truth that language cannot approach.[11]

Every art "reveals the nature of feelings" in its own, particular way, and the major function of every work of art is to do precisely that. It would not be possible to make this assertion if the word feelings were interpreted in a narrow sense, as emotion or as a shading of emotion called mood. The many new departures in contemporary art, for example, are not in any sense negating or denying human feeling; they are, instead, opening up

---

[11]Susanne K. Langer, *Philosophy in a New Key* (New York: Mentor Books, 1942), p. 191. Reprinted by permission of Harvard University Press.

whole new dimensions of responsiveness for exploration and under-standing. Far from being antihuman, as so often asserted by its critics, con-temporary art is showing, perhaps more dramatically and abundantly than ever before, the staggering potential for responsiveness of which the human organism seems capable. In this sense, new departures in art, *when successful,* expand the possibilities of human self-understanding by presenting new experiences of the seemingly limitless realm of subjec-tivity.

Every good work of art, no matter when it was made and no matter how it was made, is good because its artistic qualities succeed in captur-ing a sense of human feeling. The depth of feeling presented by a work of art can range from the most superficial to the most profound. Any success at all in capturing and presenting a sense of expressiveness, that is, of feel-ing, is artistic success to that degree. If a particular piece of music is genuinely expressive—if it presents in its musical qualities a sense of feel-ing—it is a good piece of music. A simple song which is lovely (by which is generally meant that the song is expressive) is a good piece of music. The deeper the sense of feeling captured by a piece of music, the more profound its expressiveness and the more powerful its presentation of insights into subjectivity, the better is the work. At some point along the scale of good-ness a work can be called great. Of course no simple number scale can be applied to the differences in quality between art works, but the combined judgments of sensitive people can serve as a rough guide to the level of goodness of particular works, ranging from good to great. If no sense of feeling is presented by the work, it can be called either bad art or nonart. (This idea will be developed further in Chapter Seven.)

Notice that no stipulation whatsoever is being made about what *kind* of feeling a work should present. Goodness is not a function of kinds of ex-pressiveness, in which there are good feelings or bad feelings. The entire realm of human experience is open to exploration and understanding through art. People often limit their experiences of art to a particular kind and to a particular level of goodness. But no such limitations can be placed on art itself, which is as limitless as is human responsiveness itself.

The Absolute Expressionist position suggests that the formed qualities in a work of art embody a set of dynamic interrelationships. These vital energies, including and influenced by any implications from the cul-tural environment presented by the work, are similar in quality to the felt quality inherent in all human experience. When one shares the expressive qualities contained in a work's artistic content, one is also sharing in the qualities of which all human experience is made. The relation between the qualities of the art work and the qualities of human experience is felt by the perceiver of the work as "significance." To the degree that an art work contains qualities which are convincing, vital, and profound, and to the de-gree that these qualities can be experienced by the perceiver, the significance of the experience—the relation of the artistic qualities to the qualities of life—will be convincing, vital, profound. The residue of sharing the significant artistic qualities of the art work is a deeper sense of the nature of human life as sentient.

Many words have been used in aesthetics to explain this notion. The following is a summary of the more common ones:

Art:

is expressive of	subjectivity
is analogous to	subjective reality
is isomorphic with	the quality of experience
corresponds to	the emotive life
is a counterpart of	the patterns of feeling
has the same patterns as	the life of feeling
is a semblance of	sentience
gives images of	the depth of existence
gives insights into	the human personality
gives experience of	the realm of affect
gives understanding of	the patterns of consciousness
gives revelations of	the significance of experience
brings to consciousness	the vitality of experience
makes conceivable	the dynamics of felt life

All these terms convey the same sense, that the experience of art is related to the experience of life at the deepest levels of life's significance. This is what the poet Robert Frost meant when he said "Poetry [art] is a way of taking life by the throat."

One can share the insights of art not by going outside of art to non-artistic references *but by going deeper into the intrinsic qualities the art work contains.* It is in the artistic content of the art work that insights can be found, and the deeper the experience of the artistic qualities, the deeper can be the sense of significance gained. If the experience of art is to be significant for life, the experience of art must be artistic experience, generally called "aesthetic experience." (Chapter Six will discuss its specific characteristics.)

What is the value of such experience? First, if any experience in human life can be valued intrinsically—for the sheer, sweet sake of the experience itself and our unique capacity to be aware that we can experience our aliveness—then surely artistic experience is of this sort. In this sense, to ask what the value of such experience might be is like asking what the value of the experience of love might be. To experience love is to be profoundly what we as humans are capable of being. That is a value requiring no other to justify or explain it. It is the same with artistic experiencing, which raises to the highest possible levels our capacity to experience for the sheer sake of being experiencing creatures. To require other justifications is, in a way, to demean the very nature of the human condition.

But in another sense we can reflect about the value of artistic experiencing as a major way to fulfill our capacities for richness and depth in our lives. Because experiences of art yield insights into human subjectivity the arts may be conceived as a means of self-understanding, a way by which our sense of our human nature can be explored and clarified and grasped. Among the many writers who have reflected about the human need to understand our own nature, and the value of such self-understanding, are John Dewey, who termed the value "self-unification"; Leonard B. Meyer, "individualization"; Abraham H. Maslow, "self-actualization"; Paul Tillich, "integration of the personality"; and many others. All attempt to signify the humanizing value of self-knowledge. There are few if any values deeper than this. And the arts are, or are among, the most effective means known to us to realize this value.

MUSIC EDUCATION AND FEELING

The major function of art is to make objective and therefore accessible the subjective realm of human responsiveness. Art does this by capturing and presenting in its intrinsic qualities the patterns and forms of human feeling. The major function of education in the arts is to help people gain access to the experiences of feeling contained in the artistic qualities of things. Education in the arts, then, can be regarded as the education of feeling (7, p. 8).

The major function of music education is the same as that of all the arts in education. One way of stating this function (others will be suggested in succeeding chapters) is that music education is the education of human feeling through the development of responsiveness to the intrinsically expressive qualities of sound. The deepest value of music education is the same as the deepest value of all the arts in education: the enrichment of the quality of people's lives through enriching their experiences of human feeling.

How would one teach music in order to realize its deepest value?

Several principles suggest themselves. First, the music used in music education at all levels and in all activities should be good music, which means genuinely expressive music. Because of the belief that only certain *kinds* of expressiveness are good, music education has tended to use music which is generally "polite"; which is safe, bland, sweet, well behaved, these qualities reflecting the values of most educators. But if music education is to widen people's understanding of the possibilities of human responsiveness, a more open, more freewheeling, more adventuresome attitude needs to be taken toward "proper" musical materials. Music of the many ethnic and cultural groups in American society, music of the past and much more music of the present, music of various types—jazz, rock, folk, as well as concert—all should be considered proper sources for finding expressive music.

Second, opportunities must constantly be provided for the expressive power of music to be felt. This means that the experience of the work as a unified thing must come first and last. If the expressive quality of music is the most valuable part of music and if this is the part which is to be made accessible to learners through the efforts of teachers, then music's expressiveness should not be obscured by methods which concentrate so exclusively on its details that total its impact is seldom if ever experienced.

Third, the most important role of music education is to help students become progressively more sensitive to the elements of music which contain the conditions which can yield experiences of feeling. These elements—the musical qualities of melody, harmony, rhythm, tone color, texture, form—are objective; they are identifiable, nameable, capable of being manipulated, created, discussed, isolated, reinserted into context. There is nothing mystical about musical events and how they give rise to a sense of significance. While the affective response to the elements of music is indeed ineffable, the elements which can arouse the response are not. They are the teacher's stock in trade, constituting the basic materials for teaching and learning at every level and in every activity.

Finally, the language used by teachers should be appropriate for their purpose, which is to illuminate the expressive content of music. An appropriate language is one which is descriptive and never interpretive. Words must be chosen carefully for their power to call attention to the events in music which present the conditions for feeling. But words should never stipulate what that feeling should be. Only one thing can properly cause feelingful responses to music: the sounds of the music themselves. Words which attempt to influence feeling inevitably intrude themselves between the music and the perceiver, preventing the music itself from working its own power. No one has a right to place himself between music and people—least of all the music educator.

These principles are the most germinal of the many which can be drawn from the position that music education should be primarily the education of feeling. They will be repeated briefly after the next three chapters, each time viewed in the light of that chapter's particular concern. Chapters Eight and Nine will apply them to the music education program, showing them in operation as guides to effective education in music. Chapter Ten will apply them in the context of a total arts program.

SUPPLEMENTARY READINGS

1. Baensch, Otto. "Art and Feeling." In Susanne K. Langer, ed., *Reflections on Art,* pp. 10–36. New York: Oxford University Press, 1961. Probably the clearest statement of the view that art objectifies the subjective.

2. Best, David. *Feeling and Reason in the Arts.* Boston: Allen and Unwin, 1985.

3. Dewey, John. *Art as Experience.* New York: Capricorn Books, 1958, pp. 58–70. Other sections of Dewey's classic book on aesthetics will be listed after following chapters.

4. Ducasse, Curt J. "The Aesthetic Feelings." In Eliseo Vivas and Murray Krieger, eds., *The Problems of Aesthetics,* New York: Holt, Rinehart and Winston, 1965. pp. 368–76.

5. Fry, Roger. "Pure and Impure Art." In Melvin Rader, ed., *A Modern Book of Esthetics,* pp. 304–09. New York: Holt, Rinehart and Winston, 1962. This is an excellent example of the recognition by a supposed Formalist of the feelingful nature of art as defined in the present book.

6. Hospers, John, ed. *Artistic Expression.* New York: Irvington, 1971.

7. Langer, Susanne K. "The Cultural Importance of the Arts." In Michael F. Andrews, ed., *Aesthetic Form and Education,* pp. 1–8. Syracuse, NY: Syracuse University Press, 1958. An accessible but profound explanation of aesthetic education as the education of feeling.

8. Langer, Susanne K. *Problems of Art.* New York: Charles Scribner's Sons, 1957, Chapter 2, "Expressiveness," pp. 13–26. Other chapters of this useful book will be listed as appropriate.

9. Meyer, Leonard B. *Emotion and Meaning in Music.* Chicago: University of Chicago Press, 1956, pp. 6–22. Meyer further develops, in this section, his view on the relation of art and affect.

Creating art

4

ART AS THE BEARER OF EXPRESSIVE
(OR ARTISTIC OR AESTHETIC) QUALITIES

Much of the world in which humans live can be regarded for its intrinsically expressive, or aesthetic, qualities, whether or not it was intended for that purpose. All of nature can be regarded aesthetically. Things made by people, such as machines, which are intended to serve other than expressive purposes, can also be regarded aesthetically. A work of art is a thing made by a person, and its primary purpose is to be regarded for the expressive qualities it contains. The work may serve many other important functions: it may earn a living for the person who made it, it may be part of a social ceremony, it may provide pleasant personal contacts for people engaged in its production, it may be a good financial investment, and so on. But the peculiar thing about a work of art—the characteristic which makes it different from things in nature or other things made by people is that the expressive qualities it captures and presents can be regarded as the major reason for its being. When art is regarded as art, rather than as social or political commentary, as an item of trade, as a means to any nonartistic ends, it is as a bearer of expressive or artistic or aesthetic quality that it exists in the first place.

The interest of this book is in art as art and in the value of art for people through education. While it is obvious that art also serves nonartistic ends, it is with art's artistic or expressive function that education in the arts should be concerned. This point of view leads to the question of how, precisely, the expressive qualities in a work of art are created. If education in the arts is to sensitize people to the expressive conditions created in works of art, and develop their capacities to create art themselves, it is important for those who teach the arts to have a clear understanding of how the process of artistic creation works.

Several notions about artistic creation have already been discussed. It was maintained, for example, that art is not "self-expression" or "expression of emotion." This means that the process of artistic creation is not a process of releasing emotional energy by making something which is a symptom of how one happens to be feeling at a particular moment. The process of creation is not, therefore, a "working off," but is, instead, a "working out." But how does one "work out" expressive qualities so that they are captured into something called a work of art?

ARTISTIC CREATION CONTRASTED
WITH COMMUNICATION

A helpful way to approach this question is by contrasting the process of communication and the process of artistic creation. In the difference between these two processes lies the unique power of artistic creation to capture a sense of the patterns of subjectivity—a power not available in the process of communication. Mixtures of the two processes will be discussed after an explanation of how each works as a separate phenomenon.

Several conditions must exist in order to call a process "communication." First, the communicator (say, a person), must select from all possible messages a particular message which is to be transmitted. The message may be some information, an opinion, an emotion, a command, and so on.

The message is then encoded into a signal[1]—words, dots and dashes, bodily movements, numbers, and so on—which transmit the message to a receiver (say, another person). The receiver then changes the signal, or "decodes" the signal back into the message (the signal "please close the door" is decoded into a message about a desired action). All this may happen instantaneously as in normal discourse, or it may be a prolonged process as in the writing of a book. In the latter case, the author selects a

---

[1]A signal is what we have previously called a conventional symbol. Discussions of the communication process commonly use the more technical terms "signal" or "sign." All these words will be discussed in more detail in the next chapter.

particular set of facts, opinions, assertions, and so on, and encodes them into words which are transmitted by means of ink and paper. The reader decodes the inkmarks on the paper back into words which give him the author's message.

For communication to be successful, a minimum of interference should be involved between the communicator's message and the receiver's understanding of it. Interference may occur at every step along the way. For example, the communicator could choose a poor signal for his message. Instead of saying "please close the door," which is the message he wants to transmit, he might say "no one ever cares about privacy around here." The receiver may indeed get the message that the door should be closed, but a great many other possible decodings could take place instead. Because of the ambiguity involved we could say that poor communication is taking place.

Another opportunity for interference in the communication process arises in the "decoding" phase. A guest in a foreign country, being left in his hotel room by a bell-hop, may say "please close the door." The bell-hop cannot decode the signal because he does not understand English. He looks puzzled, trying to figure out what message is being transmitted. Again, poor communication is taking place.

If communication is to be *good* communication, the communicator must begin with a clear idea of what is to be transmitted; he must translate the message into signals which exactly represent his message; and the signals must be decoded in just the right way by the receiver. If all these things happen the message will have gotten from the communicator to the receiver intact. Good communication will have taken place.

Here is a diagram of the process of communication:

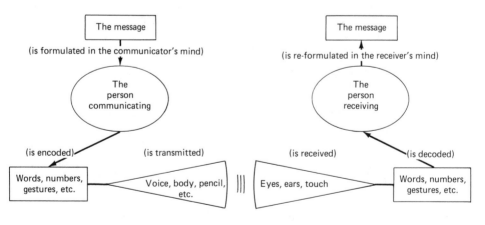

Nothing about the process just described applies to the process of artistic creation.

The first important difference between communication and the creation of art is that the artist does not begin with a message. What starts the process of creation is an "impulse," often in the form of an artistic idea such as a melody or a combination of words or a set of contrasting colors. Whatever the initial impulse, it is not a formulated message—conceptual or emotional—which then is encoded into a signal. Instead, it is a tentative motion—a sense of possibility—a germinal idea which seems to have the power to grow. The act of artistic creation lies precisely in the growth process, and this process is radically and fundamentally different from the process of choosing proper signals to transmit a preexistent message. In fact, to the extent that an artist follows the communication process rather than the creation process his work will turn out to be nonartistic: "music that is invented while the composer's mind is fixed on what is to be expressed is apt not to be music. It is a limited idiom, like an artificial language, only even less successful."[2]

The growth process which is the essential characteristic of artistic creation is a process of *exploration*. It is a searching out and discovering of expressiveness. The exploration into feeling takes place through an exploration of the expressive possibilities of the medium in which the artist is working. There is no way for an artist to explore the realm of feeling except through exploring the feelingful qualities of things—words, sounds, colors, shapes, movements, acts. Artistic creation explores and forms the feelingful qualities of a particular medium. And this exploring-forming process is in no way, shape, or form a process of encoding messages:

> Creation in the fine arts is, no doubt, not a process in which an idea springs forth in the artist's mind, to be mechanically worked out in some material; it involves feeling out the possibilities inherent in the stone or the pigments.[3]

Two typical statements by composers apply this notion directly to musical creation. Aaron Copland says,

> Every composer begins with a musical idea—a *musical* idea, you understand, not a mental, literary, or extramusical idea.... The idea itself may come in various forms. It may come as a melody...or...as a melody with accompaniment...or, on the other hand, the theme may take the form of a purely rhythmic idea....Now, the composer has the idea. He has a number of them in his book, and he examines them in more or less the way that you, the listener, would examine them if you looked at them. He wants to know what he has.... Every composer keeps in mind the possible metamorphoses of his succession of notes. First he tries to find its essential nature, and then he tries to find

[2]Susanne K. Langer, *Philosophy in a New Key* (New York: Mentor Books, 1942), p. 195.
[3]Monroe C. Beardsley, *Aesthetics* (New York: Harcourt Brace, 1958), p. 33.

what might be done with it—how that essential nature may momentarily be changed.[4]

Compare this statement by Roger Sessions:

The process of execution is first of all that of listening inwardly to the music as it shapes itself; of allowing the music to grow; of following both inspiration and conception wherever they may lead. A phrase, a motif, a rhythm, even a chord, may contain within itself, in the composer's imagination, the energy which produces movement. It will lead the composer on, through the force of its own momentum or tension, to other phrases, other motifs, other chords.[5]

Another musician, not as sophisticated as Copland or Sessions but no less insightful, who also describes this process of interaction, was Sidney Bechet, the famous Dixieland jazz clarinetist. Bechet called himself a "musicianer." He said (in an informal interview),

A man, he gets into all sorts of things in a life; things that he can't be sure what they are till he gets them thought about. A musicianer, he's like that. All sorts of things happen to him and he don't know what all it was till he gets it into the music. That's where you find out. You tell it to the music, and the music, it tells it to you.

Still another description of the way an artist and his materials are interdependent is given in an interview with the playwright Harold Pinter, who discusses writing his play Betrayal (later made into a movie). Betrayal begins after a love affair has already ended, and each successive scene takes us back in time. The final scene of the play shows the first meeting of the two people who were to become lovers. (The interviewer is Mel Gussow, for *The New York Times*, December 30, 1979.)

GUSSOW: *What was the initial image for BETRAYAL?*
PINTER: Two people at a pub...meeting after some time.
GUSSOW: *A man and a woman?*
PINTER: Yes, yes.
GUSSOW: *Did you know who they were?*
PINTER: No, truly didn't. Found out. (Pause) I remember when I wrote *No Man's Land*, I was in a taxi one night coming back from somewhere and suddenly a line, a few words came into mind. I had no pencil. I got back to the house and wrote those lines down. I can't remember

[4]Aaron Copland, *What to Listen for in Music* (New York: McGraw-Hill, 1957), pp.23–25. With permission of McGraw-Hill Book Company, Inc.

[5]Roger Sessions, "The Composer and His Message," in Brewster Ghiselin, ed., *The Creative Process* (New York: The New American Library, 1955), pp. 45–49. Copyright Princeton University Press, 1941.

exactly what they were, but it was the very beginning of the play, and I didn't know who said them.

GUSSOW: *With BETRAYAL did you actually see two people sitting in a pub or was it an imagined event?*

PINTER: No! God knows what it was! I mean you often see two people sitting in a pub.

GUSSOW: *Yes, but you don't often write plays about two people sitting in a pub.*

PINTER: No, I didn't see a particular couple, but I see people in pubs all the time. All the time. I spend quite a lot of time in pubs, and I never carry a notebook around with me. I'm really at my happiest, I think, sitting in a pub in England, or a pleasant bar in New York, of which there seem to be fewer than I remembered. I don't eavesdrop. It's much more a visual thing.

GUSSOW: *When did you decide to go backward in time instead of forward as usual?*

PINTER: After I found out what they were talking about. They were talking about the past. So, I thought I'd better go back there.

GUSSOW: *In OLD TIMES, you stayed right in the present. You didn't show us what happened. You talked about what might have happened.*

PINTER: In this case, when I realized the implications of the play, I knew there was only one way to go and that was backwards. The structure of the play seemed to dictate itself. When I realized what was going on, this movement in time, I was very excited by it.

These examples (hundreds more are available) illustrate that in the process of discovery which constitutes the act of artistic creation, the artist himself is introduced to new possibilities of feeling. His own understanding of subjectivity is expanded and deepened through his work:

> As the painter places pigment upon the canvas, or imagines it placed there, his ideas and feelings are also ordered. As the writer composes in his medium of words what he wants to say, his idea takes on for himself perceptible form...the physical process develops imagination, while imagination is conceived in terms of concrete material.[6]

How, exactly, does an artist discover feeling as she creates? As soon as the artist does something imaginative—moves her brush on the canvas, writes a poetic phrase, sketches the beginning of a melody—she immediately takes the position of a respondent or perceiver or audience to her own act. She immediately *undergoes*, in feeling and critical judgment, the effect of what she has done. "Is it OK?" "Does it work?" "Does it feel right?" "Does it go where it seems to need to go?" And, as an essential component of this subjective/critical response, "What does this lead me to do next?" So as the artist works on the material, the material immediately *works on the artist*, and the artist, with her sensitivity and imagination

---

[6]John Dewey, *Art as Experience* (New York: Capricorn Books, 1958), p. 75.

and craftsmanship, responds and decides and carries the act forward. An intimate, reciprocal relationship is established between artist and material. The art work grows and develops through the guidance of the artist's sensitivity to the feelings she recognizes, and imagination of their further potentials, and craftsmanly shaping of the material in which the expressive encounter is being embodied.

A diagram of the artistic creation process would look like this:

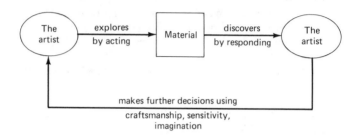

It is clear, then, that the communication process, which consists of choosing unambiguous signals (symbols) to carry a preexistent message, is quite different from the process of artistic creation, which consists of an exploration of the expressiveness of a particular medium. Communication tries to get a message from the sender to the receiver as directly as possible with as little interference as possible from the thing (the signal) which carries the message. The signal (words, noises, gestures, etc.) is of interest only insofar as it transmits the message. The expressive or artistic qualities of the signal are quite beside the point for communication. In fact, if the transmitting medium is too interesting in and of itself, it can only get in the way of good communication.

The diagram of artistic creation indicates the reciprocal effect of the artist and his medium. The artist works on the medium and the medium works on the artist. This ongoing interchange is precisely the condition which allows for exploration to take place. In the quality, intensity and profundity of the interchange lie the conditions for the quality, intensity, and profundity of the thing created out of it. If the artist's involvement with his medium as he explores its expressive potentials is of high quality—sensitive and skillful and imaginative; if his involvement is intense—strong and keen and vivid; and if it is a profound involvement, calling into play the artist's deepest sense of the nature of feeling; the product—the art work—is likely to be of high quality, intense expressiveness, profound insightfulness. The thing created contains its quality and intensity and profundity *because of the interaction* between artist and medium. This is far removed from the communication function of signals chosen to carry a message with a minimum of interference.

The process of artistic creation explained and diagrammed here is called "communication" by some writers about art. These writers (John Dewey and Leonard B. Meyer, among others) are very well aware of the distinction between actual communication and artistic creation, of course, but choose to continue to use the word communication as descriptive of the particular kind of creativity which takes place in the art process. Readers must exercise their own judgment about the gains and losses in using a word with a commonly accepted meaning to describe a process which is not at all like what the word is commonly taken to mean. Because of the importance of the distinction between actual communication and artistic creation for techniques of teaching art, the word communication will be avoided in this book. It is also suggested that teachers of art avoid the word communication in their teaching because of the inevitable confusion it arouses. Students of every age have some notion of what communication is or should be and very naturally expect art to comply when art is described as communication. It is no wonder, therefore, that so many people seek in art for what is not there—communicated messages—and are confused and disappointed when they do not find them. Arts educators can help dispel this confusion and help people look for what *is* in art, by judicious use of words which at the very least do not confuse the issue. Langer's statement in this regard about music is equally applicable to all the arts and should be taken seriously by all teachers of the arts: "Not communication but insight is the gift of music; in very naive phrase, a knowledge of 'how feelings go.'"[7]

ARTISTIC CREATION CONTRASTED WITH MAKING
AND DOING NONARTISTIC THINGS

Artistic creation is different in degree from "making." The difference between making something (say, a bookcase) and creating a work of art is that in the process of artistic creation the involvement with the medium is essentially for the purpose of exploring and capturing its expressive potential. Any nonexpressive concerns are quite peripheral. In making a bookcase the essential concern is its functional character while any expressive qualities it displays are peripheral. If the bookcase shows a high degree of concern with its appearance as an expressive object, we begin to call it a "creation," acknowledging that its purely artistic qualities are an important component. Similarly, if a so-called nonfunctional thing (say, a song) is very weak in artistic quality but strong in nonartistic concerns, such as the "clean, fresh taste" of the cigarette it extols, we hesitate to call the song a creation but are likely to regard it as being as manufactured as the

[7]Langer, *Philosophy in a New Key*, p. 198.

product it is serving. If the song is so interesting artistically that people forget the product in their enjoyment of the purely musical qualities of the commercial (a rather unlikely occurrence), the song-writer could justifiably be accused of being "too creative."

Between the two poles of purely artistic creation and purely utilitarian making are many points where things contain both qualities. A well-designed automobile should be a delight for the eye as well as a safe, efficient means of transportation. A well-designed couch should provide visual enjoyment in addition to being a comfortable place to sit. A piece of utilitarian writing—a newspaper editorial, for example—is essentially communication, but can also contain a great deal of artistry in its use of words.

If we move a little further along the line between pure utility and pure expressive quality, we eventually come to a point where we call a thing a work of art even if at the same time it has a utilitarian function or a communicative function. A novel (say, Hemingway's *The Sun Also Rises*) is a work of art, but it also, secondarily, communicates. A piece of program music (say, Berlioz' *Symphonie fantastique*) is a work of art, while at the same time it communicates some specific, nonartistic information.

On this continuum from pure works of art having no possible function except to be expressive (a Mozart symphony) to pure nonart having no expressive qualities whatsoever (an automobile carburetor), where does one draw the line between art and nonart? How much utilitarian or nonexpressive or nonartistic function can a thing or activity have and still be regarded as art? Or, to put it the other way, how much artistic quality must a utilitarian thing or activity have for it no longer to be regarded as primarily utilitarian?

Unfortunately there is no simple measuring device for categorizing things as art or nonart. Judgments must be made. The key to the making of useful distinctions in this situation is *the degree to which artistic decision making determined the final result.* As the discussion of artistic creation suggested, artistic decisions are those which are made to carry forward the process of exploring and discovering the expressive potentials of some materials. An artistic decision is a decision about expressiveness—about the intrinsic qualities of an object or event that can potentially cause a feelingful response. *The basic thing an artist does is to make artistic decisions in the act of creation.*

This idea can be applied usefully in a variety of situations. An architect is an artist who makes decisions about the expressive qualities (visual, spatial) of buildings. She must make a great many decisions in addition to artistic ones, but she is an artist to the degree that she is responsible for making artistic decisions. But the builder who then carries out the architect's plans is not an artist. The bricklayer building the wall of a building cannot (or *better* not) start making artistic decisions ("I'm supposed to make a straight wall, but wouldn't it look lovely if I just made a few curves in it?"). The bricklayer may have highly developed skills, but they are not used for artistic decision making. We can call him an "artisan" but not an artist.

Sculptors who create large-scale works often employ fabricators to build them. These are also highly skilled people, but they make no artistic decisions so we do not call them artists. Similarly for workers who make multiple editions of an artist's print, or carpenters who build stage sets, or printers who set poems, or welders who put together the frames of pianos. They are all connected to the artistic enterprise, but they are not artists because they do no create artistically; that is, they do not primarily make artistic decisions.

PERFORMERS AS CREATIVE ARTISTS

What about performing musicians, conductors, dancers, actors, scene designers, movie directors, costumers, lighting directors, and so forth? These people are indeed artists for precisely the reason that they must and do make creative, artistic decisions. They all work with artistic materials already created by someone (composer, choreographer, playwright, etc.) but not yet fully actualized. The performing arts require a second level of creative involvement—exploring and discovering expressive potentials in the yet-to-be-finished work of art and bringing those potentials to fruition in the performance of it. The diagram of artistic creation earlier applies equally to the performing artist except that the material in which expressiveness is being explored and discovered is a work of art ready to be actualized. The performer explores a potential in the material (plays the first measures, recites the first lines, etc.), discovers possibilities by responding to what she has done, decides how to carry it forward using her craftsmanship, sensitivity, and imagination. The "carrying forward" of the creative act is the making of artistic decisions. *That* is why performers are artists.

Many other people who do things or make things are called artists or call themselves artists even though artistic decision making is entirely absent or largely absent from what they do. The words "art" or "artist" are applied inappropriately, according to the mistaken ideas that (1) anything that requires skill must be art or (2) things done inexactly or despite limited knowledge must be art. Examples of the first sort are the "art" of golf or football or plumbing or accounting or installing floorboards or driving a truck or cleaning a house and on and on. People seem to love to call what they do "art": it probably makes them feel a bit special or more glamorous. But these instances and hundreds of others that do indeed require skill do not in any way depend primarily on that unique interaction with material in which the essential characteristic is the making of decisions about intrinsic expressive qualities. There may be some artistic quality attached to the action (a nice, smooth golf stroke; a graceful pass reception), but those qualities are not the necessary, fundamental point of the entire endeavor, as they are in art.

Similarly for the second sort of activity claimed to be art. Ironically (and painfully for those devoted to art), the notion seems to be that the more bewildered one is about what one is doing, the more "artful" the activity must be. When doctors don't know what is going on in a medical situation, they are likely to say "Well, medicine is an art as well as a science, after all." Teaching is mistakenly called an art for largely the same misguided reason: "We have to make so many decisions out of sheer intuition." Such activities do require intuition—a leap beyond the information available—but the point is that doctors do not make decisions on the basis of intrinsic expressive qualities: ("You've taken so many blue pills, maybe we should add a bit of red and yellow." "Wouldn't the incision look nicer if it was curved around and then swept upward?"). Neither do teachers, except, of course, when they are aesthetic educators actually creating a work of art, in which case they are both artists *and* teachers: "Listen to that crescendo again, woodwinds. How soon should it reach its peak? Do we need to hold back a bit at the beginning of it?" (artist). "Kids, you've been working real hard. Everybody stand up and move around to get the kinks out" (teacher).

Some activities seem to straddle the midpoint between art and nonart because artistic decision making is one of the major factors but not the only major factor. Ice skating is a sport, but it becomes art when expressive movement is a dominant or major factor in what is being decided. Some gymnastic events require an artistic presentation of the required moves and are judged for the intrinsic beauty of the organization as well as the correctness and skill of specific maneuvers. Cooking sometimes is guided as much by the visual beauty of presentation as by nutritional or economic factors. In those and many other cases, the principle that art exists when artistic decisions are *the* major point or at least *a* major point can be a useful guideline for clearer discriminations.

ARTISTIC SHARING AND COMMUNITY

As an artist "works out" the expressive possibilities of his medium, he is at once embodying his understanding about the nature of feeling and exploring new possibilities of feeling. The thing he creates contains his insights into subjectivity, capturing both what he brought as a person to the act of creation and what he discovered during that particular act of creation. The art work, then, contains the artist's insights as they exist up to and including that particular work.

The perceiver of the work, upon experiencing its expressive qualities (Chapter Six discusses the characteristics of aesthetic experience), both *shares* the artist's subjectivity captured in the work's expressive qualities and *explores* new possibilities of feeling opened to him by the work's exploratory nature. So the experience of the work is both a sharing and a discovering. In this sense it is also a *creative* experience for the perceiver, in that new experiences of feeling are made possible as he grasps more and more of the work's expressive subtleties.

But note that the "sharing" which takes place between the artist and the perceiver is not in any sense an outcome of *communication* between the artist and the perceiver. The art work is not a signal of a message being transmitted by its creator. If one regards an art work as a bit of code it would be proper to ask the artist what he intends to communicate by means of that code. The artist, of course, did not intend to communicate at all or he would not have made an art work. Instead, he would have chosen some proper signal to transmit his message clearly and unambiguously. If regarded solely as communication a complex work of art can only be judged a complete flop. It lacks everything good communication ought to have. This is why many people become very annoyed with an art work when they cannot figure out what "message" it might be transmitting. They are likely to ask, about a complex poem, for example, "Why doesn't the poet just come right out and say what he means?" The fact that the poet might have labored long and hard to get the poem to be just what it turned out to be, and that it would have been a simple matter for the poet to state a message if that was his intention, escapes anyone who goes to a work of art expecting to find communication.

What takes place between the artist and the perceiver, then, is not communication but "sharing." The sharing occurs by means of the art work, which contains an embodiment of feeling, this embodiment capable of giving rise to feeling on the part of the perceiver. The perceiver's feelings cannot be precisely those of the creator. In the first place the creator has not made a simple statement of an emotion but a complex set of expressive qualities capable of giving rise to many and varied feelings. In the second place the creator is one person and the perceiver is another. Each will respond differently to the expressive qualities created or perceived in the work by virtue of their different lives. At the same time, each will share a sense of significant human feeling by virtue of their sharing of the common human condition.[8]

It is precisely in this sharing of feelings common to the nature of humanity that art exercises its communal effects. There is no more powerful way for humans to explore, embody, and share their sense of the significance of human life than through the making and experiencing of art.

[8]Compare Dewey, *Art as Experience*, p. 54.

When the act of creation has taken the artist deep into the nature of human affect, when the perceiver similarly but individually shares the sense of human subjectivity embodied in the art work, both creator and perceiver have been carried below the surface differences and divisions of daily life to a point where the common humanity of people can be glimpsed and felt:

> The secret of artistic creation and the effectiveness of art is to be found in a return to the state of *participation mystique*—to that level of experience at which it is man who lives, and not the individual, and at which the weal or woe of the single human being does not count, but only human existence. This is why every great work of art is objective and impersonal, but none the less profoundly moves us each and all.[9]

The power of art to cut through the surface of life and to give a sense of life's depths makes art our most effective tool for deepening the experiences of people into their shared nature. "In the end, works of art are the only media of complete and unhindered communication [sharing] between man and man that can occur in a world full of gulfs and walls that limit community of experience."[10] This sharing is, in essence, socializing, for it allows people to know—through actual experiencing rather than through preachments—about the common sentient condition of humans.

If education is to have positive social effects, it can do so more effectively through art than through any other means. For art education to provide a sense of community with other humans, it must be primarily *aesthetic* education. That is, education in the arts must help people share the insights contained in the artistic qualities of art works, for that is where the insights into shared human subjectivity lie. The insights are available in the work of art itself, and the function of education in the arts is to make those insights available by showing people where and how to find them. One does not find them by asking their creator what he was trying to communicate. One finds them *by going deeper into the artistic qualities of the created work.* It is "inside" art that we find our deepest sense of community, as we feel deeply and empathize with others who also feel. The social nature of music activities, involving people in a common endeavor, is surely socializing also, but literally hundreds of equally social activities exist: we don't need music or art for that, pleasant as it is. The communal function of the arts is far more profound than as a group activity—it is the evidence art gives of our being in community because we all share the human condition of subjectivity.

[9]Carl G. Jung, *Modern Man in Search of a Soul* (New York: Harcourt Brace, 1933), p. 195.

[10]Dewey, *Art as Experience*, p. 105.

STUDENTS AS CREATIVE ARTISTS

The reason for emphasizing the idea that artistic decision making is necessary for art to exist is its educational implication. *When students are being involved in creating art, they must be involved in making artistic decisions.* It is precisely because they are *not* so involved in many instances of music making that such instances are inherently noncreative. When performance group directors or classroom teachers are directing the music making of students but make all the decisions *for* them ("Trumpets, play those two measures louder," "Sing the beginning of the song with shorter notes," "Altos, you're getting that rhythm mixed up; do it like this," "Hold that trill longer, then fade out," and on and on forever), those *directors* are creating, but their students are surely not. The students have been forced to be artisans, used for making art but permitted no involvement in artistic creation. The noncreative nature of much that passes for arts education stems directly from the denial of the artistic decision making function to those who need to experience it most—young people who need to feel what it is to be artistically creative. That teachers of art often neglect such experiences or prevent them is among the most serious flaws of arts education in the schools. And it may well be that music education, because of its heavy emphasis on performances directed by teachers, is the most seriously deficient of all the arts in the level of opportunity afforded youngsters to be genuinely creative. This point will be expanded later and in subsequent chapters.

MUSIC EDUCATION AND ARTISTIC CREATION

It has been suggested that the major function of education in the arts is to promote the fullest possible sharing of the conditions of human subjectivity as they are embodied in the artistic qualities of things. In light of the discussion of artistic creation in this chapter, that suggestion takes on an additional dimension in its implications for music education. Music education should help people share as fully as possible in the created expressive qualities of pieces of music, so they can experience the explorations and discoveries of feeling captured in those pieces. Music education should also involve people in the creation of music to the fullest extent possible, to experience their own explorations and discoveries of feeling through the act of creation.

How can music education provide these opportunities? The four principles articulated at the end of the previous chapter can supply the answer.

First, the musical compositions chosen for study, at all levels and in all aspects of the program, should be rich with expressive potential. Not every piece will be or need be at the masterpiece level of musical excellence and profundity; such pieces will always be exceptional. But every piece to be experienced should be marked by the qualities that testify to the presence of genuine musical creativity: craftsmanship in its construction, sensitivity in its expressive impact, imagination in its freshness, authenticity to its own musical demands and to the style of which it is an example. These qualities of excellence exist in the simplest as well as the most complex compositions, and in every period of music and every style of music. So there is little if any excuse to involve students in musical experiences that are deficient in potential for richness in expressive sharing.

In this sharing the experience of the expressive values of the music must be first and foremost, with the process of systematic study being the *means* to such experience rather than ends in and of themselves. This suggests that teaching-learning episodes be balanced between wholes (an entire piece or larger section experienced in its totality) and parts (study of details as they relate to the larger whole). The piece of music will not be experienced more accurately and therefore more richly if its artistic details are not better grasped, so study is essential. One cannot simply play or sing or listen to a piece as a whole, over and over, and expect to get very far into its complexities. But in the work on details—performing, analyzing, conceptualizing, evaluating—a sense of the larger whole to which they add should pervade the effort, so that the details can be perceived in their larger function. Good rehearsals, good classes, and good lessons are good because progress has been made both in understanding pieces in their total impact and in mastery of the technical-musical details that contribute to that impact. A good teacher knows how to balance the overall experience with the "digging in." That requires real musicianship, excellent teaching craft, sensitivity to the students at that age level and at that particular moment in time, and imagination to keep the episode lively and rewarding. There are few if any teaching challenges more demanding than this.

The second principle enabling music education to be effective in bringing people closer to the creative nature of music is that students must be presented many opportunities for being musically creative. There are three basic ways this can occur. The first is often not included among creative activities with music; that is, listening. It is sometimes assumed that listening is passive, requiring no real action on the part of the listener; listening as part of music education is often referred to as "merely listening." This is a complete misconception of what takes place in musical experiencing, which, when it is not used as a sedative ("Put your heads down on your arms, children, and take a little nap while I play some nice music"), is among the most demanding mental-emotional tasks the human species is capable of. In musical listening the perceiver actively and creatively engages himself or herself in the expressive unfolding of the work, "For to perceive, a beholder must *create* his own experience."[11] Since the major interaction most people have with music is as listeners, the task of help-

[11]Dewey, *Art as Experience*, p. 54.

ing them become creative in this most fundamental of musical behaviors is perhaps the most important in all of music education. This idea will be expanded in the following chapters, especially Chapter Eight.

The second way that people can experience music creatively is through composing. While some progress has been made in recent years toward effective methods of involving students in musical composition, this aspect of music education, along with teaching for creative listening, remains a major piece of unfinished business for the profession. Because we have done relatively little with composition as compared with performance, we are often and quite justifiably criticized by our visual art education colleagues as being an inherently uncreative field (an easy criticism, of course, in that their art essentially requires no performance).

We must take seriously our deficiencies in past efforts to teach composition to our students, these efforts having been severely limited to simple types of music or restricted to trivial levels of music. The nature of our art, which has always required an extremely high degree of technical proficiency in notational skills and knowledge of the complexities of instruments and the voice in order to compose, has mitigated against widespread involvements in composition, so it is surely understandable that our level of success in it has been so low. Now, for the first time in history, we are beginning to be able to set our sights at a totally new level of expectation because of the invention of technologies—computers, synthesizers, microchips as part of electronic keyboard instruments, and the like—that will enable us to bypass the burden of musical notation and engage ourselves directly and richly in artistic creation at the same levels and in the same direct ways as can those in the visual arts. Ironically, it may be technology that allows compositional creativity to become a reality for the masses of people. The present uses of computers and related technologies in music education, often limited to noncreative skill development, can expand to new horizons of musicality if they fulfill their potential of giving people direct access to creative decisionmaking with sounds, storage and instant retrieval of those sounds, and devices to alter and refine the previous decisions: all the conditions that would enable genuine compositional creativity. Chapter Nine will discuss the new opportunities for creative musical involvements afforded by recent technological advances.

The third way to involve students with musical creativity is through performance, for, as pointed out earlier, musical performers are artists who make expressive (aesthetic) decisions about the pieces they are bringing to completion. The problem, of course, is the limited degree to which performers in groups can contribute their own creative decisions as opposed to the unifying decisions made by the conductor, whose job it is to mold a coherent performance that is true to the piece itself. So, by the very nature of musical performance in large groups, the conductor is in a position to make far more creative choices than the players or singers. Since the conductor is the teacher, and often a teacher working under severe pressure to produce the maximum possible level of performance in a minimum of time available, the result is usually that the performers do what they are told, with little if any personal, artistic involvement in either making musical decisions or being led to understand why those decisions were made.

That is why so many school music performances are at a high level of technical proficiency and have the gloss of musicality supplied by the director but are inherently uncreative, reflecting the reality that the performers are not essentially young artists but instead artisans doing what they have been told to do. When this common music education syndrome is surpassed, in that the performers, in rehearsals, have been led to understand why they need to produce just such and such expressive values, and are allowed to experiment with appropriate and inappropriate alternatives to enhance their understanding of the more musically authentic ones, the creative act becomes internalized in every student's mind and feelings. The result is that still-too-occasional event in which real music happens, and the excitement and gratification of artistic creation is shared by conductor, performers, and audience. All of us have been touched by such shining moments: perhaps we are music educators because of them, for their power can transform our lives and dedicate us to sharing this power with others. But we must learn the essential lesson that the expressive impact of music cannot be experienced when those making the music are not steeped in that expressiveness themselves as they are producing it. We have a long way to go to make all musical performance in educational settings creative rather than just proficient. To understand that there is a big difference between making the correct sounds and being involved in an act of creation, to employ the methodologies for making that truth come alive in the real experiences of our students, and to be guided by that goal—the goal of creative music making rather than that of competitive musical dexterity—remain among our most pressing needs as a profession.

The third principle of music education related to the enhancement of creative involvements with music is that teaching must concentrate on those conditions in music which contain the possibilities for artistic interactions. In all that music teachers do, at all levels from preschool through adulthood, a major focus of study must be on the expressive organization of sounds through the interrelations of melody, rhythm, harmony and counterpoint, tone color, dynamics, texture, form. That is, musical learning should be guided toward deeper interaction with the qualities of sound about which artists make creative decisions. That interaction, mindful and feelingful, is what musical experience is all about.

Finally, the techniques and the language used by the teacher to focus attention on the expressive qualities of music should never intrude themselves between the students and the music. If a technique distracts attention from the artistic qualities of the sounds in a particular piece, that technique is a hindrance to musical education. An example of this is the technique of having children draw pictures "illustrating" a piece being listened to. Aside from falsely assuming that the artistic qualities of one medium can be translated into another, this technique ensures that attention to the sound itself will be at a very gross level. It does nothing to call attention to the subtle qualities of sound which are most affective but instead redirects attention to something quite extrinsic to the music itself.

It is also possible for language to get in the way of fuller musical sharing. Teachers who in their zeal try to get their students to feel what the teacher thinks they *should* feel, by the use of emotion words which influence feeling, can only undermine the unique value of musical creation and musical sharing, which must be allowed to be as truly personal as anything in human life can be. The availability of helpful, descriptive language makes the use of obstructive, interpretive language quite unnecessary.

Two more dimensions will be added to these principles as the next two chapters raise issues about two more dimensions of aesthetic education in music—the dimensions of the meaning of music, and of the experience of music. The more broadly conceived the principles become, the richer will be their implications for the music education program.

SUPPLEMENTARY READINGS

1. Copland, Aaron. *What to Listen for in Music*, rev. ed. New York: McGraw-Hill, 1957, Chapter 3, "The Creative Process in Music." Although written for nonmusicians, some helpful insights into various aspects of the musical process are given in this book.

2. Dewey, John. *Art as Experience*. New York: Capricorn Books, 1958, pp. 70–81. While practically everything in the book is relevant, these pages are particularly so for the topic "aesthetic creation."

3. Kneller, George F. *The Art and Science of Creativity*. New York: Holt, Rinehart and Winston, 1965. A useful summary of writings on general creativity.

4. Langer, Susanne K. *Problems of Art*. New York: Charles Scribner's Sons, 1957, Chapter 10, "Poetic Creation." Rich implications for all the arts are present in Langer's treatment of poetry.

5. Scruton, Roger. *Art and Imagination: A Study on the Philosophy of Mind*. New York: Methuen, 1982.

6. Sessions, Roger. "The Composer and His Message." in Brewster Ghiselin, ed. *The Creative Process*, pp. 45–49. New York: New American Library, 1955. In addition to Sessions' short selection, this book contains forty others by artists on artistic creation.

7. Sessions, Roger. *The Musical Experience of Composer, Performer, Listener.* New York: Atheneum, 1962. Chapter III deals with "The Composer," but the entire book is helpful for clarifying aesthetic creation in music.

8. Sircello, Guy. *Mind and Art: An Essay in the Varieties of Expression.* New Haven: Yale University Press, 1983.

9. Tomas, Vincent, ed. *Creativity in the Arts.* Englewood Cliffs, N.J.: Prentice Hall, 1964. Various essays on aesthetic creation, the most useful being the last, by Tomas, entitled "Creativity in Art."

The meaning
of art

5

Do works of art mean anything? Do they give us any kind of knowledge? These questions are central ones in aesthetics, and they are particularly important for the arts in the schools. Education, after all, consists of the development of people's ability to share meanings about humans and their world, or, to put it another way, education increases knowledge so that life can be more meaningful and productive. Do the arts have something to contribute to this endeavor? This chapter will answer these questions by explaining how the arts mean, how they are a basic source of knowledge, and why education in the arts is essential if we are to produce people who are well educated.

Unfortunately, teachers of art are often confused about whether, or how, the arts mean, and about the kind of knowledge the arts produce and share. It is necessary for teachers of the arts to be clear about these matters because they constantly deal with them whether they are aware of that or not. Whenever a comment is made by a teacher about a work of art, whether being created by a student or having been created by someone else, some ideas about the meaning of it all are implied. There is no escaping the question of artistic knowing: teachers can only be more confused or less confused about it, their effectiveness reflecting their level of confusion or understanding. To the degree teachers are clear about how art means, they can help students produce meaningful art effectively and gain the meanings available in works created by others.

REFERENTIALISM, FORMALISM, AND EXPRESSIONISM ON MEANING

The question "What does art mean?" is answered differently by Referentialists, Absolute Formalists, and Absolute Expressionists. The views of Referentialists and Formalists on this question are contradictory, as they are on most if not all other aspects of art. For the Referentialist, art acts as communication, transmitting messages containing the same kind of meanings as those which exist outside of art. It is perfectly proper, according to Referentialism, to ask what a work of art means and to expect an answer which stipulates more or less exactly what the meaning is. For those works of art which do not transmit obvious meanings—which contain no representational subject matter or "program"—one must "interpret" the meaning. The primary way to enjoy art, to understand art, to benefit from art, to teach art, is to focus attention on the nonartistic meanings which art communicates, either by decoding if this is possible or by interpreting.

The Formalist insists that the meaning of art is totally artistic, having no relation whatsoever to any kind of meaning outside the boundaries of particular art works. Art means itself, which is to say that each work of art is a self-contained system with its own, separate, distinctive meanings. If one is sensitive to the formal relationships in a particular work one can perceive its significance or "significant form." This significance is a function of mutually relevant artistic events, meaningful only within the context of the work.

Expressionists would agree that art *can* communicate nonartistic meanings and that art *can* present mutually related events which are meaningful within the context of art. There is an element of truth in both Referentialism and Formalism, but neither explains the experience of meaning which most people seem to have when creating or responding to art works. This experience contains two elements, which, because of their interrelation, seem to be of a different dimension from either ordinary meaning or exclusively artistic meaning. They are (1) that the sense of meaning in art comes from the *artistic qualities* of art, whether or not these include some nonartistic meanings, and (2) that the artistic meaning perceived in art is meaningful for human life, even as it retains its intrinsic artistic quality.

How can a work of art be meaningful *as art* and at the same time be meaningful for human experience? A key idea will help us unlock the answer to this question. This is the distinction between conceptualization and aesthetic perceptual structuring. But before explaining that distinction, a few previous questions must be asked.

THE MANY MODES OF KNOWING

Is there only one way that humans can know? Or is human knowing multifaceted, in that different areas of experience and different mental-physical-psychological operations yield different ways of knowing?

The word "know" stems from the Greek root *gno* which forms the basis for many words relating to knowing and meaning—prognosis ("knowing beforehand"), diagnosis ("knowing by analyzing"), agnostic ("without being able to know"), cognize ("to perceive"), cognoscenti ("those in the know"), and so on. The most important word of this sort for education is cognitive, or cognition—"the act or process of knowing." Our questions can now be stated a bit differently: Is there only one form of cognition? Or is cognition multifaceted?

One of the major developments in recent thought about the human mind and human meaning is the renewed interest in and recognition (another *gno* word) of the many ways cognition is manifested in human experience. For example, an influential book by Philip H. Phenix (11) identifies six fundamental patterns of meaning which emerge from distinctive modes of human cognition. He calls these (1) symbolics (languages and languagelike systems), (2) empirics (sciences dealing in empirical truths), (3) aesthetics (primarily the arts, which present unique objectifications of the subjective), (4) synnoetics ("direct awareness" or "personal or relational knowledge"), (5) ethics (moral meaning expressing obligation), and (6) synoptics (comprehensive, integrative meanings as in history, religion, philosophy).

As mentioned in Chapter One, another explanation of how the human mind operates in different cognitive realms is Howard Gardner's pathbreaking *Frames of Mind: The Theory of Multiple Intelligences* (4), which, to review, proposes that there are seven major realms of intelligent human functioning: the linguistic, the musical, the logical-mathematical, the spatial, the bodily-kinesthetic, the interpersonal, and the intrapersonal. Each of these intelligences has distinctive characteristics reflecting the differences in each cognitive domain. Musical functioning, in this view, is not just a matter of "talent," with its implication that some people just happen to be born with this special, peculiar gift, but instead is a manifestation of the ability to know—to operate cognitively—in the knowledge domain music deals with. Music is a way to know the world—to create and share meaning in the world—and to function effectively in this mode of cognition, one's musical intelligence must be developed. Music education, then, is the systematic development of a major domain of intelligence, dealing with one of the basic cognitive realms in human experience—the musical.

The growing awareness that cognition is diverse rather than unitary has begun to have its impact on education. Chapter One mentioned the 1985 Yearbook of the National Society for the Study of Education entitled *Learning and Teaching the Ways of Knowing* (3). That book, you will remember, argues that there are several distinctive realms of knowing, including the aesthetic, the interpersonal, the intuitive, the narrative-paradigmatic, the formal, the practical, the spiritual. Each of these requires systematic attention in education if education is to develop human beings who are as fully actualized as they are capable of being. The implications of this argument, and of Gardner's insistence that human intelligences are varied and can be developed through education, are enormous. Such ideas may well lead to a system of education in the future that recognizes, finally, that no form of intelligent functioning is more "basic" than any other but that each child's profile of inherent intelligences must be developed optimally. The humaneness of that idea, and its implications for the essential role of the artistic intelligences, can motivate arts educators in entirely new ways and at entirely new levels of expectation for what the future of the arts in education might be.

THE DOMINANCE OF CONCEPTUALIZATION

But at the present time we are still in a historical period in which the most widely recognized, most influential, most highly valued mode of cognition is that called "conceptual." So powerful is the influence of conceptualization on traditional ideas of what knowledge consists of and how the human mind can know, that it is assumed by a great many people that cognition and conceptualization are one and the same. To know anything is to have a concept about it. If a concept cannot represent something in the world or something in our experience, that thing is not knowable and is certainly not knowledge. The realm of cognition, in this still widely accepted view, is unitary: there is conceptual knowledge and there is mindlessness, into which category falls everything having to do with experiences not able to be put into the form of concepts. Most of present-day cognitive psychology, for example, is concerned with conceptual functioning and assumes that cognition and conceptualization are identical.[1] For another example, the influential *Taxonomy of Educational Objectives* (1) classifies educational goals into three domains: the Cognitive, which deals exclusively with con-

---

[1]Howard Gardner, *The Mind's New Science* (New York: Basic Books, 1985). A discussion of the need for cognitive science to broaden its views of the nature of cognition is given in the concluding section.

ceptual knowing, and the Affective and Psychomotor, which are not, apparently, cognitive. Such examples can be magnified a hundredfold.

The implications of this narrow view that equates knowing exclusively with conceptualizing have been profound in Western culture and education. To be intelligent, in this view, is to be able to conceptualize well. To reason is to use concepts as the sole mode of mental functioning. Conceptualizing is assumed to be the only possible way to be logical, to be rational, to be intellectual (the intellect, in fact, is equated with conceptual functioning), to comprehend, to be sensible. So far does this identification of knowing with conceptualizing extend that it is often accepted as a given that human mentality itself, thinking in its broadest sense, consists essentially of the process of conceptualizing.

The inadequacies of the traditional idea that the intellect consists of conceptualization and that the world can be known only through conceptualization have been recognized by major thinkers for many years. For example, Carl G. Jung argued that

> We should not pretend to understand the world only by intellect; we apprehend it just as much by feeling. Therefore the judgment of the intellect is, at best, only a half-truth, and must, if it is honest, also admit its inadequacy.[2]

John Dewey was especially impatient with those who equated intelligence and thinking entirely with conceptualization, leaving the arts, which do not conceptualize, in a secondary, inferior position.

> Because perception of relationship between what is done and what is undergone constitutes the work of intelligence, and because the artist is controlled in the process of his work by his grasp of the connection between what he has already done and what he is to do next, the idea that the artist does not think as intently and penetratingly as a scientific inquirer is absurd. A painter must consciously undergo the effect of his every brush stroke or he will not be aware of what he is doing and where his work is going. Moreover, he has to see each particular connection of doing and undergoing in relation to the whole that he desires to produce. To apprehend such relations is to think, and is one of the most exacting modes of thought. The difference between the pictures of different painters is due quite as much to differences of capacity to carry on this thought as it is to differences of sensitivity to bare color and to differences in dexterity of execution. As respects the basic quality of pictures, difference depends, indeed, more upon the quality of intelligence brought to bear upon perception of relations than upon anything else....
>
> Any idea that ignores the necessary role of intelligence in production of works of art is based upon identification of thinking with use of one special kind of material, verbal signs and words. To think effectively in terms of rela-

[2]Carl G. Jung, *The Collected Works*, Vol. 6, Bollingen Series XX (Princeton, N.J.: Princeton University Press, 1971), p. 495.

tions of qualities is as severe a demand upon thought as to think in terms of symbols, verbal and mathematical. Indeed, since words are easily manipulated in mechanical ways, the production of a work of genuine art probably demands more intelligence than does most of the so-called thinking that goes on among those who pride themselves on being "intellectuals."[3]

But these were voices in the wilderness: the vast majority continued to define intelligence in the traditional way. No wonder, then, that education has been and remains dominated by the attempt to improve conceptual abilities through the subjects exemplary of this mode of cognition, the subjects called "basic." No wonder that subjects such as the arts, which are nonconceptual in essence, have been considered secondary or even trivial in that they do not involve reasoning or intelligence or the intellect or logic or rationality or even *thinking*, as these have been understood by this limited and outdated position as to the nature of cognition. And no wonder that those devoted to the arts can now begin to breathe more freely as it is being recognized that this older position is unsupportable. We are coming to understand that the narrow view it represented was a gross distortion of how the human mind works and how it produces knowledge. And we are better able to understand the special cognitive status of the arts and the authentic, essential ways they involve people in intelligent, reasoned, mindful experiences that yield powerful forms of knowledge of their outer and inner worlds.

A DEFINITION OF A CONCEPT

To explain these ideas, it will be necessary to take a closer look at how conceptualization works as a mode of cognition and then to contrast that with how the arts work as a cognitive mode. A good starting place is a clear, unambiguous definition of a concept, which, as those who have tried to find one know very well, is extremely hard to come by. Here are two excellent definitions, both saying the same thing in a slightly different way:

> A concept is a sign which points to a commonality in events and which permits the concept user to make relatively stable responses to those varied events. The signs which are vehicles for the concept are largely linguistic and conventional. The commonality in events may range from simple similarities to regularities to law-like invariance.[4]

---

[3]John Dewey, *Art as Experience* (New York: Capricorn Books, 1958), pp. 45, 46.

[4]D. Bob Gowin, "The Structure of Knowledge," in Harold B. Dunkel, ed., *Philosophy of Education* (Edwardsville: Southern Illinois University Press, 1970), p. 6.

A concept is a triadic relation uniting a marker, counter, or vehicle, with stability in response on the part of the inquirer, and some common feature of a range of events.[5]

A diagram embodying the three essential characteristics of a concept would look like this:

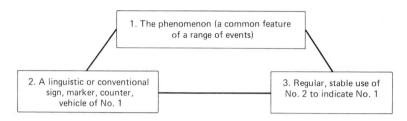

1. The phenomenon (a common feature of a range of events)

2. A linguistic or conventional sign, marker, counter, vehicle of No. 1

3. Regular, stable use of No. 2 to indicate No. 1

THE NONCONCEPTUAL NATURE OF ART

What is needed for a concept to exist is, first, something that is manifested more than once. A singular instance of something cannot be a concept. A particular person, say, Ludwig van Beethoven, is not a concept. However, if you notice that a piece of music is "Beethovenian," you have identified a common feature of at least two pieces and therefore are dealing with the first aspect of a concept. A particular thing, say, an apple, is not a concept. However, if you notice something about it that it has in common with other things ("fruit," "round," "edible," etc.), you are dealing with the first aspect of a concept. A particular event, say, a walk through the woods, is not a concept. However, if you notice something about it that is like other events ("path," "hill," "blackbird," "shadows," etc.), you are dealing with the first aspect of a concept.

The second thing needed for a concept to exist is some sort of sign, or symbol, or name, or indicator of the common feature being noticed. When you are experiencing a piece of music by Beethoven, *no such linguistic or conventional device need be part of the experience whatsoever.* No words or any other symbols need be present for you to be immersed in the ongoing experience. However, if you choose to call attention to some common feature of the sounds by giving it a name (motive, theme, repetition, counterpoint, etc.), you are now dealing with a concept in two aspects: (1) a common feature within the sounds and (2) a name for it.

Similarly for the examples of the apple and the walk. No words or any other symbols need be present as you eat the apple or take the walk, and so long as no such vehicles are present, the experience is nonconcep-

[5]Eugene F. Kaelin, "Response to Gowin," in *Philosophy of Education*, p. 19.

tual. This is not to say, however, that the experiences are not meaningful or mindful or insightful or intelligent. As a matter of fact, it is now being recognized that our minds are actively structuring our experiences in all sorts of complex ways which often never become named by symbols. These ways are not lesser than conceptualization; they are of a different order.

Some of these mental structurings can lead to conceptualization because they deal with common features. But many others are not of this sort at all in that they are responses to particular, immediate instances which are themselves deeply meaningful. Spiritual experiences, for example, are resonant with complex, profound meanings captured in the depth and height of a singular moment—a "now" that seems timeless because of the powerful sense of significance contained within it. Such an experience is "vertical" in its affect: it is rich with knowing as a singular presence rather than as a horizontal commonality with similar things. The knowing or awareness or import or comprehension in such an experience is nonconceptual in all three dimensions of a concept. Experiences of love share this nonconceptual status as do many other interpersonal and intrapersonal meaningful, cognitive experiences. In all these the richness and complexity of *what is felt* is the essential characteristic and content of their meaning.

Experiences of art also yield this verticality of the "now" felt as significance. But in art this comes from a structural presentation embodied in materials—an object (a painting, a sculpture, a building, etc.) or an event (a piece of music, a play, a poem, etc.). These structures of interrelated phenomena are very much like the first condition for a concept in that there are many features of art works that are common across a wide range of events both within a particular work and from one work to another. We hear a theme in a symphony as a unified feature of sounds and recognize the connections when it is restated, varied, extended, contrasted. We see shapes in a painting and recognize their commonalities as a structuring unit in the composition. We follow the progression of a metaphor in a poem as it grows and changes in imagery. But there are two essentially different characteristics of such mental operations from the operations in conceptualization. First, no linguistic or conventional sign is applied. We experience the embodied structure directly and immediately, that is, with no intermediating signs, symbols, or vehicles, as are *required* in conceptualization. Second, the perceived structure is inseparable not only from its embodiment in materials but from *what is felt* in the act of perceiving it. Structured materials are experienced simultaneously as both structured material and structured feeling, one inseparable from the other.

The ability of our minds to process the complex structures of works of art—to notice their embodied interrelationships and to feel what we are noticing, all without the use of any intervening symbols or signs—has been given the name "intuition."[6] This word has a passive ring to it, as if it were something that just happens; a kind of gift from on high or from biology. Aesthetic educators know that this ability can be developed through all the activities that good arts education provides. So it would seem more useful to conceptualize this mental process as being one of "perceptual structuring" to contrast it with conceptualizing. A particular phenomenon occasioning the perceptual structuring process, say, the musical function of the motive in the first movement of Beethoven's Fifth Symphony, may be called a "perceptual construct." These terms emphasize the active, educable nature of this form of cognition, and they are also more true to what this complex function of the mind consists of.

The third aspect of a concept has to do with how well a person associates a particular symbol or name with the phenomenon to which it refers. If a person regularly names a thing with a correct symbol even though the thing exists variously across a range of common qualities, the person "has the concept." For example, if a child is shown a red apple and she says "apple," one is led to infer that the child has the concept of what an apple is. If, however, you show her a green apple and she says "grape," you would have some reason for doubt. If you continued to show her different shapes and colors of apples and continued to get different names, you would be convinced that she did not, in fact, have a concept of "appleness." If, however, she were able to notice that all the variations were of a common set of qualities, and demonstrated that noticing by correctly identifying all the different kinds of apples as apples, you would be convinced that the concept had been attained.

In music, a person able to (1) notice the common features of the sounds of Beethoven's music, (2) give the proper name to that noticing ("that's Beethoven"), and (3) do so regularly whenever a piece of Beethoven is played can be assumed to have the concept of "Beethovenness." And so on for all concepts no matter how simple or how complex.

In all cases, then, a concept is a mechanism by which one can refer to a noticed phenomenon. A concept is always *about* the phenomenon. It does not constitute the phenomenon itself or the internal experience of the phenomenon. A child may be taught that all things with certain qualities are called apples, and she may get the concept perfectly. But the experience of an apple when she eats it is of a different order. The concept is *about* the apple. The eating is *of* the apple.

Concepts always and forever yield *knowledge about* (*ab*, Latin = "away from"). They never yield *knowledge of*. Works of art yield *knowledge*

[6]Rudolf Arnheim, "The Double-Edged Mind: Intuition and the Intellect," in Elliot Eisner, ed., *Learning and Teaching the Ways of Knowing* (Chicago: University of Chicago Press, 1985). The active nature of artistic intuition is explained and richly discussed in Susanne K. Langer, *Problems of Art* (New York: Charles Scribner's Sons, 1957), Chapter 5, "Artistic Perception and 'Natural Light.'"

of. The experience they exist to provide is of the immediate, singular, un-named, dynamic interplay of structured forces embodied in their elements. In the experience of them we are engaged in a process of affective/perceptual structuring. Such an experience is not "about" anything. It is "of " a particular occurrence yielded by a particular expressive form at a particular moment in time.

A diagram of the "knowledge of " character of art, as contrasted with the "knowledge about" character of concepts, diagrammed earlier, is as follows:

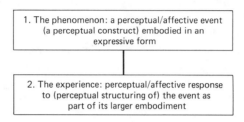

THE DISTINCTIVENESS OF EACH COGNITIVE MODE

We are constantly engaged in the meaningful perceptual structuring of our world nonconceptually. The arts are our most highly developed mode for such structuring, in their depth, breadth, subtlety, and complexity of non-conceptual cognitive potential. Because of this the argument has been made that the arts are the best underpinning for conceptualization. The arts, in this view, develop the structuring capacities of the mind most directly and most richly, so that concepts can then be built on this enhanced base of mental functioning. For example,

> The Arts involve the conscious and systematic comparison and organization of forms. The arts, then, are responsible for the elaboration of these forms whether verbal or visual. Once elaborated, this "language of forms"...is then available for the more declarative representation of objects and events....The arts develop, elaborate, and refine language, and then the language is used for representation. In this way, art precedes and leads both ordinary and scientific cognition.[7]

This claim, that artistic thinking leads to better nonartistic think-ing, is made by many people in many ways. It is very probably not true. What we are learning about mental functioning is that it is more diverse than we had thought and that its many realms of meaning are more dis-

---

[7]David Olson, "The Role of the Arts in Cognition," *Art Education,* 36, no. 2 (March 1983).

parate than we had thought. Thinking in one mode develops the capacity to think in that particular mode but has little influence on other modes of thought because each is distinctive. As a matter of fact, that is probably true within the arts themselves, because within the general domain of the aesthetic, each art requires a distinctive mode of thought peculiar to the cognitive subrealm it embodies. That is why people who are accomplished (intelligent) in one art do not necessarily or even usually manifest such accomplishments in another: when they do, it is considered remarkable. The implications of this situation for the arts in the schools are profound: we cannot simply teach "the arts" as if they were all one and the same. Each art must be learned as the special cognitive subdomain it exemplifies, its uniqueness being preserved and honored in teaching and in experience. This can be done cooperatively, in an interdisciplinary program that explores both the larger realm of meaning that makes all the arts "art," and the subrealms of meaning that make each art different. Chapter Ten will offer guidelines for accomplishing this.

But in the matter of the relation of thinking in the arts to thinking conceptually we must be very cautious in making claims that cannot be substantiated. As Howard Gardner asserts, "It appears probable that the ways we deal with...syntax in language share few fundamental properties with our transformations of special images or our interpretation of musical expressiveness." There is likely to be in psychology "separate studies of language, music, visual processing, and the like, without any pretense that they fit into one supradiscipline."[8]

The argument that the study of the arts will pay off in better conceptual functioning is intended to build a stronger advocacy position for the arts in the schools. But if the argument is based on a false premise, it cannot do anyone any good. Even if there was some measure of overlap among these cognitive domains, the argument would still be suspect, first, because it would work both ways, that is, conceptual learnings would be as helpful for artistic learnings as the reverse, the arts then requiring *less* time rather than more, and second, because it still does not recognize that the arts exist not to cause nonartistic learnings but to provide profound human meanings unavailable in any other way. Developing this mode of mentality through education is essential if education is to help children become what their human condition enables them to become. If other purposes are served by this primary value, that is fine, but as in all other claims for the value of the arts in education we cannot rest, philosophically and professionally, until we have uncovered that which is unique and essential to art, which at bottom is their function as a nonconceptual mode of cognition.

[8]Gardner, *The Mind's New Science*, pp. 132, 133.

CONCEPTUALIZATION CONTRASTED
WITH AESTHETIC PERCEPTUAL STRUCTURING

The differences between the meanings yielded from conceptualization and those from the perceptual structuring process required by art will become clearer by contrasting them directly. The following chart will guide our discussion. (Each set of terms, 1 through 8, is discussed in order following the chart).

CONCEPTUALIZATION	AESTHETIC PERCEPTUAL STRUCTURING
1. conventional or genuine symbols; signs, signals	expressive or organic or significant or dynamic forms (works of art)
2. information	experienced subjectivity
3. designative, indicative, denotative	embodied, intrinsic, immanent
4. consummated, closed	unconsummated, open
5. generality, abstraction	particularity, concreteness
6. communication, intermediate	sharing of expressiveness, immediate
7. discursive form	presentational form
8. meaning as "knowledge about"	meaning as "knowledge of"

1. As pointed out in the definition of a concept, an essential element of conceptualization is a sign or other device that indicates, in a regular way, the phenomenon being conceptualized. Such devices, or indicators, are called by a variety of names, the most common being signs, signals, or symbols. Because the term "symbol" has a variety of meanings (it is used as the indicator for several different phenomena), it should be qualified to mean, here, the kind of symbol that has an agreed-upon or conventional reference. The most common conventional symbols (also called genuine symbols) are words. Numbers, graphs, musical notation, codes, and so on, all are systems of conventional or genuine symbols, or signs, or signals.

Science is the prime example of symbol meaning, in that the most careful, most controlled use of symbols occurs in this field, yielding basic knowledge about the world and how it seems to work. The power of carefully used symbols to explain, to predict, to manipulate, to show relations, is the basis of scientific activity and the basis of our knowledge about the empirical world.

But science is not the only realm of knowing which depends on conventional symbols. Philosophy, history, social studies, all are symbol-using, symbol-knowing fields. The kind of knowledge about ourselves and our world which comes from the humanities is symbol knowledge, dependent on the use of words (primarily) as a means of discourse. While the nonscience realms of symbol knowing deal with issues different from those which occupy the primary attention of science, they are alike in that the use of conventional symbols is the basic mode of producing meaning.

The arts are unique in that the meanings they produce come from their nature as expressive forms (or organic or significant or dynamic forms) rather than as conventional symbols. The nature of an expressive form is such that a single agreed-upon meaning acceptable to everyone is neither possible nor desirable. This is quite the opposite of symbol meaning, which *depends* on agreement as to the meaning of each symbol. One basic difference between conventional symbols and expressive forms, then, is the necessity for agreement about meaning in the former and the impossibility of agreement about meaning in the latter. This must not be taken to mean that conventional symbols are precise and that expressive forms (art works) are imprecise, however. Each is precise in its own realm but very imprecise when shifted to the other. Expressive forms, as compared with conventional symbols, are quite powerless to give precise knowledge about the factual world. But conventional symbols of any sort—words, numbers, tables, graphs, and so on—are quite powerless to give us precise knowledge of human subjectivity as compared with art, which can do so more precisely than anything else.

2. The product of conceptualization is information. The information may be about the physical world, about attitudes, about beliefs, about psychological, social, political phenomena. In any case the information given through concepts is primarily of a factual nature. Concepts yield data, simple or staggeringly complex. To all of it the word information is applicable.

The product of aesthetic perceptual structuring is an experience of subjectivity. This is the apprehension of the quality of feeling as presented in the artistic quality of something. This kind of discernment yields a "sense of " rather than "information about." The sense of the nature of subjectivity given by an art work is not available through concepts.

3. The symbols that are an essential ingredient of concepts point to things other than themselves: they "designate" (or de-*sign*-ate). The number-symbol "3" indicates something or denotes something quite different from the curved line one sees. We do not look at that curved line and experience it for its own, intrinsic, visual qualities. A traffic light turns green. Green designates or signals or indicates or denotes "go now." We do not sit there experiencing (perceptually structuring) greenness as an intrinsically compelling color. (We had *better* not.) Because of the precision with which symbols designate phenomena, they allow us to deal with the objective world very precisely. If it were not for the designative, indicative, denotative power of symbols, we would not be able to make conceptual sense of our world.

But some areas of human experience, by their very nature, are not capable of being conceptualized, that is, cast into the mold of the three dimensions required for a concept. The only way to form and present an experience of subjectivity is to embody its dynamic patterns in the dynamic patterns of some object or event. When the intrinsic qualities of that object or event (that work of art) are perceived (perceptually structured), they are experienced as structured feeling. The expressive qualities of an art work do not point to or designate or denote feelings; they contain them as "immanent," as "indwelling" in the qualities themselves.[9] In a painting, for example, the curves of the number 3, its size, the thickness of the line, its color, its placement on the canvas, its interaction with other curved lines of particular thicknesses and sizes and colors, all are of essential import in the experience. A circle of green in a painting (even if it is in a depicted traffic light) is perceptually structured for our experience in its greenness, its shape, its size, the way it repeats or contrasts with other colors and shapes, and so on. So we can deal with the same stimulus (3, a green circle) conceptually or aesthetically. Each cognitive mode gives its distinctive meaning.

4. Conventional symbols must be used with regularity to indicate the phenomenon being conceptualized: you can't call a piece of fruit an apple one time and a shoe another. In that sense, symbols are "closed" with respect to what they can indicate. "Apple" can only mean a class of fruit that shares common qualities. (Or, if the word is borrowed by another concept, a class of computers that shares common qualities.) Within the concept the meaning of the symbol is "consummated," or brought to completion, when it indicates what it has been agreed upon to indicate.

Perceptual constructs—particular events within works of art—do not have a regular, agreed-upon meaning. A curved line in a painting cannot be given an assigned referent and held to that referent regularly. Every curved line in every painting is part of a dynamic, organic form in which it plays a dynamic, organic part. It does not mean one, specific, regular thing, but is a source of many possible ways to feel depending on who is experiencing it and what that person brings to the experience at that particular moment. The meanings in aesthetic perceptual structure

[9]The terms immanent and indwelling are used often in the literature of phenomenology, a philosophical approach that studies the nature of experience itself. An excursion into phenomenology would take this book too far afield for its purposes. Readers interested in the subject should consult, to begin with, Thomas Clifton, *Music as Heard: A Study in Applied Phenomenology* (New Haven, Conn.: Yale University Press, 1983); F. Joseph Smith, *The Experiencing of Musical Sound: Prelude to a Phenomenology of Music* (New York and London: Gordon and Breach, 1979); Mikel Dufrenne, *The Phenomenology of Aesthetic Experience*, ed. and trans. by E. S. Casey (Evanston, Ill.: Northwestern University Press, 1973); Maurice Merleau-Ponty, *The Phenomenology of Perception*, trans. by Colin Smith (London: Routledge and Kegan, 1962); and Alfred Pike, *A Phenomenological Analysis of Musical Experience and Other Related Essays* (New York: St. John's University Press, 1970).

are "open" or "unconsummated" in that agreement on a single meaning is impossible.

This is the case even when a conventional symbol is used in an art work. We can say with confidence that the curved line in a painting by Stuart Davis is a 3, or that the golden circle over the head of a saint in a medieval painting is a halo, or that those pieces of fruit in a Cezanne painting are apples, or that the words in poetry are, in and of themselves, conventional symbols. The crucial point is that the concept meaning of a symbol in an art work is never its aesthetic meaning. Of course many art works include concepts, but conceptual meaning must always give way to aesthetic perceptual structuring if the work is to be experienced aesthetically. The 3 or the golden circle or the apples or the words become aesthetically meaningful when, beyond their conceptual function, they are experienced as embodied in the dynamic form in which they play their expressive part. Conceptually we can all agree that those apples in the painting are apples. But when a person looks at the painting and says "Those are apples," we can be sure he has seen the *picture* but not yet the *painting*. Aesthetically, the apples' shapes, colors, textures, placements, interactions structurally within the painting, yield meanings that dwell within their intrinsic being, and are shared by us when we perceive and feel their artistic significance.

That is why, of course, a profound sense of aesthetic meaning can be given by a work of art that uses unimportant concepts (apples) or why a work with very important concepts (love) can be trivial aesthetically. Aesthetic meaning is never limited to any conceptual meanings a work may contain. In art, conceptual meanings are always a means to artistic ends. As Lucius Garvin explains in his discussion of poetry,

> Most poems...have subject matter. But such subject or meaning, when treated aesthetically, is not, in strictness, the meaning of the poem in the sense that it is something external to the poem that the poem symbolizes. It is the very stuff of the poem; not the whole stuff, but a part which enters into and fuses with the phrases and words and their assonances and rhythms to constitute the poem as an aesthetic organism.[10]

Many statements similar to Garvin's will be found in the Supplementary Readings listed at the end of this chapter. Their implications for understanding art and for teaching art are summarized in a single sentence by Langer: "Representational works, if they are good art, are so for the same reason as non-representational ones."[11] That is, *whether or not* an

---

[10]"The Paradox of Aesthetic Meaning," in Susanne K. Langer, ed., *Reflections on Art* (New York: Oxford University Press, 1961), p. 64.

[11]Langer, *Problems of Art*, p. 125.

art work contains conventional symbols, it must be understood and taught as an expressive form.

When teaching focuses on a work's symbolic content as separate from the work as an expressive form, the teaching is not yet aesthetic. This is not to suggest that teaching will *ignore* the symbolic content of art works, for to do so would be to ignore an important element in many works of art. It is to point out, however, that so long as attention is being paid to the symbol *as symbol*, teaching has not yet become aesthetic teaching. When the use of the symbol as contributing to the total expressive effect of the work is attended to (when, for example, the program is regarded as an inseparable part of the music's melody, harmony, rhythm, tone color, form), teaching is indeed aesthetic.

5. Because concepts must be consummated or closed in their meanings, and art works are always open to a variety of experiential meanings, it might be assumed that concepts deal with the particular and concrete while art deals with the general and abstract. This is a common misconception, leading to the very harmful idea that art is vague and inexact. The fact is that concepts are always generalities which abstract ("to draw or take away") from the particularities they deal with, indicating only the general common qualities of phenomena. A concept is always an abstraction; that is, it is "conceived apart from concrete realities, specific objects, or actual instances." Science is a method of creating better generalizations and abstractions about the world:

> To know a science is to be able to formulate valid general descriptions of matters of fact....Science is characterized by descriptions which are essentially *abstract*. It does not deal with the actual world in the fullness of its qualitative meanings. Rather, certain carefully defined aspects of the experienced world are selected as the basis for scientific descriptions. Different sciences deal with different aspects of the experienced world, using different schemes of abstraction.[12]

Art, on the other hand, deals with particular, concrete instances. It never generalizes about or "draws away from" the specific qualities it displays. The feelings art presents are "objectified." They are captured in the art object itself, in the artistic conditions (melody, rhythm, and so on in music; color, line, and so on in painting; and so on) each work is made of. Phenix explains it this way:

> The chief feature distinguishing esthetic meanings from symbolic and empirical meanings is the *particularity* of the former. Symbolic meanings are *general* in the sense that the conventional forms are devised to serve as

---

[12]Philip H. Phenix, *Realms of Meaning* (New York: McGraw-Hill, 1964), pp. 95–96.

bearers of meaning in an indefinite number of instances. Symbol-systems are formal types in which the structural pattern alone matters and not the particular concrete instance of utilization. Similarly, science is general in the sense that the particular data of observation are not the goal of inquiry, but only the raw material for generalization and theory formation. Knowledge in language is primarily of general patterns of expression, which may be used in a great variety of particular contexts. Knowledge in science is ideally of general laws and theories, connected with observable particulars by way of prediction and verification.

In the esthetic realm, on the other hand, the object of knowledge is the singular particular form, the primary concern is not with types of things—not with kinds and classes of things—but with unique individual objects....Each work of art contains its own meaning and speaks for itself. Its significance cannot be embodied in separable symbolic patterns, as in the sciences. Knowledge in science is *about* kinds of things in certain of their aspects. Understanding in the arts is *of* particular things in their wholeness. Scientific knowledge is *mediated* by general symbolic forms. Esthetic understanding is *immediate*, referring directly to the objects perceived. Empirical knowledge is mediated by general *concepts* Esthetic understanding is attained in direct *perception*. The content of scientific knowledge is expressed in *propositions*, statements that may be called true, false, or probable, or as holding within certain limiting conditions. Esthetic understanding is not contained in propositions, but in particular presented objects. While esthetic objects may contain propositions, as in the case of poetry and drama, these propositions merely contribute to the content of the work of art, and their truth or falsity is not the measure of the esthetic meaning of the work.[13]

6. The expressiveness of an art work is contained in its artistic qualities rather than being pointed to in something outside itself. Conventional symbols have no intrinsic meaning but refer to meanings extrinsic to themselves. Concept meanings can be communicated (by means of symbols), but the meanings in a work of art are available only through an immediate apprehension of specific qualities. Such apprehension (perceptual structuring) is essentially a private adventure, in which the potential for feeling is shared by the person responding to the work. The work does not communicate something—it embodies artistic qualities that can be experienced by someone who is aware of them and feels their expressive potential.

Conventional symbols are intermediaries for meaning—they are "go-betweens" that show one where to find the meaning they refer to. Art works can give meaning only if we become immersed in their own, singular qualities, with no intermediary between the qualities and the perceiver of them. In this sense the experience of art is "immediate," that is, directly felt with no intermediate thing or step between the apprehended work and its expressiveness:

[13]Phenix, *Realms of Meaning*, pp. 141, 142, 143.

We never pass beyond the work of art, the vision, to something separately thinkable, the logical form, and from this to the meaning it conveys, a feeling that has this same form. The dynamic form of feeling is seen *in* the picture, not through it mediately; the feeling itself seems to be in the picture.[14]

7. The telescoping of form and import into a single, immediate experience is a special characteristic of art. A system of conventional symbols—a language—operates in another way. All languages consist of "strung-out" symbols; one symbol follows another in single file, accumulating meanings as they go along. This characteristic of language—its "single-file" form—is called "discursiveness." Everything speakable or thinkable by means of language must be spoken or thought of in this linear, discursive form, symbol after symbol after symbol.

According to some people, anything which cannot be stated discursively cannot be known. Nothing is accessible to the human mind, according to this view, except that which can be put into discursive form, that is, into symbol languages (sign languages) (9, pp. 66–69). Everything else in human experience is sheer emotionalism, incapable of being handled objectively or of being known in any real sense.

If this point of view were correct, the immediate, expressive, concrete, unconsummated, embodied insights given by art could not be described as "knowledge." But human experience has a dimension of meaning beyond that or different from the meaning available through discursiveness. Art works also give meanings, but they do so by gathering up their constituent parts and presenting them for immediate apprehension and response. In art the meaning does not come from discrete, intermediary, communicative, abstract, consummated, designative bits of information, as in conventional symbols. The "all-at-once" quality of art is called "presentational" form, to distinguish it from "discursive" form. (Art works existing in time, such as music, drama, dance, and literature, are presentational rather than discursive, even though the "all-at-onceness" is spread out from beginning to end of the work.)(10, pp. 76–79)

Presentational forms—expressive forms—are the natural mode of articulating subjectivity, bringing it into the realm of knowing. Humans *can* experience more of their affective nature and therefore of their humanness. But they cannot do so through the use of concepts, which are powerless to capture and present the qualities of things. Expressive forms have this power. Upon being aesthetically experienced, expressive forms yield insights into the qualities of feeling, and such insights are meaningful in a way that information cannot be.

8. Because the words meaning and knowledge have been so limited to the idea that they can exist only through conceptualization, some people

---

[14]Langer, *Problems of Art*, p. 34.

prefer to give up those words as applied to art and use others, such as "import," to describe the product of aesthetic sharing. But those words are too powerful, especially in education, to let go of just because of traditional prejudices. Those in the arts must insist on their right to use the words and to expect the older, narrower view to broaden sufficiently to recognize that human meaning and knowledge are available in a variety of ways. That will help people to be open to meaning in their lives beyond the single mode of concept meaning. If a distinction must be made, it should be between conceptualization as "knowing about," and aesthetic perceptual structuring as "knowing of." Both are authentic, essential realms of meaning that all humans must be helped to assimilate through education. (The role of concepts as a means to know more "about" art so that more can be known "of " it will be explained in the next chapter.)

GAINING AESTHETIC MEANING

It is now possible, in light of this explanation of conceptualization and aesthetic perceptual structuring, to make a pivotal assertion about art and the teaching of art: pivotal because it is a culmination of this book to this point and will serve as a basic idea in the chapters following. The assertion is that *in all teaching-learning interactions with art, aesthetic meaning should be sought.* That means that whenever teachers and students approach a work of art it should be approached (1) as an expressive form, (2) that is capable of yielding an experience of subjectivity, (3) embodied in its intrinsic, immanent qualities, (4) that will be open to a variety of possible ways of feeling, (5) but will always be caused by the particular, concrete events in the work, (6) that are apprehended directly and immediately from those events as a sharing of their expressiveness, (7) through the presentational form, (8) that is the bearer of meaning as "knowledge of " the inner feelings of human life as lived and experienced. (Whew!)

Further, whenever teachers and students are engaged in perceiving and responding to a work of art, creating a work of art, judging a work of art, analyzing and discussing a work of art, their purpose should be to gain more meaning from it as (1) an expressive form, (2) that is capable of yielding...(and so on for the rest of the previous heroic sentence). This exercise in applying the terms in the right-hand column on page 86 to teaching the arts should make very clear that art requires to be treated very differently from subjects that are taught for their conceptual meanings. If the arts in education are to be meaningful as art, they must be taught aesthetically.

A DEFINITION OF ART

The distinction explained here between conceptualization and aesthetic perceptual structuring, and the different modes of cognition each provides, can be used to distinguish things which are art works from things which are not. A statement that stipulates such a distinction can be regarded as a definition of art. But because definitions in the aesthetic realm raise such severe philosophical-linguistic problems it is much more reasonable to regard what look like definitions of art not as final, inclusive, conclusive laws, but much more modestly, as "seriously made recommendations to attend in certain ways to certain features of art."[15] It is as such a recommendation that one may regard the definition offered by Susanne K. Langer: art is "the practice of creating perceptible forms expressive of human feeling."[16]

There are three essential elements or aspects of art suggested in Langer's recommendation. The "perceptible form" aspect requires that some material be involved—some stuff that can be presented for perceptual structuring, whether sounds as in music, movements of the body as in dance, colors, shapes, lines, and so on as in visual arts, and so on. Second, the "creating" aspect requires that these materials be organized in some way, that some decisions be made about what to do with the sounds, movements, colors, and so on. Finally, the materials must be organized for an expressive purpose, that is, to capture in their dynamic interrelations a potential for that dynamicism to be experienced subjectively. Materials (sounds) organized (telephone ring) for other purposes (signal to answer the phone) are not works of art. All three conditions must be present if the result is to be called art. This leads to a simplified version of Langer's definition or description of art: *art is material organized to be expressive.* (Please review the discussions in Chapter Four under the headings "Artistic Creation Contrasted with Making and Doing Nonartistic Things" and "Performers as Creative Artists," which give examples of when this definition of art applies and when it does not apply.)

Some people are unwilling to accept as art anything that is even touched by nonintrinsic, nonexpressive concerns. Others are willing to call art anything that has even the tiniest bit of intrinsic quality. In the middle ground between those things that are clearly and unambiguously "material organized to be expressive" and those that are just as clearly not, there are things about which hard and fast rules are difficult to apply.

---

[15]Morris Weitz, "The Role of Theory in Aesthetics," *The Journal of Aesthetics and Art Criticism*, XV, no. 1 (1956), p. 35.

[16]"The Cultural Importance of the Arts," in Michael F. Andrews, ed., *Aesthetic Form and Education* (Syracuse, N.Y.: Syracuse University Press, 1958), p. 2.

Both history and current events should teach us that people's capacity to invent new modes of exploring, embodying and sharing aesthetic meanings is seemingly endless. It would be easy and safe for arts educators to stick to well-established art works, but doing so deprives students of the exploration which is, after all, one of the exciting qualities of being involved with art. A safe attitude also brands the teacher as a reactionary, looking backward wistfully and forward fearfully. And it removes the opportunity for critical judgments to be made about problem art works. So, while teachers of the arts should not be without guidelines for judgment making, they should be leaders, openers of doors, seekers of aesthetic adventure among the new while at the same time helping to make available the proven values of the old.

It is important to notice that in this definition of art nothing has been said about how good a thing must be in order to qualify as art. A work of art can be good, bad, or indifferent—it is still art. Art is a kind of thing, just as food is a kind of thing. Food can be good, bad, or indifferent according to the criteria of judgment being applied. Criteria of judgment can also be applied to art, and it is important in arts education for students to learn what the criteria are that can help them judge whether a particular work of art is good or bad or mediocre. Chapter Seven will discuss this matter in some detail. The point to be made here is that when young people are engaged in organizing material to be expressive, whether they are painting, singing, playing, dancing, writing poems, or whatever, *they are being artists and they are creating art*. They may be doing it poorly or brilliantly (taken as a whole, it can be counted on that they are doing it on a normal curve from bad to good) but they are surely "doing art." That is why it is essential that all students be engaged in the process of perceptually structuring material organized to be expressive, whether they are doing the organizing themselves or are responding to someone else's creation. Doing so engages them in the experience of aesthetic meaning—the payoff of aesthetic education.

MUSIC EDUCATION AND THE MEANING OF ART

The primary function of aesthetic education, in light of the concern of this chapter, is to help people share the meanings which come from expressive forms. How can music education be aesthetic education? That is, how can music education help people share the meanings available in musical expressive forms? The same four principles applied in previous chapters can serve as guidelines.

First, music which is genuinely expressive in its characteristics must constitute the core of material for studying and experiencing. Since aesthetic meaning is not conceptual, it cannot be designated, so it is impossible, because of the very nature of art, to choose works according to their meanings. Instead, one chooses art works because of their artistic quality, knowing that the higher this quality the more satisfying, the richer, the more powerful can be the meanings shared.

It often happens that an art work's conceptual content is so obtrusive in and of itself that, at least for some people, it prevents the work from being responded to as an expressive form. Examples would be a sensuous nude painting or sculpture used in a junior high school art class, or a heavily sacred Christian play used in a Jewish neighborhood, or a novel condescending to blacks used in an inner-city school or *any* school, or art songs with very romantic words used in the upper elementary grades, and so on. It is true that in each of these cases the work of art should be approached, perceived, responded to, judged, and taught as an expressive form rather than as a symbol, that is, for its aesthetic characteristics rather than for its nonaesthetic designations. But that is easily said. Good sense would suggest that care be taken before placing such severe obstacles in the way of aesthetic education. One cannot simply ignore the world in which people live as one goes about helping them become more sensitive to the aesthetic qualities of the world. A bit of sensible strategy would seem in order, to avoid fruitless barriers to aesthetic learning while at the same time helping to make more and more of the aesthetic components of the world accessible to all children.

Second, the experience of music as expressive form is the be-all and end-all of music education, for such experience is the only way of sharing music's aesthetic meaning. This indicates that musical experience itself should come first and last. The payoff of music education—the sharing of music's aesthetic meanings—should be central, with all means focused toward that end and actually producing that end at every possible moment as learning proceeds.

Third, the study of music—the means for reaching aesthetic ends—should concentrate on those characteristics of sounds which make them expressive. The embodied, expressive, unconsummated, presentational character of sound can be taught for systematically, both as a component of all music and as the specific content of particular pieces. The skillful teacher will help students get closer and closer to the sounds of music, so that the sounds themselves—the tone conditions of melody, harmony, rhythm, tone color, texture, form, which embody musical meaning—can exert their affective power.

Fourth, the language and the techniques used by the music educator must be true to the nature of music as an expressive form. It would be a great mistake—perhaps a fatal mistake—for teachers to assume that because the meaning of an expressive form cannot be verbalized, words are therefore not useful for teaching aesthetically. Language remains a basic means toward aesthetic ends. The best language for this purpose, paradoxically, is the most symbol-like language, giving useful information, designating precisely the important components of musical events, making helpful generalizations about how music works, communicating specific data about the conditions of sound which can yield aesthetic meaning.

The role of the music educator as aesthetic educator, which is to make accessible the aesthetic meanings of music, is an active, directive, involved one, calling for a high degree of musical sensitivity and pedagogical expertise. To help people share aesthetic meaning is no simple task, but it is perfectly capable of being fulfilled by good teachers. In this, aesthetic education is no different from any other kind of education.

SUPPLEMENTARY READINGS

1. Bloom, Benjamin S., et al., eds. *Taxonomy of Educational Objectives, Handbook I: Cognitive Domain.* New York: David McKay 1956; Krathwohl, David R., Benjamin S. Bloom, and Bertram B. Masia. *Taxonomy of Educational Objectives, Handbook II: Affective Domain.* New York: David McKay, 1964; and Harrow, Anita J. *A Taxonomy of the Psychomotor Domain: A Guide for Developing Behavioral Objectives.* New York: David McKay, 1972. These well-known taxonomies predate recent thinking about the breadth and diversity of human realms of meaning and knowing.

2. Dewey, John. *Art as Experience.* New York: Capricorn Books, 1958. The chapter "The Expressive Object" treats aesthetic meaning in a most interesting, incisive way.

3. Eisner, Elliot W., ed. *Learning and Teaching the Ways of Knowing.* Chicago: University of Chicago Press, 1985. Chapter II, by Eisner, is on "Aesthetic Modes of Knowing." It provides a helpful supplement to this chapter.

4. Gardner, Howard. *Frames of Mind: The Theory of Multiple Intelligences.* New York: Basic Books, 1983. Explains musical intelligence as being one of seven. The theory that intelligence is multifaceted is beginning to influence thinking about needed changes in the traditional school curriculum and in traditional ways to measure intelligence.

5. Garvin, Lucius. "The Paradox of Aesthetic Meaning." In Susanne K. Langer, ed., *Reflections on Art.* New York: Oxford University Press, 1961. pp. 62–70. A short but extremely useful discussion.

6. Goodman, Nelson. *The Languages of Art.* Indianapolis: Hackett, 1976. A very influential book raising important issues about art and meaning.

7. Langer, Susanne K. *Mind: An Essay on Human Feeling.* Baltimore: Johns Hopkins University Press, 1967, Chapter 3, "Prescientific Knowledge." In this volume, the first of a three-volume work, Mrs. Langer's views on human feeling reach a high point of articulation. Chapter 3 is a storehouse of ideas about aesthetic meaning.

8. Langer, Susanne K. *Problems of Art*. New York: Charles Scribner's Sons, 1957, Chapter 3, "Creation." Among the important ideas in this chapter is that of the "sensory illusion," a key to understanding Langer's concept of aesthetic meaning. See also Chapter 9, "The Art Symbol and the Symbol in Art." In informal language Mrs. Langer discusses art as expressive form and the existence of conventional symbols in art.

9. Langer, Susanne K. *Feeling and Form*. New York: Charles Scribner's Sons, 1953, Chapter 3, "The Symbol of Feeling." This keystone book in Langer's edifice of thought contains her most detailed explanations of each major order of art. Chapter 3 lays some groundwork for all the arts as she understands them.

10. Langer, Susanne K. *Philosophy in a New Key*. New York: Mentor Books, 1942. Chapter 4, "Discursive and Presentational Forms," makes very clear the incapacity of discursive languages to conceptualize all that humans can know.

11. Phenix, Philip H. *Realms of Meaning*. New York: McGraw-Hill, 1964. Although the chapter on music (pp. 141–151) is too elementary to be of use, its first four pages give a fine overview of some of the unique qualities of aesthetic meaning.

12. Ross, Stephen D., ed. *Art and its Significance: An Anthology of Aesthetic Theory*. Albany: State University of New York Press, 1984.

13. Sontag, Susan. *Against Interpretation*. New York: Farrar, Straus & Giroux, 1961. In this widely discussed and immensely interesting book, Mrs. Sontag, in the first chapter, explains the irrelevance of "interpreting" works of art. (Her famous essay "Notes on 'Camp'" is contained in this volume.)

Experiencing art

6

The previous chapter attempted to explain how aesthetic perceptual structuring is a mode of cognition enabling people to understand the intricacies of their subjective nature. The understanding in this mode of cognition comes from "knowing of " rather than "knowing about." Another way of expressing this idea is that this mode of cognition depends on a particular kind of experiencing—a way to apprehend objects and events that will yield a special kind of experience of them. We can experience any objects or events that way. Works of art are objects and events specifically created to be experienced that way.

What is that experience like? How can one get from art the special experience it exists to give? And how can one help *others* get more of that experience from art? No questions are more important than these for people responsible for teaching the arts.

FORMALISM, REFERENTIALISM, AND EXPRESSIONISM
ON EXPERIENCING ART

For the Absolute Formalist the experience of art is different in kind from any other experience in life. When one discusses the way people respond to the intrinsically expressive qualities of things one is discussing a totally isolated area of human response having its own special character and its own special value. Not everyone is likely to be able to respond this way.

The Referentialist, at the other extreme, takes the position that the experience of art is not essentially different from many other kinds of experience. Communication is communication, no matter what symbol system happens to be used. So one should not treat aesthetic response differently from how one would respond to any communicated messages, nor should the values of aesthetic experiencing be understood as any different from the values of communication.

The position to be taken here, consistent with those the Absolute Expressionist takes about other major issues in aesthetics, is that the experience of art is indeed a particular kind of thing having characteristics which give it an identifiable quality of its own. At the same time, this particular way of experiencing permits a major component of human life—subjectivity—to be more fully known, or to be more fully shared.

The connection between the experience of art and the realm of human feeling or subjectivity is so close and so profound that it is impossible to discuss one without implying the other. So it will be helpful at this point to look more closely at the idea of subjectivity explained in Chapter Three, and then work our way back to a description of how subjectivity is experienced through art.

LIVING AND FEELING

Every living thing shares the same basic condition: an interaction between the thing and its environment. This interaction consists of a constant process of accommodation, of impulses received and given, of movement and countermovement. The characteristic quality of life is an ongoing state of flux in which the organism moves from imbalance to balance, from tension to relaxation, from agitation to stasis, from need to fulfillment, from action to rest. As long as an organism continues to respond to its surroundings it is alive. When interaction stops life has stopped.

Human life is permeated with the movement—the rhythm—of organic existence. At the cellular level myriad changes take place in constant movement between growth and decay. Muscles and organs play their part in the ongoing flux of living. At the preconscious level hundreds of occurrences exhibit the fact that the organism lives: eyes blink, lungs fill and empty, sensations are received and responded to. At the lower levels of consciousness countless small acts exhibit the rhythm of life: we sit, stand, reach, grasp, chew, stretch, walk, bend, look, hear. As we organize the sensations of life into conscious constructs the scope of life's rhythm gets larger. We sit down to a meal, eat, and finish. A class starts, the hour progresses, the class ends. An evening begins, several people meet, go out, come home. Morning comes, the day starts, many things happen during its course, night comes, the day is over. Monday morning rolls around (inevitably), we go through the week, the weekend comes, another week has passed. The curve of life's rhythm becomes broader as larger sections of life are lived: the passing of the seasons, the passing of the years, the time of childhood, of youth, of middle age, of old age. The totality of a life is itself an overarching curve of movement, containing beneath it an infinite number of smaller and smaller rhythms. And all earthly life together can be conceived as the broad arch of livingness, under which all separate lives play out their separate but common rhythms.

Because of the intimate connection between movement (taken in the broad sense of vitality or ongoingness or interaction) and life itself, anything which exhibits a rhythmic motility seems to be touched with significance. We watch the waves moving in from the sea or lake, gathering energy, dashing on the shore, retreating with energy spent. The fascination of this sight goes much deeper than its sheer sensuous pleasure. We get a sense, wordless but strong, of "the way things are." Similarly for many other rhythmic phenomena: the gathering storm, its energy, its dissolution; the fading of day, the sunset, the coming of darkness; the first signs of spring, the budding of trees and flowers, the greenness of summer. All give a sense of the essential quality of life itself.

Two characteristics of human beings lead from the conditions of livingness to the experience of art. First, humans are capable of perceiving movement intrinsically as a bearer of significance. This kind of perception is quite different, for example, from seeing an egg in the sand along a barren seashore and knowing that life exists in a seemingly lifeless place. The egg is a sign of life, the word sign being used in light of all the information given about it in the previous chapter. The significance of movement, on the other hand, is not a sign or symbol of life, but *an embodiment of the conditions of livingness*. As in every such embodiment, the significance, or import, or insight, or expressiveness, is inseparable from the very shape and form of the thing which embodies the movement. The expressive form does not "point to" life, as does the seabird's egg, but presents embodied conditions which are immediately (without an intermediary) grasped as significant. The ability to respond to the intrinsic significance of expressive forms is a basic, pervasive, peculiar characteristic of human beings.

The second human characteristic which leads to the experience of art is an extension of the first. Humans are not only capable of responding to things as intrinsically expressive, they are capable of transforming their sense of the significance of movement into expressive forms. Human beings create and respond to expressive forms not as an adjunct to their lives—as a pleasant activity for spare moments—but as an essential component of their nature.

Art works are expressive forms in which the vital conditions of living-ness have been captured so that people can regard them and experience them. The conditions of life—the rhythms of organic existence—are embodied in the artistic qualities of art works. In music, for example, the qualities presented by melody, harmony, rhythm, tone color, texture, and form are expressive of or analogous to or isomorphic with the patterns of felt life or subjectivity or the conditions of livingness. (Other terms for this notion are given in the list on page 52.) When we perceive these conditions embodied in the qualities of a thing, and react to the expressiveness—the feelingfulness—of these qualities, we can share the sense of "aliveness" they present. To the extent that the expressiveness of a work is deep and vital, and to the extent that we can share that expressiveness by perceiving and reacting to the conditions which embody it, our sharing of a sense of organic life will be deep and vital. This experience of the vitality of life, through perceiving and reacting to qualities which are expressive of the vitality of life, is called "aesthetic experience."

The position being taken here as to the biological or "natural" basis for aesthetic experience is very strongly based on the thought of John Dewey (2) and Susanne K. Langer, among a great many others. Langer especially built her system of aesthetic thought on a "naturalistic" base, the most profound statement of her position (and perhaps the most important treatment of the biological basis of the arts in the entire literature of aesthetics) being the three-volume *Mind: An Essay on Human Feeling.*[1] The reader wishing to expand his or her understanding of the relationship between art and life should spend some time with Langer's books. The point of calling attention to them here is to establish the position that art is not esoteric or rarified or removed from life, but is a basic means for *making contact with life.* The particular way one makes such contact through art is by aesthetically experiencing it.

CHARACTERISTICS OF AESTHETIC EXPERIENCE

Although human experience in general is a complex, shifting mixture of countless elements and influences, several characteristics which are peculiar to aesthetic experience can be identified. Whether these characteristics can exist in a pure state entirely separated from other elements of experience is an interesting but academic question. It seems clear that unless these elements are present to some degree the experience would not

[1]Susanne K. Langer, *Mind: An Essay on Human Feeling* (Baltimore: The Johns Hopkins University Press, 1967, 1972, 1982).

be described as aesthetic. A clearer notion of what these elements are can help differentiate aesthetic experience from nonaesthetic experience.

One important characteristic of aesthetic experience is "intrinsicality"(5).[2] This indicates that the value of the experience comes from its own, intrinsic, self-sufficient nature. Aesthetic experience is not a means toward nonaesthetic experience and serves no utilitarian purpose. It is experience for the sake of the experience in and of itself, unlike practical experience, the value of which is that it procures something other than itself.

For an experience to be intrinsic it must be removed from practical, utilitarian concerns, so that it can be enjoyed for itself. In this sense aesthetic experience is "disinterested"—not lacking in interest but lacking in concern about pragmatic outcomes. Another term for this is "psychical distance," which indicates that the person must be sufficiently removed from practical involvement with the experience to be able to lose himself in its own, immediate power.

But while aesthetic experience is intrinsic, disinterested, distanced, it is also involved, outgoing, responsive. Aesthetic experience is much more than detached recognizing or identifying. One's interest and reactions must be absorbed by or immersed in the expressive qualities being attended to, calling forth a feelingful reaction (please remember the enormous scope of "feelingful") to the perceived qualities. A common term for this involvement is "empathy," which means an identification with or a self-projection into the qualities of the thing to which one is responding. Another phrase indicating the same idea is "tension in repose," the tension being the involvement or empathy, the repose being the distancing or practical disinterestedness.

Aesthetic experience is involvement with expressive qualities rather than with symbolic designations. The involvement is with the embodied qualities of a thing, which have absorbed any designative material which might be present. The experience of the embodied qualities is immediate, that is, direct. The particular, concrete, expressive nature of the presented form is what is responded to, rather than any generalized, communicated information the thing may contain. One's attitude in aesthetic experience is to regard a thing as an expressive form rather than a symbol, to expect to get what one gets from an expressive form rather than a symbol, to be interested in the thing as an expressive form rather than a symbol. This "aesthetic attitude" is consciously cultivated by the elaborate social behaviors surrounding museums, concert halls, theaters, helping to put people into a frame of mind which encourages aesthetic experience to take place. But the perfectly natural, informal, ever-present need for aesthetic

[2]Several of the terms used here are treated more fully in Schoen's chapter.

experience makes it a very common, very everyday kind of occurrence in addition to its occasional formalization into institutional molds.

Finally, aesthetic experience always comes from involvement in the qualities of some perceptible material. There is always a sensuous element in aesthetic experience—a presentation to the actual senses. The material may be sounds, words, colors, movements, shapes, spaces, acts, but there must be formed material which contains expressive qualities to be perceived and responded to.

AESTHETIC EXPERIENCE CONTRASTED WITH OTHER EXPERIENCES

Let us see how these conditions work in practice as a guide for distinguishing aesthetic experience from other kinds of experience. Suppose, for a moment, that several people have happened to park their cars at the same time by the side of a mountain road. One is a geologist from a nearby university. A second is a farmer who owns land in the valley below. A third is a clergyman. The fourth and fifth are a couple on their honeymoon. The sixth is a music educator (no doubt on his way to a convention). All are looking at the scene below but each perceives something different from the others and reacts according to what is perceived.

The geologist thinks "What an interesting example of glacial movement. The shape of that end of the valley and the way the river runs through it seem to confirm the Schmidt-Eisenson theory of valley formation. I wonder if I should bring my graduate seminar up here to see it." The geologist's experience is scientific in the sense that knowledge (information) is its major component. The scene is perceived to be a bearer of scientific information and the reaction is appropriate to that perception.

The farmer looks at his fields below and starts to worry. "Just as I feared," he thinks. "Dry as a chip. I'll have to double the irrigation pipes and this will put me into the red. Maybe I had better go into chicken farming." His perception is of particular signs of growth or the lack of it, and his reaction is a function of what he has perceived. His experience is practical.

The clergyman finds himself awed by the grandeur of the scene. "God's works are magnificent," he thinks, and begins to recite a prayer of thanksgiving. Perceiving the valley as an instance of Divine creation, the clergyman's reaction is to offer thanks in an act of worship. His experience is religious.

The couple stands there arm in arm. "We're together," they think, "and we're finally alone. Now we can begin to build our lives together. We can share all our experiences like this." They hold each other lovingly. Their experience is relational. (The other people avert their eyes.)

The music educator (aesthetic to the core) perceives the interplay of colors, of shapes, of the texture of the clear sky against the roughness of forest and sparkle of water, of the mass of mountains against the horizon, framing the entire valley. The perceived qualities of the scene are enjoyed for their intrinsic delight. The scene is felt to be beautiful—to give a sense of pleasure, of significance, of immediately present import. "How lovely," he thinks. And in wordless absorption he loses himself in the expressive qualities presented to his vision. His experience is aesthetic.

These experiences were described as if they were pure. While they certainly can be so, they also are likely to be mixtures of components of each and of many others. The six people might actually be one person, perceiving differently from moment to moment and reacting differently according to what is perceived. Nevertheless, real differences do exist. The differences are important because they clarify the distinctive nature of aesthetic experience. The clearer we are about its special features the more effective we can be in cultivating them through education.

Let us suppose now that six people, counterparts of those on the mountain, are standing in front of a painting in a museum. An art historian might regard the painting as belonging to a particular style period and try to decide whether it is an early or late example. An art dealer could perceive the painting as just what one of his wealthy clients is looking for. "How can I get the museum to sell it to me?" he wonders. A religious devout might regard the painting—say, a crucifixion scene—as a religious statement, his experience focusing on the representation in the painting as an event with profound religious meanings. Our couple is holding hands. "Marriage is great," they're thinking. "Much better than everyone told us it would be." (They're still on their honeymoon.) The music educator perceives the painting as a complex set of visual qualities. Colors, shapes, lines, masses, bodies are perceived as intrinsically expressive through their dynamic interrelations.

Again, these experiences—scholarly, practical, religious, relational, aesthetic—are in actuality likely to be far less pure than described. And they are not without influence on each other. Each kind can influence the others and alter them in some way. Our concern is to differentiate the particular qualities of experience which make it aesthetic so that we can influence these qualities in appropriate ways.

A final example. Our subjects are at a concert. The scholar, a musicologist, perceives that the full orchestra is being used to play an early Mozart symphony. "How inappropriate," he thinks. "This conductor certainly doesn't care much about authenticity." Next to him sits the conductor of an orchestra from a nearby city. "If I could pay this concertmaster enough I'm sure he'd come to my orchestra," he thinks. "Then I could schedule that violin concerto I've been wanting to do." At his side sits a Nun. "This movement sounds like a part of the Requiem," she says to herself. "The Lord's power is in everything." Our couple is necking in the back row—their attention is surely not on Mozart. Finally we come to the music educator (who has had a very busy day). He perceives those qualities which make sound expressive—melody, rhythm, harmony, tone color, texture, form—and their fusion in a work which is significant by virtue of its musical qualities. His reaction is to the embodied expressiveness of the sounds. Through immersion in those conditions of sound which can produce feeling he responds by sharing the sense of feeling contained in those sounds. His experience of the music, unlike that of his fellow listeners, is aesthetic.[3]

The characteristics which make experience aesthetic can be present in relatively pure form as with our hypothetical music educator but they can also exist to some degree in experiences which are not dominantly aesthetic. Some people would take the position that unless the experience satisfies the conditions of aesthetic experience entirely it should not be called by that name. They would argue that it is possible for an experience to have some aesthetic characteristics without being, properly speaking, an aesthetic experience. A Ford, by way of analogy, has some of the characteristics of a Mercedes Benz but is not a Mercedes Benz. An apple has some of the characteristics of a potato but is not a potato. A hand has some of the features of a foot but is not a foot. A mathematician working at her desk may be intrinsically interested in the developing idea she is manipulating. She may be absorbed in their interrelations quite apart from any practical use they may have. She may feel that her ideas are beautiful because of their balance, their progression, their interlocking implications. Can this experience be called aesthetic?

Some people would prefer to say that while her experience has some aesthetic features, it lacks a necessary component of aesthetic experience—a "formed substance" which embodies intrinsically expressive events. Ideas in and of themselves do not qualify as material presented to sense nor are they intrinsically expressive.

Others would be perfectly willing to call aesthetic experience any experience which has even the smallest amount of aesthetic character. This debate is similar to the one about what can be called a work of art (page 94). There is no pressing need for a solution to this argument because the purpose of aesthetic education remains the same no matter what position one takes about how purely aesthetic an experience should be in order for it to qualify as aesthetic experience. The purpose of aesthetic education is to develop the ability of people to perceive the embodied, expressive qualities of things and to react to the intrinsic significance of those qualities. To the degree that people can perceive and react that way they

---

[3]The following chapter will discuss musical aesthetic experience in some detail.

can share the special kind of experience presented by the aesthetic components of things. Some of that special kind of perception and reaction must be present for any aesthetic experience at all to take place. The task of aesthetic education is to influence that "some"—to make it "more" as a result of teaching and learning.

AESTHETIC PERCEPTION × AESTHETIC REACTION = AESTHETIC EXPERIENCE

A particular kind of perception, called aesthetic perception, and the particular kind of reaction it causes, called aesthetic reaction, are the two necessary behaviors involved in any experience which can be called aesthetic. Aesthetic perceptual structuring consists of an interaction of the two. The perception and the reaction are simultaneous and interdependent. The perception is not a separate process which later produces reaction but is inherently reactive in nature. What is perceived is perceived *as expressive*, the response being an integral part of the perception. The reaction or response does not take place in isolation. It is dependent on perception of expressive qualities or conditions which can produce reaction in the first place.

It is possible to have a high level of perception with no reaction: this does not qualify as aesthetic experience. Music students taking dictation in theory class are exercising musical perception but are not reacting to the expressiveness of the musical qualities perceived. Few people would call this experience aesthetic.

It is possible to have a high level of reaction with a bare minimum of perception: this only minimally qualifies as aesthetic experience. The person who goes into ecstasies about a piece of music, and who at the same time hasn't the vaguest notion of what went on in the music, can be said, perhaps, to have had an aesthetic experience. But the experience is more self-absorbed than music-absorbed: the expressive events in the music itself were of little influence on the experience.

The interaction between perception and reaction in aesthetic experience exhibits the same qualities as the interaction between perception and reaction in artistic creation. It will be remembered from the discussion in Chapter Four that artistic creation was described as a process of exploration—a searching out and discovering of expressiveness through the manipulation of some medium. The creator works on the medium and the medium works on the creator.

In aesthetic experience we find the same kind of interaction, except that the "searching out and discovering" part does not lead to the creation of a thing. Nevertheless there *is* a searching out and discovering, and this is what has been called "aesthetic perception." Aesthetic perception is an active, outgoing "doing," which intensely involves the person in the expressive qualities of the thing being regarded. The expressive qualities of the thing, in turn, work on the perceiver as he becomes involved with them, as they do on the creator as he is shaping them. The "doing" becomes an "undergoing," as reaction takes place to what is perceived. The doing—undergoing process, then, is common to both artistic creation and aesthetic experience (2, pp. 53–55).

In the sense of searching out (doing) and reacting (undergoing) an aesthetic experience is a creative experience. It involves a person actively in the creation of new feelings through searching them out in the qualities of something in which they are embodied. To expect that the experience will be identical for all people who happen to be regarding a particular thing, say, a symphony, is to misunderstand the essentially creative, personal aspect of aesthetic experience. Certainly there will be a sharing of feeling because all people share in the common human condition. At the same time the individuality of every person will insure that his or her experience has a personal dimension. It is this unique combination of the personal and the superpersonal which is one of the most satisfying, most fulfilling characteristics of aesthetic experience, in that it promotes a sense of individuality and of commonality at one and the same time. This combination reaches to the roots of the human condition.

Aesthetic perception, as the term is being used here, is a complex behavior composed of many subbehaviors. When a person perceives the intrinsically expressive qualities of a thing he combines behaviors of recognizing, recalling, relating, identifying, differentiating, matching, subsuming, comparing, discriminating, synthesizing, and a host of others. None of these are conceptual during the aesthetic experience in that all these processes are a "noticing without naming." The mind is structuring the perceived events but not according to concepts. That the human mind can operate at such incredibly complex levels of perceptual integration is among its greatest marvels.

Aesthetic reaction is just as complex. Every bit of perceptual processing taking place has its affective dimension, inseparable from the noticing taking place. That our minds can feel in these infinitely complex, subtle, discriminative ways is equally marvelous.

THINKING ABOUT, THINKING WITH

As explained here and in Chapter Five, the expressive events embodied in a work of art are perceived nonconceptually when they are aesthetically experienced. But these events can be identified by attaching a sign or symbol to them, transforming them from perceptual constructs into concepts. When we focus on a particular artistic event embedded in a work of art, say, the four sounds that begin the Beethoven Fifth Symphony, and want to call attention to their unity as an expressive gesture and their use as a structuring device within the first movement, we can give them a name— "motive." Now, having made the percept a concept, we can discuss it, analyze it, generalize about it, even test for it in a variety of ways. We can do all these things only when we conceptualize. So long as the motive is perceptual it cannot be extracted from the experience itself. Conceptualizing allows us to change the aesthetic "knowledge of " the motive to conceptual "knowledge about" it. Now we have a tool—a concept—by which to compare this motive with others, ask students to create pieces using motives, find motives in pieces they know, and on and on. As pointed out at the ends of the preceding three chapters, the careful, descriptive use of language, or concepts, is an essential tool for heightening awareness about the way music works.

But such awareness is always a means, never an end. The end is the special "experience of " that the arts exist to provide, called aesthetic experience. So it is important that many opportunities be given for the concepts, which allow "thinking about," to become immersed in the nonconceptual experience itself, in which they are transformed to "thinking with." This is the case with all learnings—there is nothing particularly different about heightening aesthetic awareness. In learning to play an instrument, for example, every aspect must be brought to conceptual awareness: "hold your arm higher," "relax your wrist," "pull your jaw back," "that's a quarter note," "it's flat," and on and on (forever). But those "thinking abouts" are only effective when they have become so integrated that they have become "thinking withs." We really know something when its operations have become internalized, or tacit. Such is the case with aesthetic knowing, when concepts have served their purpose as pointers and that to which they point is experienced directly with aesthetic perception and aesthetic reaction.

But it is important to understand that the *perception* dimension of aesthetic experiencing is what is capable of being conceptualized and therefore taught objectively and systematically. The *reaction* aspect cannot be conceptualized because there are no conceptual pointers available for feelings—they are truly ineffable. (Please review the discussion about feelings and emotions in Chapter Three.) The feelings that come from aesthetic perception cannot be named except in the most superficial terms, which, as explained in Chapter Three, are worse than useless in describing their actual nature. Aesthetic reaction cannot be isolated for inspection; in short, it cannot be taught as separate from the artistic events which embody them. To attempt to do so, by discussing people's emotions (feelings, by definition, cannot be discussed), by trying to inculcate particular emotions, by suggesting emotion-producing ideas, by any other device which attempts to bypass the necessary and intimate relation of aesthetic feeling with aesthetic qualities perceived, is to violate the nature of aesthetic experience. Nothing more effectively cancels out or distorts the creative, personal, subjective response which is the most valuable characteristic of aesthetic experience than to try to influence that response separately. Only one thing can properly influence aesthetic reaction. That is the artistic qualities of things themselves. To the extent that a person can perceive artistic qualities keenly, subtly, precisely, sophisticatedly, sensitively, his reaction can be keen, subtle, precise, sophisticated, sensitive.

The major task of aesthetic education, in light of this discussion, is to influence the ability of people to have aesthetic experiences. The ability to have aesthetic experiences can be heightened by education if education concentrates on teaching what is teachable—aesthetic perception—in contexts which encourage creative, personal reactions to that which is being perceived. It is quite possible (and not uncommon) for aesthetic perception to be taught in ways which prevent aesthetic reaction rather than promote aesthetic reaction. This practice is hostile to aesthetic experience because it makes perception a cold, sterile thing and gives the impression that it should be so. To keep in fruitful balance the aesthetic behaviors which can be taught and those which can not, to encourage feelingful responses without doing so nonaesthetically, to guide perception directly enough to make advances while not so intensively that it becomes separated from expressiveness, are teaching tasks as delicate and as difficult as any in the field of education. But while aesthetic educators have a particularly challenging job to do, the rewards of success are concomitantly great, both for the teacher, who is dealing with one of the most fulfilling aspects of human life, and for students, who are gaining more and more of that fulfillment.

AESTHETIC EXPERIENCE AND ELITISM

The ability to have aesthetic experiences; that is, the ability to perceive aesthetically and react aesthetically, can be called "aesthetic sensitivity." Far from being mysterious, aesthetic sensitivity consists of behaviors which are quite identifiable and quite amenable to being developed. The notion that aesthetic experiences and the ability to have them are like exotic flowers, blooming very rarely and only under elaborate hot-house conditions, is unfortunate and untrue, reflecting an "aestheticism" too often cultivated by artists, writers about art, and teachers of art. Aesthetic experience is a hardy weed, growing abundantly and sturdily wherever humans exist. Given conditions friendly to its growth aesthetic sensitivity will flourish, spread, and bear joyful fruits. Under conditions of ugliness (which means conditions devoid of aesthetic qualities), of lack of concern about the quality of people's experience of life, of low expectations for significance as a normal component of experience, aesthetic sensitivity can become stunted and weak.

Whatever the conditions under which it operates, aesthetic education must provide more fertile ground for the growth of people's aesthetic sensibilities than would have existed if there were no aesthetic education. Certainly this is easier under conditions already positive toward the aesthetic in experience. But to think that aesthetic experience is for the privileged, that the pleasures and satisfactions of the aesthetic realm are limited to and proper for particular people only, is to misconstrue the nature of aesthetic sensitivity and the nature of human potential. Aesthetic sensitivity exists to some degree in all human beings, can provide the same delights for all human beings, is capable of development for all human beings. The task of aesthetic education is to deepen the aesthetic sensitivity of all human beings.

The elitist notion that aesthetic experiences are only for some people carries over into the equally elitist idea that aesthetic experiences can be gotten—or should be gotten—from only some kinds of art. There are two key issues relating to this aspect of elitism. The first has to do with criteria of excellence. Should the same criteria be applied to all art, or should some art—"popular" art, for example—be judged according to different standards than "serious" art?

The elitist view is that standards should differ. Popular art or folk art, after all, cannot possibly be attempting to do what serious art attempts, which is to embody human subjectivity in expressive materials, yielding aesthetic experiences. Popular or folk art should be judged only according to entertainment value or relaxation value or hobby value. It should certainly not be taken seriously or be evaluated according to the same measures by which "quality" art should be judged.

This condescending attitude denigrates much of the world's art as well as the people who delight in it. It assumes that some human feelings are serious and some are not or that some people can have worthwhile feelings and some cannot so they only respond to art which is not worthwhile. It reserves artistic goodness to only "acceptable" kinds of art so that other kinds need not stand up to expectations of quality. So ingrained are these elitist assumptions that many people who hold them think they are being liberal or democratic to so generously let "art of the people" off the hook. But what they are being is superior. If they had appropriate respect for art as art they would realize that *all* art does the same thing and that *all* art can be and should be judged by the same criteria for success. Chapter Seven will discuss what these criteria might be.

The second issue relating to elitism about art is an extension of the first. If one accepts that it is condescending and elitist to apply different criteria to different kinds of art, wouldn't one have to apply a single set of universal criteria to all art on a single scale? Wouldn't a jazz piece have to be compared with a symphony? Wouldn't a popular song have to be compared with an operatic aria? Wouldn't a comic book have to be compared with Picasso? Wouldn't a country fiddler have to be compared with Itzhak Perlman?

Underneath the elitist's "generosity" in proposing different criteria for different kinds of art is the secret assumption that all art should be judged on an absolute scale rather than allowing each kind of art to be judged on its own scale. If all art must be put on the same scale, as elitists assume, surely the first of the pairs just mentioned would lose out as compared to the second. That probably wouldn't be fair, so why not just judge them differently? That gets elitists out of the uncomfortable position of looking too elitist. But their problem is the assumption that all works of art must be lumped together and be compared indiscriminately with one another. That is not true, in art or in many other aspects of life.

A nonelitist or populist point of view accepts one set of criteria for excellence in art, insists that the criteria be applied across the board, but also insists that works in each kind (genre, style, type, etc.) of art be judged in terms of its excellence relative to the characteristics inherent in that kind. It is irrelevant—and elitist—in this view, to compare a popular song to an operatic aria. A popular song is excellent, in fact, an exemplar, when its artistic value is at the outer reaches of potential in that genre, as represented by popular songs that are "classics." Comic book art is excellent and classic when it fulfills the artistic potentials of that genre, not Picasso's genre. Ethel Merman is a classic exemplar of her type, not Maria Callas's type. On artistic criteria applied genuinely, Louis Armstrong playing "When the Saints Go marching In" is at the outer reaches of excellence achievable in that genre. The falseness of putting him on an absolute scale as compared with a performance of the Hummel *Concerto for Trumpet*, or of putting Merman in competition with Callas singing a Verdi aria, is to imagine the Boston Symphony playing "Saints" (there is, in fact, a condescending, painful recording by the Boston Pops) or Callas trying to sing "There's no business...." Art, and artists, in the populist view, must be judged for excellence relatively to what they are creating.

The populist view is pervasive in all aspects of American life, in which excellence is sought openly across the broad spectrum of culture. The search for the best has become a way of life, whether it is the best hamburger, ice cream, automobile, movie, and so on. Those who would argue that a good hamburger is to be judged against an elaborate French dinner are implicit elitists. They would win the argument on those terms—it is just that we don't have to buy in to those terms.

Elitism is deadening to culture because it is unable to enjoy the great variety of life's good things. It is pernicious, of course, when it claims that access to culture should be limited according to social class, race, financial status, and so on, a position untenable in a democracy. The unfortunate consequences of elitism are not quite so blatant. The worst of these is an attitude, usually hidden, that denigrates the tastes, pleasures, and choices of "the masses." Some arts educators take the attitude that even though the masses hold "high art" in contempt, they are, after all, capable of enjoying it if given the chance. Well, all people are capable of enjoying art beyond what popular culture provides which is why art of all kinds, including the classical masterworks ("high art"), must be included in schooling. But the contempt some of "the masses" hold for high art is not of the art—it is of the attitude of those elitists who, overtly or covertly, express that those who don't hold their value are to be sneered at at worst or educated out of their ignorance at best. It is unsupportable to argue that only some art—"high art"—exists to give aesthetic experiences while other kinds of art are only functional or social or in other ways "lesser." All successful art, whether or not intended for the quiet contemplation of the museum or concert hall, is artistic, that is, expressive of inner subjectivity. To argue that aesthetic experience is passive, that it is limited to only a certain kind or level of art that most people are not interested in, that most people use art for purposes other than its intrinsic beauty, is to emasculate the active, freewheeling, broad-ranging nature of aesthetic experience, to denigrate folk and popular and informal musics as somehow not artistic, and to underestimate both the need and the capacity of all people to enjoy whatever art they choose and to enjoy the beauty—the richness of feeling— it adds to their experience.

People know when they are being condescended to and know quite rightly that elitists in arts education intend to pat them on their heads for their quaint tastes and to give them the beneficent opportunity to change those tastes. That is different from what can and should be done—to recognize the standards of excellence that can be applied no matter what kind of art is being explored, with the attitude that kinds of art are not in competition with each other and every person has the right—even obligation— to value those kinds of art he or she finds fulfilling, based on a broad-ranging acquaintance with art of all kinds.

AGE AND AESTHETIC EXPERIENCE

A strange notion exists among some people about age as a factor in the ability to have aesthetic experiences. Childhood, according to this view, is a period of preparation for the coming of some glorious future time when one will be "able" to have aesthetic experiences. A proper education, then, consists of preparation. "You may not understand why I'm having you learn this material; you may not find it of any immediate relevance, but take it from me—when you are ready you will be glad I made you learn it." This position, which is not at all rare, is based on a view of children as non-human beings in training to be human beings. Nothing prevents the growth of humanness so effectively. Especially is this the case in the aesthetic realm. Unlike some experiences in life, which, according to law or custom a person must be at least 18 to have legally or morally, aesthetic experience is normal for children and necessary for children. The first-grader delightedly singing "Twinkle, twinkle, little star," perceiving its lovely contour of melody, its rightness of harmony, its ongoingness of rhythm, its balance of form, and feeling the expressiveness of the song as musically artful, is having the same *kind* of experience—aesthetic experience—as the crustiest old musicologist absorbed in the complexities of Beethoven's Ninth. The only difference is in *degree*. The job of aesthetic education is to influence that degree, and it must do so whatever the age of the students involved.

LIKING AND JUDGING IN AESTHETIC EXPERIENCE

It should be noted that no mention has been made of liking or judging as elements in aesthetic experience. This is because neither is a proper component of aesthetic experience. It is a very common idea that what one is supposed to do when confronted with a work of art is to evaluate, to decide whether it is any good, and even more importantly, whether one likes it or not. So people often go around an art exhibit as they would go around a smorgasbord table, sampling a bit of this and that and saying "I like that one. No, this one I don't like. Oh, I love that one. This one I don't care for at all." The snap judgment is a function of snap perception and snap reaction. Few people are capable of an instantaneous, deep, sophisticated perception of and response to an art work's complexities. In the vast majority of cases, quick judgments reflect a superficial level of aesthetic experience.

But more important than that, the idea that one's experience of art should be one of liking or judging actually *gets in the way* of aesthetic experience. Aesthetic perception should be unhindered by concern about judgment making. It should be a free, open, uncluttered giving up of oneself to the expressive qualities being regarded. The less concerned one is about having to decide about the goodness of the work one is attending to, the more likely one is of being able to share openly and fully in its artistic qualities. And the less worried one is about one's own subjective evaluation of the work the more can one's reaction consist of a sharing of the expressiveness of the perceived qualities. Aesthetic reaction should consist of what aesthetic perception causes. It should *not* consist of something brought in as an extraneous factor, for this only prevents fresh, direct reaction to the expressive content of the work.

Art does not exist in order to be liked, in the sense of providing simple, transitory pleasures. It makes sense to like vanilla ice cream better than chocolate, or to like peaches better than plums. Concern about liking art usually puts it on that superficial level. Art contains insights to be shared; it offers self-knowledge of a very basic sort. This is true of simple as well as complex art. The way to share art's power is to aesthetically experience it—not to taste it to find out whether it pleases the palate. Yet it is this latter, superficial kind of experience which teachers actively promote when they constantly ask "Did you like this song?" "Did you like this painting?" "Did you like this poem?" As if it *mattered!* What matters is, "Did you hear what happened in this song and did you feel what you heard?" "Did you see more in this painting and did you feel more of what you saw?" "Did you grasp more of the subtleties of this poem and did you feel more subtly as a result?" In the sense of perceiving more and reacting more, the central question is "Did you *understand?*"

> ...art, like science, is a mental activity whereby we bring certain contents of the world into the realm of objectively valid cognition...it is the particular office of art to do this with the world's emotional content. According to this view, therefore, the function of art is not to give the percipient any pleasure, however noble, but to acquaint him with something which he has not known before. Art, just like science, aims primarily to be "understood." Whether that understanding which art transmits then pleases the feeling percipient, whether it leaves him indifferent or elicits repugnance, is of no significance to art as pure art. But since that of which it makes us aware is always of an emotive character, it normally calls forth, more or less peremptorily, a reaction of pleasure or displeasure in the perceiving subject. This explains quite readily how the erroneous opinion has arisen that the percipient's delight and assent are the criteria of art.[4]

When art is experienced aesthetically and understood aesthetically, it delights in a way that few experiences in human life provide. To share *that* delight, which is the delight of experiencing more fully the potentials of human subjectivity, is the important job of aesthetic education. In talking about the literary form of tragedy, Susanne Langer says

> Few people know why tragedy is a source of deep satisfaction; they invent all sorts of psychological explanations, from emotional catharsis to a sense of superiority because the hero's misfortunes are not one's own. But the real source is the joy of revelation, the vision of a world wholly significant, of life spending itself and death the signature of its completion. It is simply the joy of great art, which is the perception of created form wholly expressive, that is to say, beautiful.[5]

---

[4]Otto Baensch, "Art and Feeling," in Susanne K. Langer, ed., *Reflections on Art*, (New York: Oxford University Press, 1961), pp. 10, 11.

[5]Langer, *Feeling and Form*, p. 405.

To share the joy of art—the perception of expressive form—one must help people experience art aesthetically, free from the strictures of liking or judging. Let judgments come later, as reflection after the fact, about particular aesthetic experiences. Aesthetic education can and must help such reflection be sensible and therefore to promote better aesthetic experiences for the future. But such reflection, including the self-analysis of liking or disliking, should be purged from aesthetic experience itself.

MUSIC EDUCATION AND AESTHETIC EXPERIENCE

If, as has been suggested, the goal of aesthetic education is to improve the ability of all people to have aesthetic experiences; that is, to heighten all people's aesthetic sensitivity, how would music education contribute to this goal? Again we ask the central question of this book: How can music education be aesthetic education? The previously discussed four principles can guide us again.

First, teachers must use musical works which are capable of being aesthetically perceived and reacted to by the particular students with whom they are working. It should not be assumed, however, that every piece of music should be so simple that *all* of its artistic qualities can be perceived by those studying it, listening to it, performing it. Good works of art are likely to contain so much expressiveness that few people will perceive all possible subtleties and complexities. Partial understanding is probably the rule rather than the exception. If one accepts the fact that not all of a work is likely to be perceived, one can use music of a much more sophisticated sort than if one assumes that all music must be so simple that every learner can get every bit of its musical quality. Of course some reasonable balance is needed, but our errors have been in the direction of over-simplicity and therefore of minimal excitement and minimal involvement. We can be bolder about musical materials—not disregarding the age and experience of students but not underestimating their capacities or their willingness to accept aesthetic challenge.

Second, teaching and learning must be arranged so that aesthetic experiencing is central and other learnings play a supporting role. Every possible opportunity must be provided for aesthetic perception to take place in contexts which encourage, or, at least, allow for aesthetic reaction to occur. Music education, for many people, consists of material learned and skills gained. It is being suggested here that music education should consist of musical aesthetic experiences. Of course reading, writing, practicing, talking, and testing are legitimate and necessary components of music education. But when they become separated from musical experience itself they have become separated from that which provides their reason for existence.

In the "study" part of music education—the part used in the service of deepening aesthetic experiences of music—attention should be focused on that which, if perceived, can arouse aesthetic reaction. The conditions of sound which are expressive can be revealed to students of all ages. The responsibility of music education, at every level and in every part of the program, is to reveal more fully the musical conditions which should be perceived and felt. The qualities of sound which make sound expressive— melody, harmony, rhythm, tone color, texture, form—are the objective "data" with which music teachers systematically deal. Illuminating these "data" in musical settings is the task of musical teaching.

Such illumination requires, in addition to the handling of musical stuff itself through performing and composing, conceptualization about that which is to be perceived. As pointed out previously, conception is a major means for developing perception. A constant interaction between conception about expressive qualities of music, and perception of those qualities, should pervade every aspect of musical study. This requires a careful use of language because language is the indispensable mode of conceptualization. Language becomes a powerful tool for increasing aesthetic sensitivity when it is devoted to the refinement of aesthetic perception in contexts which present perception as an integral part of expressive music to be felt. The music program is the means for arranging for aesthetic perception and aesthetic reaction—aesthetic experience—to take place systematically.

SUPPLEMENTARY READINGS

1. Broudy, Harry S. "The Structure of Knowledge in the Arts." In Stanley Elan, ed., *Education and the Structure of Knowledge*, pp. 75–106. Chicago: Rand McNally, 1964. Also Ralph A. Smith, ed., in *Aesthetics and Criticism in Art Education*, pp. 23–45. Chicago: Rand McNally, 1966. This essay would also be appropriate as a supplementary reading for Chapter Five. It is listed here because of its rich implications for developing aesthetic perceptivity.

2. Dewey, John. *Art as Experience*. New York: Capricorn Books, 1958, Chapter 1, "The Live Creature," and Chapter 3, "Having an Experience." These two chapters are directly concerned with aesthetic experience and have been extremely influential on modern notions of what constitutes aesthetic experience.

3. Langer, Susanne K. *Feeling and Form*. New York: Charles Scribner's Sons, 1953. Chapter 4, "Semblance," is a penetrating discussion of the "illusion" presented by art works for aesthetic experiencing. Chapter 21, "The Work and Its Public," contains some of Langer's most direct statements about aesthetic experience, as well as some thoughts about aesthetic education.

4. Langer, Susanne K. *Problems of Art*. New York: Charles Scribner's Sons, 1957, Chapter 4, "Living Form." The ideas presented in this chapter are developed in *Mind: An Essay on Human Feeling*, but are more easily accessible here.

5. Schoen, Max. *Art and Beauty*. New York: Macmillan, 1932, Chapter 6, "The Experience of Beauty," especially pp. 133–149. An old but still very useful treatment of various views of aesthetic experience.

6. Scruton, Roger. *The Aesthetic Understanding: Essays in the Philosophy of Art and Culture*. Methuen, 1984.

Experiencing music

7

A MUSICAL VIEW OF THE ARTS

The position about art being taken in this book is, essentially, a "musical" one. The assertion that all the arts should be approached as expressive forms, perceived as expressive forms, responded to as expressive forms, judged as expressive forms, taught as expressive forms, is an assertion heavily colored by a musical outlook toward art.[1] The presentation of artistic qualities in a self-sufficient, self-complete way can be more easily achieved in music than in other arts, which often require a context of conventional symbols against which or through which the artistic expressiveness is presented. This does not mean that music is therefore the best or the highest or the purest art (although music educators often assume this to be a self-evident truth), but simply that the peculiar nature of sound lends itself very naturally to totally artistic use. Walter Pater acknowledged this fact in one of the most famous (and most misquoted) statements ever made about music as the most "artistic" art (the famous sentence is italicized—by Pater—in the following excerpt):

[1]That the art of music is regarded by Susanne K. Langer as the touchstone art for understanding all art makes her writings particularly relevant for music education. This is one important reason for the influence of her writings on this book and for her extensive influence on music education at the levels of philosophy and practice.

...music [is] the typical, or ideally consummate art, the object of the great *Anders-streben* ["other-striving"] of all art, of all that is artistic, or partakes of artistic qualities. *All art constantly aspires towards the condition of music.* For while in all other kinds of art it is possible to distinguish the matter [symbol] from the form, and the understanding can always make this distinction, yet it is the constant effort of art to obliterate it. That the mere matter of a poem, for instance, its subject namely, its given incidents or situation—that the mere matter of a picture, the actual circumstances of an event, the actual topography of a landscape—should be nothing without the form, the spirit, of the handling, that this form, this mode of handling, should become an end in itself, should penetrate every part of the matter: this is what all art constantly strives after, and achieves in different degrees.[2]

Every art work which achieves the status of an expressive form is successful to some degree as art. The old argument as to whether the presence of nonartistic material increases or decreases the impact of art need not be belabored. What is of importance is the recognition that the artistic qualities of things are what have aesthetic value. We turn our attention now to how the art of music presents artistic qualities to be experienced for their intrinsic expressiveness; that is, how experience becomes musical. While many ideas about musical experience have been implied in the preceding chapters, they can now be made explicit. The following diagram will help focus the discussion.

Categories of Experiences of Music

Nonmusical (nonaesthetic) experiences	Musical (aesthetic) experiences
Functional	
Practical, religious, therapeutic, moral, political, commercial, etc.	Sensuous
Referential	
Association	
Intrasubjective	Perceptual
Character	
	Creative
Technical-critical	

While the number of actual experiences of music is doubtlessly as large as the number of people who have ever responded to music, several categories of common experiences can be identified.[3] The categories listed

[2]Walter Pater, *The Renaissance* (London: Macmillan, 1910), pp. 134–35.

[3]Several of these categories have been adapted from the studies described in Max Schoen, *Art and Beauty* (New York: Macmillan, 1932), Chapter VII, "Beauty in Music."

are conceived broadly, as guidelines for discussion rather than as an exhaustive, rigid framework into which all possible musical experiences must fit. Also, as with all complex human behaviors, instances of pure experiences unmixed with bits and pieces of others are probably the exception. Nevertheless it is helpful to map out groupings of experiences to provide a manageable structure upon which ideas can be organized.

The nonmusical experiences are so called because they are not primarily focused on the two necessary components of any experience which can be called aesthetic: aesthetic perception and aesthetic reaction. For an experience to be musical the perception must be of the artistic qualities of sound and the reaction must be caused by the expressiveness of those qualities. The responses in the left-hand column do not exist to fulfill these conditions.

FUNCTIONAL USES OF MUSIC

The practical, religious, therapeutic, moral, political, commercial, and so on, experiences of music are not dominantly caused by artistic qualities of sound which are inherently expressive. At a political rally, for example, a candidate's theme song might be played before he appears at the podium. The song is perceived as a symbol of the candidate, who has propounded an exciting policy for improving American government. Perceived for its designation, the song is reacted to appropriately—with stirrings of pride, hope, dedication to American ideals. The song will probably be of a generally exciting sort suitable to its purpose of arousing excitement for the candidate, but the embodied, expressive, presentational, unconsummated meanings (page 86) of the sounds as artistically organized (expressively formed) are peripheral to the experience if they are present at all. The song is a symbol, perceived and reacted to as such. Certainly the song is fulfilling a legitimate and important function. That function, however, is not primarily an aesthetic one.

The use of music for utilitarian purposes—to serve ends other than musical ends—is ancient and widespread. Such uses range from the insignificant (background music in a department store, identification of commercial products) to the profoundly important (as a concomitant of worship services, as a means for therapy). And there is sometimes no clear separating point between musical experience as such and the experience of something else for which music is merely a means, in that some degree of attention to artistic qualities may accompany the nonmusical focus. The point of listing functional uses of music as an example of nonmusical or nonaesthetic experiences is that they do not intend to focus primary attention on music as music but instead to put music to use to serve other functions. There is no reason why music should not serve such functions. Indeed, it is difficult to conceive many social occasions without music as a functional component. But the position being taken in this book is that music education should be primarily *music* education, that is, education for the essentially aesthetic or musical qualities and values of music as an art.

There is really no problem in understanding music's functional, non-aesthetic uses and the values of such uses. These values are self-evident. The nature and value of music as art, on the other hand, is a complex matter requiring systematic explanation. If music education makes any claim at all to being musical education—to being aesthetic education—it is necessary to have a philosophy which explains the musical, aesthetic nature and value of music. One important aspect of that explanation is to distinguish between experiences of music which are essentially musical and those which are essentially not.

But this is not to argue that there is no room for functional uses of music in school programs. Many legitimate, socially significant values are connected to music even if they are not entirely musical, and it would be puristic to refuse to serve any of those values because they are not at the core of aesthetic education. Music educators who are secure in knowing that their primary focus is artistic can relax and go along with reasonable and necessary musical services to other things. It is possible, after all, to be a good music educator without being a snob. We must be aware when things are getting out of hand and when there is a genuine threat to the artistic integrity of our program. We must never let that happen. But it would be equally extreme to admit no other values in one's program than strictly musical ones. It is necessary to know the difference between the two, maintain a musically solid, valid program, and then cheerfully (and expertly) serve some nonmusical ends when it is reasonable to do so. Chapters Eight and Nine will reiterate this point in connection with the general music and performance programs.

REFERENTIAL RESPONSES TO MUSIC

Functional uses of music are referential in the broad sense in that they do not focus on musical experience as such. The experiences listed here are referential strictly speaking. In these responses there are no apparent nonmusical functions being served: people may be performing or sitting in a concert hall listening to a performance or may be at home quietly listening to a record. But while the concentration seems on the surface to be entirely musical the content of the experiences is not focused on musical perception and musical reaction but on references outside the music.

In the association experience the music suggests any number of extramusical ideas or occurrences in the life of the responder. A typical statement describing such an experience might be "The music reminded me of when I was a child, and we went swimming at the beach, and a storm came up and the waves became dangerous." Or "I kept thinking about my term paper on Mozart and how I would have to work on it after the concert." Or "As soon as the music started I thought about how I got my first teaching job and had to start a chorus and a band at the same time, and we performed this piece at the first concert." The music in such experiences serves as a stimulus for memories, worries, self-conversations of all sorts. The sounds of the music get the experience going, but they are not perceived and responded to for their embodied expressiveness. The music fades from consciousness, providing a pleasant background against which to daydream.

The intrasubjective experience is an association experience in which the visual or literary imagination is stirred by the music. Rather than calling up a particular association from one's life the intrasubjective response calls up all sorts of fanciful images. A person might say "I thought of a beautiful forest, with the sun shining through the trees, and butterflies and birds were flying here and there." Or "I began to make up a story, with a prince and princess and witches and monsters." Or "It was a parade, and the bands came by and there were floats and balloons and riders on horseback."[4] Again, the music stimulates a great deal of mental activity, but this activity is only remotely related, if related at all, to what is actually going on in the music.

The character response focuses on the "mood" or "character" element of music. "It was very depressing. I felt that death was all around and all life must come to an end." Or "How happy it made me. I wanted to smile at the whole world." Or "This movement is dainty. The last one was soulful. I wonder what the next one will be." Here the most obvious mood quality of the music causes the response, with no grasp of the expressiveness of the musical events beyond the superficial level of emotional designation.

Experiences of program music and vocal music include referential elements. As has been stated many times in our explanation of how art can contain conventional symbols, the program or the words can enter into the aesthetic expressiveness of a piece when they become immersed in the expressiveness of the melody, harmony, rhythm, and so on. When this occurs the experience is musical (aesthetic) even though a nonmusical (nonaesthetic) component is present. The descriptions given above of the nonmusical responses to music assume that they remain at an entirely nonaesthetic

---

[4]The Walt Disney movie *Fantasia* gives some clear examples of intrasubjective interpretations of music, in wide-screen, stereophonic, technicolor gloriousness.

level, as they often do. Similarly for program or vocal music. Such music can be experienced aesthetically, of course, but our interest at the moment is in the (very common) nonaesthetic experiences of this music.

Nonmusical experiences of music—regardless of what kind of music—are closely related to one another and probably can be separated only artificially. They are natural responses occurring spontaneously, with no necessity for musical training or musical perceptual development of any sort. Because music is perceived and responded to as either a symbol of something nonmusical or an occasion for reminiscence or fantasy-making or mood-enhancement, there is little one can do to improve or educate such responses. Of course the teacher can encourage such responses by asking all sorts of nonmusical questions about music, such as "What do you think it means?" "What does it make you imagine?" "How does it make you feel?" "Can you tell a story appropriate to this music?" "Does it make you remember anything that has happened to you?" "Is this music sad or happy, like this painting or like this other painting, like a sunny day or a rainy day, blue or red, like butterflies or like elephants, heroic or cowardly, and so on, and so on, and so on?" All such questions will effectively call attention away from the music itself to matters referred to by the music. They will therefore force the experience of music to be nonmusical and, even more important, *teach people that nonmusical responses to music are appropriate and desirable.* In this, such "teaching" does educate. If one is not a Referentialist, but instead is an Absolutist, one can only say that such "teaching" can only miseducate.

Music education has been and is now to some degree *nonmusic* education. A stronger way to state it would be *antimusic* education. When teachers foster nonmusical experiences of music, when they give the impression that such experiences are what music is essentially for, when they prevent aesthetic experiences of music from taking place (let alone *helping* aesthetic experiences to take place), they are being nonmusic educators and are producing nonmusical people. All nonmusic education does is to get in the way of music education. But if music education is as important for human life as our philosophy has suggested, nonmusic education becomes a serious obstacle to the development of an important component—the aesthetic component—of people's lives. Of all people, music educators should not be the ones to weaken the power of music to be musically experienced.

Some people have the idea that nonmusical experiences are appropriate for younger children and can be phased out as the children grow older. What this says, in effect, is, "Let us make sure that we start children out on the wrong foot. Let us teach them, at the most impressionable time of their lives, that music is not an art, that they should experience music nonmusically, that the more nonmusical they become now the more likely it is they will become musical later. Let us prevent children from sharing the joy and delight and significance which music can add to life, for life begins later. Aesthetic experience is not for children; let us teach accordingly. Our non-aesthetic use of music will eventually lead to music as it really is. How? Somehow."

This attitude, all too common in music education and in arts education generally, has no doubt done more to block the growth of aesthetic sensitivity than any other single thing in education. If anything at all is known about how people learn, it is that people learn to do what they do. Teach children nonaesthetically and they will learn to be nonaesthetic. Teach them aesthetically and they will learn, to the level of whatever capacity they have, to be more aesthetically sensitive. If music education is to be aesthetic education, it must be, first of all, *music* education. It cannot be so if it fosters nonmusical experiences of music.

THE TECHNICAL-CRITICAL LEVEL

The technical-critical experience of music is separated from the referential experiences because it is different in kind even though it is, in and of itself, a nonaesthetic or preaesthetic experience. In this response the perception is of the technical, mechanical elements which go into the making of music and the reaction is a function of that kind of perception: "That soprano certainly has trouble in her upper register." "Did you notice how the conductor used his right hand for some of the cues?" "I heard this pianist several years ago and his style has changed a great deal since then." "The sound on this recording is blurry." "The auditorium isn't very full. I wonder if it will affect the tone quality." "The intonation is terrible in this band." "What a great vibrato."

An endless number of such responses surrounds musical activity in all its aspects. Much of this kind of perception is directly applicable to the development of perception which is musical. By itself it is preaesthetic but when used as a means to aesthetic ends is a necessary aspect of music education.

One of the major occupational hazards of being a professional musician, music teacher, or music student is that one can easily become so concerned about the techniques and apparatus of musical activity that one seldom has enough "psychical distance" to be able to experience music musically. This is too bad, but at least the professional can gain solace from the fact that he is being paid (or will be paid) for his expertise and that if he is sometimes too busy being an expert to enjoy the music this is part of the game. There is no such excuse, however, for focusing so heavily on the technical-critical level of experience that students are not able to go beyond it to the aesthetic experience of music. Many people get the impression from their musical education that the technical-critical response is the "really musical" way to experience music. This is an understandable result of the common and unfortunate separation in music education of technical learnings from musical aesthetic experiences. The next two chapters will expand on this idea.

MUSICAL EXPERIENCE: THE SENSUOUS DIMENSION

Having discussed several ways to respond to music nonmusically or premusically, the characteristics of musical experience itself can now be made explicit. Musical experiences have three major dimensions or aspects beyond and including an awareness of nonmusical references when such references exist. All three dimensions are present in all musical experiences: they are listed in order only because that is the only way language is capable of dealing with things, consecutively rather than simultaneously. Musical experience includes all three simultaneously in various mixtures.

The sensuous dimension is represented as an open-ended continuum because its range extends from the nonmusical (or minimally musical) to musical responses of a sophistication not yet fully explored or understood. In the sensuous response music is processed for its surface sound qualities with little if any attention to the inner organization and interrelation of the sounds. Rather than responding with a perceptive ear for coherent events one experiences "with the skin," the immediate sound itself—its surface texture and intensity and color—being not so much heard as felt tactilely.

All experiences of music ranging from the most naively non-musical to the most deeply musical include the sensuous element, for sound is always felt physically whether or not it is really heard. But while the sensuous element is a necessary component of all experiences of music, it can be and often is the dominant level of response. At the nonmusical end of the continuum, the sensuous experience is a mindless, undiscerning, passive wallowing in the sheer existence of sound. The sound can be the driving, hypnotic beat of rock and roll, overwhelming in primitiveness and volume, entering the pores more than the ears, vibrating every muscle (many of which oldsters have not used in years) and blotting out everything but soundsense. But it can also be equally mindless while not so earthy, as when those no longer young find their own (more restrained) physical pleasure in the tickle of Lawrence Welk's bubbling sounds, or the soothing balm of Mantovani's shimmering strings, sparkling brasses, glistening woodwinds. The "kicks" in both cases are sensuous ones, minimally musical because perception is minimal but very attractive and pleasant because sensuality is, after all, a basic human characteristic.

Bathing in warm sound is so popular a pastime (the temperature of the sound simply cools down as age advances) that a whole industry exists to supply "music to be caressed by." There is nothing wrong with such use of music except for the impression it gives that all musical experience should be tranquilizing in its effects. This tense world is so overlayed with soothing Muzak that one feels, occasionally, as if he is wading through aural molasses. This use of sound for creature comfort no doubt fills a human need, but it does make it more difficult for the music educator to use music for quite the opposite purpose, that is, to help people feel more vividly rather than less so.

It is paradoxical, then, that the sensuous response to music can be powerfully aesthetic, requiring high levels of perception and reaction. As one moves along the continuum from mindless immersion in indiscriminate sound to subtle, complex, expressive uses of the sensuous qualities of music, one enters a seemingly endless realm of artistic meaning embodied in the direct impact of sound itself. All important music, no matter when composed, depends for at least part of its expressiveness on the sensuousness of tone, and it is one of the major responsibilities of music education to help people become more sensitive to this dimension of musical affect. The means for doing so are the same as for all musical education: helping people perceive the conditions of sound which are expressive (in this case sensuously expressive) in contexts which encourage feelingful reactions to what is perceived. No matter what type of music is being used, no matter what the age of the students, no matter what the activity—singing, playing, composing, listening, and so on—musical learning will include some attention to the sensuous level of aesthetic responsiveness.

An interesting fact of contemporary life is that the sensuous level of expressiveness has expanded enormously in a very short time. In the past the sensuous component was just that—a component part of an aesthetic presentation which was organized to be perceived for its interrelated properties presented through a sensuous medium. Now, in practically every mode of art, the sensuous has been used as the major or total artistic presentation, with little or no intrinsic interrelations of expressive properties (or no *perceivable* interrelations at any rate) in the sense of coherent, related, structured, interconnected. Aleatory (chance, random) art, or art so structured that it gives the impression of randomness such as so-called "total serialization" in music (4, Chapter 7 and Part III) has no content of perceivable interrelated events and so must be responded to at the sheerly sensuous level and is usually intended to be responded to that way. But far from being a mindless, passive kind of response, this level of sensuous experience can be extremely active and perceptive. And compositions that are not random but employ continuous repetition and/or minimal goal-directedness (pieces such as by Steve Reich, Philip Glass, Gyorgy Ligeti, musics of world cultures such as India and Africa) depend less on the Western use of "movement toward arrival" than on use of "activation of ongoing energies." In such music the sensuous level plays a major role. This must not be construed as somehow inferior or less musical just because Western ears are more attuned to music that "goes some place" and "gets there." Modern works of art less formally structured than is traditional, and cultures in which art depends less on periodic contrasts and points of arrival and departure than it does in the West, illustrate the diversity of subjective experience and the richness and complexity of sensuous responsiveness as a meaningful source of artistic experience. Music educators must be aware of this and provide sufficient opportunities for students to share such meaning through performing, composing, listening to, and discussing representative types of such music.

The sensuous dimension of musical experience has special power for performers. In addition to responding sensuously to the sounds they are creating, performers feel in their bodies the actual processes by which sound is produced because all creation of sound stems from bodily effort. We know too little about the effects on musical experience of the physical making of musical sounds, but all of us who are or have been performers know that our experience of music includes a "knowing in the body" that comes from performing. This is a major reason we must provide the opportunity for performance to all children, in general music classes and, for those who choose to involve themselves further, in performance groups. Aside from and including the obvious creative and pedagogical opportunities in performance, the sensuous experience of making music is a powerful, meaningful dimension of the satisfaction a music program offers its participants.

MUSICAL EXPERIENCE:
THE PERCEPTUAL AND CREATIVE DIMENSIONS

The perceptual response includes, in addition to the ever-present sensuous dimension, (1) discernment to some degree of the constituent elements of music—melody, rhythm, harmony, and so on and (2) reaction to the expressiveness of the perceived musical interrelations. In musical terms it is a matter of perceiving, for example, the contour of a melody, the relation of the melody to its harmony, the rhythmic structure of both, the tone color of the presentation, the function the melody and harmony serve in the developing form. But this kind of perception is far from being the coldly clinical "ear-training" which characterizes the technical-critical response. The perception is itself *feelingful* perception in which the musical events are experienced, first and foremost, as *expressive* events. When musical perception becomes separated from musical reaction the experience is preaesthetic or nonaesthetic. When musical reaction is caused by other things than musical perception the experience is, again, preaesthetic or nonaesthetic. The old, belabored distinction between the so-called "intellectual" (perceptive) and "emotional" (reactive) components of aesthetic experience is a fruitless and misleading one, for when experience is genuinely aesthetic, the two become indistinguishable.

The perceptual response, then, is a "reactively perceptive" one. Some people, especially highly trained musicians, may tend consciously to identify the actual musical devices which are used to create expressiveness. ("Here comes the deceptive cadence—now we go to the authentic.") The amount of conscious-naming (conceptualizing) which accompanies musical perception and reaction will range from very much to none at all depending on the background and/or personality of the listener. But it is extremely important to understand that musical perception in no way depends on the ability to name the technical devices which cause musical expressiveness. What must be perceived, *whether or not it can be named,* is the uncertainty of the movement through that deceptive cadence and the resolution of the movement in an authentic cadence. Being able to name the device employed is extremely helpful but as a means toward the end of making the expressiveness of the device more available for experiencing.

The creative response to music is an extension of the perceptual response. It includes, in addition to the perception of expressive musical events and the reaction to the perceived expressiveness, a constant recall and anticipation of musical events. The experience is marked by an absorption in the way the music sets up expectations, deviates from expected resolutions, causes uncertainty in modes of continuation, delays expected consequences of events, satisfies musical implications. The experiencer not only perceives the melody in relation to its harmony, for example, but anticipates changes in the movement of the melody and the harmonic changes which seem to be implied. He feels the section coming to a close, anticipating a cadence which will mark the end of one section and imply the beginning of another, noticing the unexpected treatment of the movement toward the cadence, the expressive diversions, the sudden fulfillment, the much-expected new melodic idea but with a surprising carryover of harmony from the previous section. His musical perception and musical reaction are brought to bear in such a way that he is, in a real sense, *creating along with the music.* He is absorbed in the world of expressive sound, both molding the experience by his active participation and being molded by the events as they interact with his expectations. There is a sense of "oneness" with the music—of being submerged in expressiveness while at the same time influencing the amount and quality of expressiveness gained.

The perceptual and creative responses, obviously, are intense, active, extremely attentive, engaging both mind and feelings together at high levels of concentration. This is worlds apart from the "let's relax to the music" kind of response so common inside and outside of educational settings. If one is to share the experience of human subjectivity presented by the aesthetic qualities of sound, one must share them in the only way they *can* be shared—by becoming absorbed in them with one's powers of thinking and feeling.

Creative responses to music, then, are not limited to composing and performing, which are creative in the more specific meaning of that word in that they create sounds newly imagined or bring to actuality the sounds imagined by a composer. That dimension of creativity, as it is explained in Chapter Four, is the one most often thought of in connection to music (and the arts generally) and of course is essential or there would be no music (or art). The point being made here is that all musical experience is self-created whether or not a person is composing or performing. We too seldom give credit to the creativity of musical listening as such and thereby tend to denigrate it in our music programs as if it was a passive, mindless waste of time that could better be spent in "real" creativity. That is not only untrue; it is also among the most serious weaknesses in all of music education, in that it leaves too neglected the development of the one capacity on which all experience of music depends—discerning, creative listening. Opportunities to perform and compose must build on and add to the foundational creative experience of music—listening—rather than replacing it or substituting for it.

THE RELATION OF SOUND TO FEELING

The explanation of musical experience given here implies a theory of how sound can be used to give rise to feelings. For the Referentialist, musical sounds produce feelings in the same way that any other symbol systems have their effects, by pointing to that which they symbolize. The Formalist separates feeling in music from the general realm of feeling in life. In Formalism, what we feel from music is the rightness and necessity of formal relationships in and of themselves. Expressionists would agree that music can refer to feelings outside the sounds themselves and also that formal balances can be and are experienced with feeling as well as with discernment. But neither of those answers explains the expressive richness of every aspect of sounds used musically. Whatever the style of a piece of music, from the most goal oriented to the most rambling, from the most tightly knit to the most free form, from the most complex to the simplest, every moment in which sounds are being responded to as intrinsically interconnected produces concomitant subjective responses in the person involved. How and why does sound have this power to cause feeling?

We may never have an exact, complete answer to such a question. Phenomenologists continue to work toward an explanation of how humans actually experience the world (Chapter Five, footnote 9, page 88) and the literature on emotions continues to grow,[5] but we must remember that we are dealing with an issue that strikes to the very heart of the mystery of human consciousness. How and why are humans conscious *at all*? So pervasive is this question, so staggeringly complex and so closely tied to our fundamental nature as creatures, that every culture throughout history has created explanatory stories for how humans came to be created as conscious beings. There is no reason to believe that such stories will not continue to be told, whether couched in allegorical or objective terms. So in the broad sense, we have asked a question to which there is not an answer, only a groping toward enough understanding that the question will not always consume us as we go about living our conscious lives.

But in a narrower sense there have been and continue to be musical-theoretical attempts to answer the question.[6] Perhaps the clearest and most extensive explanation of the processes by which sound can be organized to produce expressiveness is that given by Leonard B. Meyer (6). With many examples and detailed analyses Meyer shows how tonal events arouse tendencies, cause expectations, produce various kinds and degrees of tendency resolutions and expectation satisfactions. When a system of sound relationships—a piece of music—is experienced aesthetically, the tone-matrix of tensions and resolutions produces tensions and resolutions within the experiencer, and these are "significant" because they are analogous to the modes of human feeling. As Susanne Langer explains,

> The tonal structures we call "music" bear a close logical similarity to the forms of human feeling—forms of growth and attenuation, flowing and stowing, conflict and resolution, speed, arrest, terrific excitement, calm, or subtle activation and dreamy lapses—not joy and sorrow perhaps, but the poignancy of either and both—the greatness and brevity and eternal passing of everything vitally felt. Such is the pattern, or logical form, of sentience; and the pattern of music is that same form worked out in pure, measured sound and silence. Music is a tonal analogue of emotive life.[7]

For technical explanations of how rhythm, melody, harmony, form, and so on produce the conditions of affect, the reader should explore *Emotion and Meaning in Music*, especially Chapters III–VII. Two implications from Meyer's treatment of musical expressiveness are so relevant to music

[5]For overviews of scholarship on emotion, see Magda B. Arnold, ed., *Feelings and Emotions: The Loyola Symposium* (New York: Academic Press, 1970); Amelie O. Rorty, ed., *Explaining Emotions* (Berkeley: University of California Press, 1980); and Klaus R. Scherer and Paul Ekman, eds., *Approaches to Emotion* (Hillsdale, N.J.: Lawrence Erlbaum Associates, 1984).

[6]Recent work in music theory, such as that by Fred Lerdahl and Ray Jackendoff, *A Generative Theory of Tonal Music* (Cambridge, Mass.: MIT Press, 1983), and other works by these authors, indicate rising interest in the problem of the relation of structured sounds to experienced feelings.

[7]Susanne K. Langer, *Feeling and Form* (New York: Charles Scribner's Sons, 1953), p. 27.

education that attention to them is warranted at this point. The first has to do with the necessity of correct style expectations. The second concerns the matter of criteria for judging the quality of music.

STYLE AND MUSICAL EXPERIENCE

For sounds to have tendencies—to arouse expectations that certain things are likely to happen—and for musical tendencies to be manipulated in expressive ways by deviations, delays, resolutions, repetitions, uncertainties, and so on, a context must exist which provides people with a commonly accepted sphere of musical probabilities. Such a sphere of probabilities, in which a recognizable degree of predictability exists, is called a "style." When melody, rhythm, harmony, tone color, texture, and form are used in characteristic ways so that some unity of expectation is possible on the part of the perceiver, a style is in operation, providing the basic set of agreed-upon "likelihoods" for musical sharing to be built upon.

Trying to respond musically to sounds in an unknown style is like watching a game being played in which none of the rules or purposes are known to the person watching. One tries one's best to make some sense out of the proceedings, both in the music and the game, but unless some probabilities are discovered—some organizing factors which provide the possibility for perceiving relationships—the experience can only be meaningless. No sharing can take place because perception is nonexistent and reaction is therefore impossible (except the reaction of frustration).

A great deal of music is meaningless to a great many people (and therefore frustrating to them) because they are ignorant of the music's style; that is, they cannot perceive and react to the aural events as being coherent, interrelated, unified, sensible. Eastern music (by which is *not* meant the Tokyo Philharmonic playing Mozart's 40th) is largely unaccessible to the casual Western listener. Jazz is a closed book to many concert music lovers, and much concert music is meaningless to many jazz enthusiasts. Music of past eras in Western culture has little or no meaning for some people, and much contemporary music makes no sense to a great many listeners. Truly, the "universality" of musical sharing is more a fond hope than a reality.

Unfortunately, music education has often contributed to parochialism by emphasizing certain music styles (those in "good standing") and neglecting—sometimes *ignoring*—certain others. This is especially true in the education of young children, where experiences have often been limited to music which the children can sing, thus narrowing the field to the style of simple diatonicism and even to music using the pentatonic scale. Serious thought must be given to the dangers of such restricted acquaintance with style at the very age when tastes are being formed and long-lasting impressions are being made.[8] This raises the question of how much reliance should be placed on performance as the major mode of music education, a question which will be touched upon in the following chapters. It is clear that anything which restricts rather than widens familiarity with the rich diversity of styles available to people should be regarded with suspicion or, at the least, compensated for by other means of providing musical experiences.

The notion that students—of *any* age—should be protected from certain styles, these usually being the more puzzling contemporary styles, is one which a more mature profession would find intolerable. A two-pronged obligation is involved here: one to our students, who deserve the richest, most diverse possible musical fare, and the other to music itself, which deserves, at the very least, that those who are dedicated to a fuller sharing of this art not inadvertently produce people with restricted tastes, built-in prejudices, provincial preferences. The surest ways to keep musical options open, to encourage wide-ranging musical interests and widely varying musical pleasures, are (1) to display in all that is done at every stage of music education a joyous, open, free acceptance of good music in many styles and (2) to help people share more of the many styles of music by skillful teaching which shows how music is expressive no matter what its style. This implies a concentration on (1) those components of sound used in all styles, such as dynamics, tempo, the various media for producing sounds, pitch direction, register, range, rhythmic patterns, pace, consonance and dissonance, phrase structure, variety, repetition, and so on, and (2) how the expressive elements of sound are used in characteristic ways in each different style. Good music teaching—*musical* music teaching—will include such concerns as the background for all activities at every grade level.

CRITERIA FOR JUDGING THE QUALITY OF ART

Given that musical experience is a function of sensuous, perceptual and creative involvements with expressive sounds, what criteria can be applied to judge the quality of particular pieces that are being experienced? We cannot judge music as good or bad artistically on the basis of functional or referential components. Music must be assessed for its value as art on the basis of its effectiveness in providing opportunity for musical experience. Music educators especially must be informed about criteria for judgment because they are constantly forced to make such judgments, in choosing music for their students to experience and in assessing the

---

[8]For some comments about the importance of an early introduction to complex contemporary music, see (7), p. 274–76.

quality of their students' handling of that music. Whether or not music educators care to think of themselves as "arbiters of taste," an inevitable degree of control over musical experiences does exist and always will exist so long as formal teaching and learning of music takes place. It is impossible to avoid making value judgments about music when one deals with music as a professional. And while any overt imposition of musical values would be distasteful to most music educators and most students, the entire music education enterprise is built on the assumption that musical tastes can be improved, that musical experiences can be deepened, that musical enjoyment can be refined, that musical significance can be made more available to all people. These assumptions, all of which are very healthy and beyond criticism, do imply a movement toward "better" musical experiences of "better" music. The question is, what makes music, or any art, "better"?

There is a popular assumption that the quality of music or art in general cannot be defined—that excellence in the arts is merely a matter of taste, and, as we all know, in a democracy everyone's taste is equal in value to everyone else's. Further, *de gustibus non disputandum* (there is no disputing about tastes). It follows, in this view, that what music educators choose for their students to listen to and perform is strictly a function of their own personal taste, which is no doubt in conflict with that of at least some people in their communities who then regard their taste as faulty if not perverse.

But the criteria for excellence in art are in fact well known and can be applied with a high degree of discrimination by people who are trained to do so. Of course subjective judgments are involved and *must* be involved. In that, the arts are no different from a great many other fields in which informed, educated, expert subjective judgments are essential, fields such as medicine, psychology, social work, business, and on and on. In all these endeavors subjectivity must be applied, but there is a great big difference between ignorant subjectivity and refined subjectivity. In the arts, as in everything else humans do, there is no substitute for professional expertise, and that requires conscious awareness of the criteria upon which we base our judgments about art and its performance, that is, the criteria upon which our taste has been developed. Further, our responsibilities in arts education include that we educate our students about those criteria so they understand what guides us and also so they can use the criteria as guides for their own judgments.

While the literature on judgments about art—the literature of aesthetic criticism—is vast and complex, a workable base of operations can be built on just four criteria for assessing the quality of any art work and, in the case of the performing arts, its performance. These four are (1) craftsmanship, (2) sensitivity, (3) imagination, and (4) authenticity.

Craftsmanship is the expertness by which the materials of art are molded into expressiveness. Each art has its own unique material—sound in music, movement in dance, language in poetry, the various visual media in the visual arts, and so on. These materials, as all materials, resist. That is why art requires materials—to set up a situation in which resistance must be encountered. The creative act in art requires a confrontation with resisting material in which a resolution of the resistances is achieved through the use of craft, sensitivity, and imagination. The depth of resistance, the degree of tension in the act of creation and therefore in the resulting work of art, is one major factor in the greatness of that work. No great art work is achieved without great work. The materiality of art is the battleground, the field of forces, upon which the creative struggle takes place.

To struggle successfully, to win through to an expressive form, requires a high degree of skill in both knowing profoundly about the material and acting with mastery upon it. This is quite different from skill in the more everyday sense, which is basically an ability to do things with some degree of dexterity. Craftsmanship includes that, of course, but reaches a level in which the resisting material is so integrated within the self as to be shaped by a unity of mind, hand, and feeling. That is why there is something almost spiritual about craftsmanship, something that so integrates our human powers that we feel elevated by it. Anyone who has ever achieved real craftsmanship in some aspect of life knows its tremendous impact. When we labor to refine our craftsmanship, by perfecting our technical skills, by identifying deeply with our chosen medium, by endless practice with its expressive potentials, all of which require time and sweat and often frustration, we are not just pursuing dexterity—we are searching for creative communion with those materials, and to the degree we achieve it we have achieved craftsmanship.

Craftsmanship exists in degrees. At one end is virtuosity, and it is no mystery why we regard with awe the chosen few who display it. But at the other end are those small moments we have all experienced when things come together—when our know-how and our insight reinforce each other and we say about something we or our students have done or are trying to do, "That's not bad." A song, a drawing, a little dance, a verse of poetry— all can embody the significance that craftsmanship gives when it is present. We must, when choosing art for use in education and when performing art as part of education, be deeply aware of the quiet "shining through" that shows that craftsmanship has touched the work. Such work touches us.

The absence of craftsmanship is signaled by shoddiness, by disrespect for material, by forcing material to do something rather than doing what it requires, by skill that is devoid of heart—skill that manipulates the material rather than serving its expressiveness. Such work demeans us.

Professional expertise means having enough craftsmanship to be able to tell the difference.

The second criterion for judging art, sensitivity, has to do with the depth and quality of feeling captured in the dynamic form of a work. Since the function of art is to give objective existence to feelings which are otherwise only private and transitory, a medium is needed—something that will hold onto the fleetingness of subjective experiences and give them outward being. The materials of art do precisely this. Sounds, movements, colors, shapes, the interplay of human forces as in a play or a novel, all these are the public counterparts of private subjectivities. As artists shape their materials into form, they are at one and the same time giving shape to their feelings.

It is precisely because artists are not giving vent to a feeling they are having but are building up an expressive complex of developed feelings (as explained in Chapter Three) that we are able to judge the success or failure of the result. We cannot judge as good or bad or fair a person who is truly expressing his feelings. Would we say "that baby cries very well," or "only moderately well," or "that lady is screaming nicely," or "she's screaming OK but I heard a lady screaming much better the other day"?

Every time an artist acts on his material, he makes a decision. Thousands of such decisions are made for every painting or poem or film or play. The decisions are made on the basis of some overall plan: a lyric poem, say, has certain ways to do what it does, a requiem mass can do certain things but not other things, and so forth. They are also made on the basis of what just happened in the unfolding work, what might therefore happen now, what it might lead to happening a little later. Sensitivity is the "in touchness" an artist has with the developing, forming feelings, so that he or she can make ongoing decisions that ring true, that convince, that grasp us by their expressive power. Some works move us a little—they take us on a pleasant journey of feeling that we enjoy. Some works plunge us so deeply into complexities of feeling and intensities of feeling that we emerge from the experience profoundly changed. All works of art that are sensitively created have the potential to touch our feelings—to take them on an adventure, small or large, that deepens our sense of self.

The absence of sensitivity is betrayed by works in which the obvious overwhelms the subtle, in which the surface of feeling is offered rather than challenges to feel more deeply. The world is full of art so called that gives immediate gratification of feeling, that condescends to our subjectivity rather than expanding it. Such art cheapens our sense of ourselves.

Professional expertise means being sensitive to the difference.

The criterion of imagination deals with the vividness of an art object and its performance. Most of our lives, moment by moment and day by day, is lived at a fairly placid emotional level. At the everyday level we may, if we're fortunate, feel a general peace, a sense of ongoing satisfaction and pleasure with ourselves and what we're doing. But we also need, from time to time, to make contact with the depths of which human experience is capable.

Art reaches for the depths. It may not try to reach very far. A Strauss Waltz, say, or a Neil Simon comedy, or a light opera, aren't intended to plunge us into the deepest reaches of feeling. But even when the intent is modest, as in such works, success requires an out-of-the-ordinary experience. No matter how small or how limited the work of art, we must be to some extent captured by it, at least for a moment and at least to a degree of feeling that dips us a bit below the surface. Imagination in a work of art is what captures our feelings.

To be captured, something must grab us. When we expect a thing to happen, and it happens, we often move right through the experience without noticing it. It is when we are led to expect something and it does *not* happen, or it happens in a way we did not foresee, or it only happens after several unexpected deviations have occurred, *that's* when we begin to pay attention. Artists constantly strive to get us to pay that kind of attention. They are experts in setting us up and then, by making a decision we would not have expected them to make, grasping our feelings and forcing us to respond. It may be the smallest change from the expected—that change is what gets us.

At every moment in the creative act, whether it consists of composing a piece of music or painting a landscape or writing a poem, craftsmanship and sensitivity combine to guide decisions that are also, to some extent, imaginative—that do not follow through in a straight, undeviating line of expectation but reach for the original solution, the unexpected event, the novel twist and turn, the unfolding of events that pull us, as we follow them, to feel more deeply because we cannot entirely predict the outcome. Great works of art present such challenges to our feelings by their richness of imagination—sometimes the audacity of their imagination—as to shake us to our foundations. Every good work of art, no matter how simple, must have enough originality to vivify our feelings, to bring them to more vibrant life. All such works, across the entire spectrum from the modest to the profound, enliven our experience.

When imagination is absent or is insufficient, a work of art betrays us. We go to it for vividness. What we get is the docile, the prosaic, the uninspired, the cliché. Many so-called art works, whether through timidity or literal-mindedness, have the opposite effect on us than art exists to have; they depress our feelings rather than excite them. Such art at best leaves us untouched. At worst it deadens us.

Professional expertise means being alive to the difference.

ART, MORALITY, AND DISCIPLINE

The final criterion for quality in art, authenticity, raises the issue of morality. This is among the most confused topics in the entire realm of aesthetics, and it cannot be treated fully in the context of this book. But a few points can be made. The major one is that morality in art, like meaning in art, has little if anything to do with the nonaesthetic content of art—with the statements art may contain or actions it may depict or events it may tell about or opinions it might offer about the world and its workings. For art all such content is raw material and as such is neither aesthetically moral or immoral. It is how the material is treated that makes the difference. A novel or a play, for example, may be filled with lust and violence and war and greed and betrayal and every other problematic behavior of human beings and yet be profoundly moral nevertheless, such as Tolstoy's *War and Peace* or Shakespeare's *Hamlet*. On the other hand a work may be full of sweetness and light yet have the effect of degrading our humanity: think of dime-store pictures of Jesus in day-glo colors on black velvet.

What then is morality in art? Simply put, it is the genuineness of the artist's interaction with his materials, in which the control by the artist includes a giving way to the demands of the material. As much as an artist shapes his material his material shapes him. The material of art takes on its own life as it begins to be shaped, making its own requirements which must be felt by the artist. To the degree the artist responds honestly, not forcing his materials to do his will but interacting creatively with the dynamics that have been set in motion, to that degree he is acting morally. It is when an artist ignores the unfolding interplay, or bypasses it to achieve something external to the needs of the developing feelings in the creative act, that he has violated his art and thereby corrupted it. As John Dewey says,

> If one examines into the reason why certain works of art offend us, one is likely to find that the cause is that there is no personally felt emotion guiding the selecting and assembling of the material presented. We derive the impression that the artist...is trying to regulate by conscious intent the nature of the emotion aroused. We are irritated by a feeling that he is manipulating materials to secure an effect decided upon in advance.[9]

In art that is immoral. What it produces is art so called that displays sentimentality rather than sensitivity, the surface appearance of feeling rather than its underlying vitality. An honest work takes us wherever it

[9]John Dewey, *Art as Experience* (New York: Capricorn Books, 1958), p. 68.

goes—to the unpleasant as well as the pleasant. No matter—it will, by virtue of its fidelity to its inner needs, ennoble our humanity. A dishonest work forces us to a foregone conclusion. We arrive at it with a nasty taste in our mouths—we know we've been used. Our feelings yearn for honesty, not for sentiment. We are honored by the genuine, no matter how tough to take. We are humiliated by the fake in art as in everything else.

Professional expertise requires that we respect the difference.

It is often claimed that the study of music trains children to be disciplined, a claim based on the narrow idea that discipline consists of forcing oneself to do tedious work, such as practicing, whether one wants to or not. The claim for the training of discipline is also based on an outmoded psychological view—"faculty psychology"—abandoned shortly after the turn of this century when it was demonstrated conclusively that human mental functioning is not a series of separate faculties (discipline, imagination, reasoning, etc.) that can be exercised in the way that muscles of the body can be exercised to strengthen them.[10] The combination of a limited sense of what discipline consists of and a long since discredited psychology as its basis makes the claim for "music study as discipline" both ludicrous and demeaning. Would we honestly set up as paragons of moral, disciplined life-styles many of the great musicians both in history and in the present? Can we say with straight faces that studying music and being involved in the world of music makes people better—more moral—than people who study and are involved in any of the world's other endeavors? Do we want to argue with coaches—at their level—that music, like athletics, "makes boys into men" (and girls into men as well, no doubt)? We can only make fools of ourselves (and probably fool some of the people some of the time) when we emphasize that music study is valuable because it imparts discipline in such senses, because in those senses, despite their popular appeal, we misrepresent what discipline is, what morality is, and what music is.

There is a sense in which music and the arts require morality and discipline in their most profound meanings. It is the sense that involvement with art calls upon one to give oneself up to the unfolding requirements of the expressive materials with which one is working, controlling one's behavior in the service of a greater good than one's own immediate needs. Discipline as inner self-control, freely exercised to serve larger ends, is discipline in the truest sense of the word, in which humans demonstrate their capacity for self-transcendence. This is what is meant by the insight,

---

[10]An excellent short history of faculty psychology and its relation to the doctrine of formal discipline (and the satire of it called "The Saber-Tooth Curriculum") is given in Robert F. Biehler, *Psychology Applied to Teaching* (Boston: Houghton Mifflin, 1971), pp. 265–67.

so often expressed, that art has a "moral" dimension. It has nothing to do with morality in the superficial sense of acting in accordance with society's rules and regulations, necessary as that is if societal order is to prevail. It is morality as only the human condition allows it to be manifested—choice within freedom, restraint because it is needed, adapting oneself willingly because it is right to do so.

Authenticity as a requirement for quality in art, along with craftsmanship, sensitivity, and imagination, calls attention to the inner integrity of the expressive core in a piece of music. No piece can be good as music without such internal cohesion, or "truth to feeling." We sense in Beethoven's Fifth Symphony the struggle he engaged in to capture the veracity of expression his self-imposed journey of creation required him to discover. We intuit that he did in this music what he sensed deeply he was required to do, the rightness of the outcome shaped by his craftsmanship and sensitivity and imagination yet also providing a demand upon them to which he consented to bend his will. The morality of this music has nothing to do with its extramusical references (there are none) or Beethoven's extramusical life (better left unmentioned). It has to do with authenticity—doing what is needed because that is what it is inherently right to do. That is discipline—that is moral—at the level which ennobles us as humans whenever we experience it.

We don't need to be a Beethoven to experience discipline in music. A child singing a song, sensing the flow of the melody and singing it as it needs to be sung, has experienced the power of music to shape her experience in order to serve its expressive demands. She has not learned "about" discipline—she has had an experience "of " it. What one knows when one knows music includes the "knowing of " the need for music to be master and us to be servant. A child practicing a piece, discovering its internal demands and yielding to them as she experiences them and shapes the sounds to capture what needs to be captured, is undergoing discipline—is being moral. Art never preaches: art requires us to experience. The joy expressed by artists who say about their work that they "serve their art" is precisely the joy of disciplined, intrinsically moral experience. Music educators do not provide discipline or teach morality. Music does.

APPLYING THE CRITERIA FOR JUDGING ART

The four criteria of quality in art—craftsmanship, sensitivity, imagination, and authenticity—provide helpful guidelines for the professional arts educator as works are chosen for study, for performance, and for experience, and as comments are made to help students improve works they are creating. And while there has never been and no doubt never will be complete agreement as to which works of art achieve moderate or good or excellent or "great masterwork" success in the level to which they exemplify the criteria, enough agreement does exist about enough examples that teachers can choose works with sufficient confidence that much can be gained from them. But should music education always aim for the top—for the established masterworks—as the only worthy examples to be studied?

It would be unrealistic and unnecessary to aim for constant use of great music in teaching and learning, partly because of the obvious limitations of students' musical capacities and partly because people, of any age, should not be expected to operate at the farthest reaches of their abilities at all times. Some reasonableness of expectations is called for, in which music of a wide range of goodness is used, providing sufficient challenge for the particular age group while at the same time providing musical enjoyment for immediate sharing. And occasionally it is helpful to use an "awful example"—a piece obviously deficient in excellence or expressiveness—as a way to make a particular point. To insist on studying nothing but the monuments of music literature, to rule out that large segment of music which, while well made and genuinely expressive is not of the *creme de la creme*, is to deprive a great many people of any musical satisfaction at all and to expect that all musical experience should be at the deepest level of involvement. This is certainly unnecessary. At the same time a heavy use of unimportant music, of "pretty" pieces with little muscle, of that vast realm of music which is not really bad but certainly is not very good, makes of music education a whipped-cream dessert, pleasant and light, but not to be considered an important part of educational fare. If the general level of musical quality is such that a constant movement toward the "better" is taking place—that is, a movement toward music of more refinement and subtlety in craftsmanship, more sensitive, probing embodiment of feelings, more challenging, wide-ranging imagination, and, as a bedrock, pieces that are authentic in their particular style and in their individuality—then music education will be fulfilling its role reasonably and responsibly.

The movement toward "better" music applies with equal relevance to the improvement of students' compositions and performances. It is especially important for children themselves to be given many opportunities to apply criteria for judgment to music they are composing and performing and experiencing. As pointed out previously (page 114-116), judgments should not interfere with immediate, open-minded experiences of music because when judgments are premature they stifle the experience rather than enhancing it. But as one begins to reflect about a piece one has heard, or about music one is composing or performing, judgments must come into the picture. Music teachers often forget that such judgments, especially about performance, are their students' business and not just their own. If students are to become independent about music, they must learn to apply the criteria by themselves; this is an essential aspect of educating them to become musical. The vast majority will never become professionals, of course, but they will have experienced how professionals and sophisticated amateurs judge music relevantly. And those who do go on to become professionals will have been given a firm foundation for whatever aspect of music they may become involved with, for no aspect of the music profession is devoid of the need for expert judgment making. To remove the prejudice that judging art is entirely subjective or whimsical, replacing it with the understanding that criteria can be identified and applied reasonably, is an important function of music education—a function far too often neglected. It is a necessary component of the music program, which must be developed as systematically as other essential skills and understandings.

THE RELEVANCE OF OLD MUSIC AND POPULAR MUSIC STYLES

Two often-debated questions about suitable music for music education can be answered by applying the conceptions in the foregoing discussion. These are the questions of (1) the relevance or irrelevance of older music for modern experience and (2) the propriety or impropriety of using popular musics in music education.

When a work of art is weak in craftsmanship and superficial in expressiveness, it is irrelevant to human experience no matter when it was made. Conversely, a work of excellence and genuine expressiveness, from any period in history, has the power to reveal a sense of feeling to all who are capable of responding to it musically. The point of using a wide variety of styles in music education is to ensure that good music of any age can be perceived relevantly and responded to feelingfully. Of course much music of the past is dated and beside the point for modern sensibilities, but always and in every case such music is irrelevant because it is "of a time" and its time has passed. Many art works are limited by their dependence on fashion. They are not so much autonomous works, valuable in and of themselves, as they are instances of the peculiar mode of expression of their time. When the time has gone the value of the work is gone. Many such works can be regarded as "camp"—as old-fashioned, banal, "arty" in the worst sense, charming in their essential irrelevance.

The better the work of art, the more it transcends its time of creation and is relevant to human experience in general. Of course styles change, but works of excellence are vital, living sources of insight into the human condition no matter how different in style from the one then current. The notion that art works should be regarded as "an expression of their time" (a popular idea in "humanities" approaches) misses the point of art's value except for the most superficial works, which really *are* little more than "an expression of their time."

It is especially true of today's culture that good art of the past is readily accessible and widely acceptable. To concentrate on the art of one's own time to the exclusion of good art of *any* time is as provincial as the opposite, that is, insisting that only old art is good art. The criteria for choosing music, then, are essentially ahistorical—that sufficient craftsmanship, sensitivity, imagination, and authenticity be present to deepen the musical experience of the particular students being taught.

Do popular musics—the variety of rock styles and other styles—qualify as a valid source of music literature to be experienced in schools through listening, composing, and performing?

First, a distinction must be drawn between the various popular musics and jazz, the latter being a musical style domain with a complex history, a well-developed literature, a rich variety and abundance of music of unquestionable excellence and profound expressiveness. While jazz still finds itself fighting the old, tired battle of its "impolite" origins, it has long since become accepted for what it is—a fascinating and valuable source of musical experience.

But what of popular music? Here the question of musical value does have relevance, and, to complicate matters, the generation gap makes it difficult for communication to take place between music educators of varying ages and between teachers and students. As a result the debate about rock and popular music in the schools often seems to have generated more heat than light. A few ideas from this chapter and previous ones might be of some help in thinking about this issue.

To rule out of court any music without regard to its inherent musical quality is to act from an irrelevant basis for judging musical value. Just because music is popular among young people does not, in and of itself, make it unsuitable for use in music education. The question to be asked about such music is the same that should be asked about *any* music: Is enough musical quality available here to help musical perception and reaction grow? An answer to this question in regard to contemporary popular musics must necessarily be based on personal and professional judgment. It can be argued—and well argued—that some popular music of the present time (an astonishing amount, as a matter of fact) is of extremely high quality in musical excellence and musical expressiveness. The best of this music is at least as good if not much better than the best popular music of any time in the past, and of a musical level which transcends its popular context and becomes, in and of itself, musically valuable. To rule out such music from music education would be not only a loss of fine material, but, even worse, an artificial, elitist mode of behavior which can only make the music education enterprise seem artificial and elitist.

At the same time it must be recognized that a vast wasteland of musical inanity exists in the popular music field because of the enormous profits to be made catering to mass desires for experiences only marginally related to music as such. Much of popular music is a vehicle for nonmusical experience and therefore has little to do with the function of school music as aesthetic education. We can bypass such music safely because few youngsters would expect or want it to be brought in to school. When we include examples of the various popular styles, we can engage students overtly in the decision-making process: What pieces exemplify the best craftsmanship for their particular style? Which are musically sensitive and imaginative? Is there an inner authenticity to the piece as well as a genuineness in its style? Explaining the reasons for our own choices, and tapping our students' (usually superior) acquaintance with good examples they can suggest, makes of the enterprise a shared exploration of potentials for high-quality musical experience. That can be a healthy balance to the teacher-dominated program we are so used to, benefiting everyone psychologically as well as musically. We expect our students to be open-minded about the great diversity of music a good program will include. We must demonstrate the same open-mindedness, judging music not by whether it is in an "acceptable" or "appropriate" style but by whether it exemplifies the qualities that make a work of art good no matter its style.

THE RELEVANCE OF MUSIC OF VARIOUS CULTURES

The diversity of musics represented in school music programs must include, in addition to music of every historical period and popular and jazz styles, musics associated with various ethnic groups and cultures around the world. Our profession has recognized this in recent years, as it has also recognized the validity of using popular literature, and has tried to incorporate a fair representation of such musics in its materials. This is partly because of our growing social awareness—our raised consciousness about the need for America's ethnic diversity to be celebrated rather than homogenized. We are also more aware of the way the world is shrinking, making our country less insulated from cultures very different from our own.

Underlying our social obligation to honor the ethnic groups represented in our schools, and our need to participate in America's growing internationalism, is an aesthetic reason for experiencing music from a variety of cultures—a reason adding artistic validity to the social imperatives. It is that, while music as a whole captures and displays the dynamics of human subjective experience, music of each ethnic-cultural subgroup manifests that experience in the particular way in which that group experiences the world subjectively. The reason the world does not have just one style of music is that each culture has its special shading of affective experience of the world. Music—and all art—is the most powerful way to explore and experience the specificity of how life is felt by each group sharing a communal subjective identity.

We are instructed, by the diversity of ethnic music styles, that human feeling is universally existent but is also expressed uniquely by each culture. That is precisely the social lesson our children must learn through their musical education; that all human beings share the basic condition of subjective awareness and that each culture experiences this awareness with a special character. Human beings are both universally alike and culturally different; that is the human paradox embodied most strikingly in art.

Honoring cultural diversity at its deepest level—the level of affective distinctiveness—requires honoring one's own culture and sharing it richly with one's children while at the same time sharing with them the flavors of cultures other than their own. It would be a serious error to neglect either, depriving children of the particularity of their own heritage or the universality of other heritages. We must not be so "multicultural" in our outlook that we forget to enrich each child's musical experience of his or her inherited subculture; that would be to ignore a precious birthright. At the same time we cannot be so ethnically delimited as to deprive children of the joy of sharing the world's multitudinous flavors, both for the sheer enjoyment of those riches and the awareness that his or her own culture is one among many. We have to achieve a very difficult, very subtle balance here—as difficult and as subtle as the human issue it reflects, in which each of us is both a member of a particular group that gives us an essential aspect of our identity, and of the larger group that is the larger human community, also giving us our identity.

Because of our devotion to "democratic principles" we can easily go to the extreme of neglecting the specific ethnic musics represented among the particular children we are teaching. That would be tragic. We need to give honor to *specific* musics, and in multiethnic communities that requires the music teacher to use all possible community resources to bolster his or her own capacities to cope. But at the other extreme the program can get so ethnically focused as to forget that (1) the United States is part of a larger culture—the culture of Western music—that should be part of the inheritance of each of our citizens, and (2) we must also experience some of the diversity of heritages from around the world.

When we are aware of our dual obligation we can keep ourselves in good balance from moment to moment. And we can get the maximum benefit from all the music we include when we remember that each piece, no matter its cultural origin, should be studied and experienced for its *artistic* power including but transcending any specific cultural references. It is, after all, as *music* that we treasure this or that piece, and it is, after all, for *musical experience* that we aim. That is where we discover both the specialness of feeling a piece exemplifies and its instantiation of feeling as being universal. There is no substitute, in the end, for being an effective *music* teacher, helping each child experience each piece in its musical veracity. That, finally, is where its cultural veracity is located.

How can music education promote musical experiences of music and therefore help share musical meaning more fully? Three major aspects of music education have evolved as the means by which musical learnings can take place: general music, performance, and music studied in company with its sister arts. The question must now be asked: How can each of these components of the program contribute to aesthetic education?

SUPPLEMENTARY READINGS

1. Beardsley, Monroe. *Aesthetics: Problems in the Philosophy of Criticism.* Indianapolis: Hackett, 1981.

2. Clifton, Thomas. *Music as Heard: A Study in Applied Phenomenology.* New Haven: Yale University Press, 1983.

3. Dahlhaus, Carl. *Esthetics of Music.* Cambridge University Press, 1982.

4. Langer, Susanne K. *Feeling and Form.* New York: Charles Scribner's Sons, 1953, Chapter 7, "The Image of Time," Chapter 8, "The Musical Matrix," Chapter 9, "The Living Work." See comment under (5).

5. Langer, Susanne K. *Philosophy in a New Key.* New York: Mentor Books, 1942, Chapter 8, "On Significance in Music." This chapter and the three listed in (4) contain Langer's most extended treatments of music. They will reward the patient reader with a great many valuable ideas about how music functions. If one chapter were to be selected, "The Living Work" in *Feeling and Form* would probably be the most immediately useful.

6. Meyer, Leonard B. *Emotion and Meaning in Music.* Chicago: University of Chicago Press, 1956, Chapter 1, pp. 22–42, and the remainder of the book. After completing his discussion of the relation of affect and musical experience (pp. 22–42), Meyer presents detailed musical analyses employing Gestalt laws of pattern perception. While the serious student will want to study this material carefully, a quicker reading will serve to introduce the principles upon which Meyer builds his theory of musical expectation.

7. More recent works by this author have expanded his original concepts to include musics less goal oriented in structure than he had previously dealt with, because he recognized that many musics of the world did not follow tendency-expectation patterns as clearly as music of the Western common practice period. See his "Toward a Theory of Style," in B. Lang, ed., *The Concept of Style*, (Philadelphia: University of Pennsylvania Press, 1979); "Exploiting Limits: Creation, Archetypes,

and Style Change," *Daedalus*, 109, no. 2 (1980); and "Innovation, Choice and the History of Music," *Critical Inquiry*, 9, no. 3 (1983).

8. Meyer, Leonard B. *Music, the Arts, and Ideas*. Chicago: University of Chicago Press, 1967. Part I contains five previously published articles on music and art, of which Chapters 1, 2, and 3 are extremely helpful discussions of various aspects of music. Chapter 5, "The End of the Renaissance?" is a most provocative treatment of randomness in art. The remainder of the book presents as lucid a discussion of contemporary artistic trends, especially of "total serialism" in music, as one is likely to find in the complex literature on this subject.

The philosophy
in action:
The general music
program

8

The premise of this book, as stated in Chapter One, is that music education is valuable because the art of music is valuable. Since so many things
are valuable, and education cannot be responsible for all of them, schools
must concentrate on those subjects that embody values regarded as unique
and essential for all students. In Western culture at this time in history
certain subjects have come to be regarded as basic in that their value seems
to be necessary for all. Auxiliary subjects are those in which the value is
not considered essential, or is considered to be relevant to only a few, or
can be gained by studying something else more important. Such subjects
are allowed in school as pleasant or useful adjuncts to the extent they do
not interfere with the basics in any significant way. Music and the arts occupy this auxiliary status. (Chapter Ten will expand on the historical
reasons for this situation.)

That a culture's values should determine its education is entirely
proper, and to the extent education is successful in both inculcating and
refining a culture's values, education may be considered successful. The
field of study focusing on values—explaining them, studying them,
evaluating them, suggesting how to apply and improve them—is

philosophy. So one can substitute the word "philosophy" for the word "values" in the first sentence of this paragraph. A culture's philosophy determines what education should include and successful education both carries out and develops the culture's philosophy.

This book has attempted to offer a philosophy which explains why the value of music and the arts for human life is unique and essential for all people, because no subject that is not essential or not unique or not relevant for all people can expect to be regarded as basic. That is the way it should be: education cannot afford to spend more than small amounts of time on the thousands of potential learnings that are positive but secondary. So to the degree that a philosophy of music and arts education can establish the case for the essentiality and uniqueness and all inclusiveness of these subjects, it will aid in having them be regarded as basic in the education enterprise.

But while a convincing philosophy is necessary if a subject is to be accepted in education, it is not sufficient. The subject must also be able to fulfill the requirements that it be teachable to all students, learnable by all students, and developmental for all students. It must lend itself to a rational plan requiring selection of essential subject matter content, an organization of that content appropriate both to the subject and to the cognitive capacities of learners, a sequence of learnings that is authentic to the subject and to the developmental abilities of young people, ways to demonstrate that learning is taking place, and adaptability to the structures and processes that define schooling in our culture. In short, the subject must be able to become a curriculum.

NONPHILOSOPHICAL DETERMINANTS OF CURRICULUM

For a variety of reasons and in a variety of ways music education in the past has (1) failed to offer a philosophy that could establish its basic value, and (2) failed to demonstrate that it is capable of becoming a genuine curriculum.

On the philosophy side, music education has offered rationales so puny, so unessential, so political, so tied to values not unique to music, as to convince many that music is little more than a pleasant, recreational hobby. Equally damaging, music education has offered bases for school programs that are not philosophical at all, thus ensuring the irrelevancy of music except as a special elective. For example, an argument has been made that school music programs should stem not from a philosophy but from a psychological theory of how children learn, or "learning theory" (a term long since abandoned by psychologists). Psychology, of course, can be applied to the learning of anything—music, cooking, driving, mathematics, house cleaning, and on and on. So anything included in schooling would have to use psychology as a means for effective teaching and learning. But psychology is incapable of differentiating among music, cooking, driving, and so on as to which should be taught to all students and what within the subject should be chosen to teach; only philosophy can do that because those are questions of value. A music program must employ psychology to actuate its philosophy. But a program cannot be built on psychology; that is dangerous to music and to students because it does not know where it is going, does not know why it is going there, and provides no rationale as to why anyone should care about what it does. A curriculum based on psychology will be mechanically correct (if the psychology it uses is among those that happen to work fairly well) and also musically trivial.

Another improper basis for the general music curriculum is an idiosyncratic theory about how children develop musically in a "natural" way from simple rhythms and intervals and scales (basically the pentatonic scale) patterned on a supposed evolutionary development in mankind. Research on children's musical development, regularly reported in our research journals, is beginning to reveal complex but useful data that must be incorporated in curriculum planning, but the realities of America's present diverse musical culture, the variety of ways children from early ages are involved with it, and the great variety of factors implicated in musical development, make any single, systematized method of induction so limited and artificial as to deprive children of the richness of musical possibilities their culture makes available to them. A curriculum, to be valid, must be inclusive of all possible musical experiences and modes of involvement and developmental patterns.

Still another invalid basis for the curriculum is that single aspect of music learning having to do with the development of vocal skills. No curriculum is likely to exist without singing and its associated skills as a component because the artistic values of music can be realized in effective ways through singing experiences. But a curriculum based on this single behavior, to the virtual exclusion of others, limits the musical experiences and involvements of students so severely as to both restrict possibilities for aesthetic experience and contain creativity within the narrowest confines. It simply misrepresents the art of music and the nature of young people when a curriculum is built on such a limited base.

These and other inappropriate foundations for a music curriculum have led to programs (a program is a curriculum in action) so narrow in goals and behaviors and involvements as to set music apart from any other subject the schools offer. Educators know that such programs are not instances of genuine curricula: little if anything about them conforms to the principles of curriculum development guiding all the basic subjects. So these programs are accepted, in those cases where they *are* accepted, as demonstrations of the "specialness" of music: of the inability of this subject to be an authentic curriculum area. The impression is given and is internalized that music is so esoteric, so unlike the "regular" subjects, so technique-skill-proficiency oriented, that there exists no basis for the ongoing development of cognitions, including skills, that any bona fide educational curriculum must provide. The nonphilosophical foundations of such programs, leading to their single-minded, restricted, method-based activities, differentiates the subject of music clearly from anything the schools will ever or should ever recognize as essential.

How can the art of music, or any of the arts individually or collectively, be organized into a program that warrants the term "basic"? Only by being broad enough and inclusive enough to be truly comprehensive. That does not mean indiscriminate. Choices will have to be made as to what can be included and what left out, but what gets included will have to represent the subject in its intrinsic structure, its significant details, and all the important ways people interact with it. Anything less than this comprehensive treatment will be inadequate in comparison with basic subjects and will keep music in its inferior position. It will also be inadequate for the musical needs of our students.

To spell out in detail the components and contents of a comprehensive music program for the schools would require at least another large book in addition to those already dealing with this issue in music education. So the intent of this chapter must be far more modest: it is to sketch the broad outlines of a general music program in the shape of the philosophy being offered. The following chapter will do the same for the performance program. While major advances have been made in music curriculum building over the past decade and a half or so in the direction of a bona fide aesthetic education program in general music[1] and to a lesser extent in the performance area, an overview of principles can help provide a basis for needed further developments. The following model of the total curriculum, and of any separate subjects within it, will organize the discussion.

A MODEL OF THE TOTAL CURRICULUM

The school curriculum as a whole consists of seven interacting phases. Each subject taught in schools, at each level of schooling, can be understood in terms of the same phases. The model appears on p. 152.[2]

---

[1] My own attempt to build a comprehensive curriculum for general music classes in grades 1–8 is the series of textbooks entitled *Silver Burdett Music* (Morristown, N.J.: Silver Burdett, 1974, 1978, 1981, 1985), written with co-authors Elizabeth Crook and David Walker (grades 1–6) and Mary Hoffman and Al McNeil (grades 7, 8).

[2] This model is an adaptation from an initial conceptualization suggested by John I. Goodlad, to whom I am grateful.

A Model of the Total Curriculum

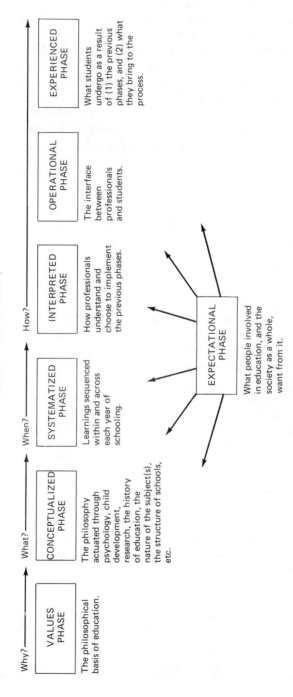

VALUES
PHASE

The philosophical
basis of education.

Why?

CONCEPTUALIZED
PHASE

The philosophy
actuated through
psychology, child
development,
research, the history
of education, the
nature of the subject(s),
the structure of schools,
etc.

What?

SYSTEMATIZED
PHASE

Learnings sequenced
within and across
each year of
schooling.

When?

INTERPRETED
PHASE

How professionals
understand and
choose to implement
the previous phases.

How?

OPERATIONAL
PHASE

The interface
between
professionals
and students.

EXPERIENCED
PHASE

What students
undergo as a result
of (1) the previous
phases, and (2) what
they bring to the
process.

EXPECTATIONAL
PHASE

What people involved
in education, and the
society as a whole,
want from it.

THE GOAL OF THE GENERAL MUSIC CURRICULUM

At the level of the total education enterprise, the starting point is always the culture's values, its answer to the question "Why and for what purpose should we educate?" To the extent that a culture is unified in its philosophy of life, the answer can be quite uncomplicated. In a culture such as that of the United States, representing maximum diversity of philosophies of life, the values issue is so complex and so ongoing and so contentious as to always be unresolved. We continually attempt to forge enough consensus that schools can have a foundational value dimension but such attempts in a democratic, multicultural society like ours will always be problematical. Simple-minded pleas that the schools should teach x or y or z specific values turn out to be straws in the wind. Yet underneath the confusion there are enough abiding beliefs, shared by enough people, to define us as a culture and to provide some essential guidelines for educational action. It is just that anyone who needs complete agreement on the "Why" question is living in the wrong country, and our system of education must always reflect that reality.

The general music curriculum must be based on the deepest values of the subject for which it is responsible. In light of the philosophy offered in this book, the overall goal or aim of the general music curriculum is to develop, to the fullest extent possible, every student's capacity to experience and create intrinsically expressive qualities of sounds. Another term for this capacity, which every student has to some degree, is aesthetic sensitivity. Another term for intrinsically expressive qualities of sounds is music. So the goal or aim of general music can also be stated as the development, to the fullest extent possible, of every student's aesthetic sensitivity to the art of music. No lesser goal or aim is capable of establishing general music as a basic component of the total curriculum.

It is one thing—an essential thing—to start with a philosophy of sufficient importance to provide a strong foundation for the curriculum built on it. It is another matter to use that philosophy as a guide for all the other decisions that must be made to create experiences that will teach learners effectively and authentically. The curriculum model makes clear how complicated the process is.

THE CONCEPTUALIZED PHASE OF THE CURRICULUM

The first step, or phase, toward actuating the philosophy is to conceptualize it according to all the real-world issues impinging on the process of education. Psychology—how the mind works, how perception occurs, how meaning arises, how motivation and interest affect our behaviors, how our social natures influence our capacity to learn, how aptitudes relate to achievements, and on and on with essential issues—must be brought in to play. None of these issues are philosophical, but all are germane to the philosophy because they will either be compatible with it or hostile to it depending on how they are addressed. For example, Behaviorism was influential in education during the 1960s and 1970s and influenced the ways music was taught. Some of these ways were relevant to aspects of aesthetic education and helped it become effective. Other ways had little to do with the art of music but influenced practices nevertheless. Now Behaviorism as a theory is largely defunct, but some of its practices hold over. A new psychological point of view, called Cognitive Psychology, has come into influence, which is changing, often radically, how teaching and learning are being approached.[3] And the new psychology will no doubt develop and change and eventually be supplanted by still another.

The same is true of child development as a field of study (overlapping with psychology of course): it is not a static body of revealed truths but a dynamic, fluid field constantly moving in new directions. That is true as well of research in education as a whole and specifically in music education, which must be applied when a curriculum is being created but which nevertheless shifts its ground constantly. As our knowledge of the history of education grows, including our knowledge of the history of music education, we come to understand ourselves differently and redefine ourselves accordingly, thereby subtly or obviously changing what we feel we can or should expect from a curriculum. And our understanding of music itself, directly guiding us in our choices of what is important to teach about it, is in a state of continual change as new theories about its nature are developed. Further, the school as an institution keeps evolving, with new ways to structure time, new ways to relate to the community, new values thrust upon it, new expectations of teachers, differing understandings of proper student behavior, and so on.

Each subject must adapt itself to these and many other realities, all of them in constant evolution. General music must be just as influenced by them as any other subject, building its own foundation of learnings grounded in a philosophy but adaptable to the best thinking in all those other fields as that thinking develops. What provides stability, centeredness, the courage to choose when choices must be made despite inevitable uncertainties given the fluidity of knowledge? The answer to that question can only be a foundational value system—a philosophy that leads one in a coherent, committed direction, guided by the best and deepest understanding one is capable of and which one's collective profession is capable of.

The need for a grounded philosophy becomes painfully apparent when one is confronted with the jumble of decisions one is forced to make to create

---

[3]The most comprehensive overview of the fall of Behaviorism and the rise of Cognitive Psychology is Howard Gardner's *The Mind's New Science: A History of the Cognitive Revolution* (New York: Basic Books, 1985).

a curriculum. What we cannot do—what no subject can do—is to retreat from this built-in dilemma by seizing on some safe, easy corner of our field and using it as a pacifier. That is what we do in general music when we give up the challenge of education and settle for training—in sight singing, for example, or instrumental techniques (recorder, guitar, etc.), or notation skills and drills, or one simple modality (pentatonic), or in singing folk songs, or learning terminology, or using movement exercises, and on and on with separate little pieces substituting for the art of music. All those particular pieces have their legitimate and even important place. All can be and should be incorporated in a general music curriculum because all have an excellent contribution to make to musical education. But each by itself, as if it was a curriculum, is insufficient for education and the challenges education presents to every subject claiming legitimacy. General music has no right to protect itself from having to deal with all the major curriculum issues and still claim its importance as a school subject. We cannot have it both ways. If we opt to become an assemblage of "methods," either singly or eclectically (a program consisting of an eclectic mixture of methodologies, each of them inadequate to be a curriculum, is never an adequate curriculum but simply a collection of inadequacies), we must then accept our status on the fringe of the education enterprise, hoping against hope that we are not allowed to drop off the edge. If we accept the responsibility of building authentic curricula, using a philosophy as a base and adapting it to the growing knowledge in each of the areas impinging on education, we will take on the complexity of what education entails but we will also take on the maturity and validity of an educational basic. There is simply not much choice here.

CONCEPTUALIZED GUIDELINES

At this period in history a general music program constituting a genuine curriculum will have to fulfill several conditions:

1. It will have to be compatible with developments in cognitive psychology, focusing on the enhancement of musical cognition, of musical intelligence, of musical thinking. It will have to be problem solving in orientation rather than rote-and-skill focused. Group learning processes will dominate, with isolated drill learning, as provided by computers, as auxiliary extensions from the base of cooperative and individual problem manipulations.[4]

2. The curriculum will have to adapt itself to post–Piagetian child development theories in that Piaget's ideas, dominant for almost three decades, are now being severely eroded by new discoveries about child

---

[4]A helpful overview of cognitive psychology principles applied to the various subject matter fields including music is Ronna F. Dillon and Robert J. Sternberg, eds., *Cognition and Instruction* (Orlando, Fla.: Academic Press, 1986).

development generally and specifically in music.[5] Conceptual development in children will have to be taken into account because of the necessary role of concepts as one means in musical learning, but specifically musical developmental principles will have to become more influential as research continues to discover them.

3. The curriculum will have to reflect the historical background of music education, such as being relevant to the needs of all students no matter their level of musical talent as potential performers, representing a wide diversity of music literature including musics of all the peoples comprising our diverse society, serving judiciously managed social-patriotic-entertainment functions as adjunctive to aesthetic learnings. But it will also have to reflect major changes in historical patterns, such as the evolution from self-provided to other-provided musical performances, the change from a musical economy of limited availability to one of overabundance requiring greater selectivity, the existence of a "supermarket" of musical styles from which everyone can choose freely and with lesser stigma attached to idiosyncratic choices, the rebalancing of importance of those musics depending on traditional instruments and those requiring newly developed electronic instruments including computers, the birth of mass composition opportunities through microchip applications to inexpensive keyboard devices.

4. The curriculum will have to choose its essential subject matter in light of all the foregoing, which means, inevitably, a focus on the inherent properties of music enabling students to have access to all specific musics and all modes of interaction with music, including performance but increasingly rebalanced toward composition and listening. The content of the curriculum will include the study of the basic elements of music (rhythm, melody, etc.), of the structuring processes that make music dynamic (sequencing, varying, extending, transforming, simultaneous and successive interaction, repeating, contrasting, building, patterning, implying, beginning, ending, and so forth), of styles as collections of pieces sharing common expectation characteristics, of specific pieces as both representative of a style but also in a real sense incomparable. All this music-focused study will be experiential, the immediate "experience of" being the point and "knowing about" being a way to help get to the point.

5. Helpful "knowing abouts" will have to be more influential in the curriculum. Students must develop an understanding of the many roles music plays in a society, both nonmusical and musical. They need to know what artistic decisions consist of so they can make them intelligently. They need to know the criteria for judging art, the differences between emotions and the sense of feeling art deals with, the difference between what com-

---

[5]See, for one explanation among many, Howard Gardner, *Frames of Mind: The Theory of Multiple Intelligences* (New York: Basic Books, 1983), pp. 17–22.

municating does and how art is shared, why art means differently from words, what is actually entailed in experiencing aesthetically as distinguished from experiencing in other ways, and so forth. These ideas are not or should never be allowed to be "academic." They will have to be tied to actual experiences that will give them tangibility and immediacy of musical meaning.

The conceptualized phase of the total curriculum of general music requires that the best thought about what young people should learn be brought to bear; anything less will produce one-sided or limited programs. This is difficult and ongoing and frustrating because new developments constantly call present practices into question. But there is no way out for a subject intending to be taken seriously in education.

THE SYSTEMATIZED PHASE OF THE CURRICULUM

Two essential factors determine the "when" of education. The first has to do with the nature of the subject. What are the aspects of a subject that most matter, that characterize the essential qualities and processes that make a subject what it is? How can those wholes be divided into meaningful parts that are manageable, learnable, developmental, so that movement toward larger wholes is fostered through increasing control of the meaningful details?

The second factor for effective sequencing has to do with human development itself. How can the internal parts-wholes of a subject be matched effectively with the modes of learning and capacities for learning specific to the age level being taught? Research is a crucial source of insight as we seek answers to this question.

INVALID BASES FOR SEQUENCE

Two very serious mistakes have been made in music curricula in the systematization or sequencing aspect of the curriculum. The first has been a tendency to abandon the nature of the subject itself—music—as an essential source for sequence decisions. This occurs in three ways.

The first is to allow music to be studied only or primarily when opportunities arise in the study of other subjects, such as social studies or science or language. Music becomes a by-product learning connected to other learnings, thereby removing any possibility for its own nature to determine the order in which it is studied.

The second way music has abandoned its selfhood as the only genuine basis for sequence decisions has been its use of nonmusical events in the school year as the organizing factor for its program. Holidays, school events, a series of in-school and out-of-school concerts and programs provide a handy excuse for a noncurriculum sequence. There's always so much to do to get ready for the next holiday or season and its obligatory program that clever general music teachers can go for years just moving right along on the wheels of "all those demands the school makes on me." The school and community get used to such a program, in which music serves a pleasant entertainment function, so a nice collusion gets built and everyone is happy. It is tempting to settle for this because one can get through grades 1–8 handily this way, churning out programs and filling any slack time in between with a bit of notation drill, some extra songs, a few filmstrip listenings, maybe a Young Audience program or two. The impression is given of a great deal of activity, while underneath, where most do not know enough to be able to look or don't even try to look because they don't expect music to have one, there is no foundation. But why complain? One need not expect any more than this, except, of course, if one has respect for young people and for the art of music. In a curriculum respectful of both, nonmusical events can be honored and catered to without the loss of curriculum integrity. But would any subjects with self-respect, such as the basics, allow themselves to be sequenced only by nonsubject community and school events?

The third way music programs in the schools have made the mistake of using an invalid base for sequence decisions is to put together a set of activities and units having no inherently musical-logical coherence. For example, for many years the general music program was based on "the five-fold curriculum," a collection of activities (singing, playing, creative activities, listening, moving), that, in and of themselves, constituted the total program of studies. All those activities are essential, of course, but as means for learning about how music works as an art and how it is experienced by people. Activities are instrumentalities within a curriculum; they are not a curriculum.

The same invalidity applies to series of units related tangentially but not essentially to music. Some programs used to be and still are organized by units such as "Water in Music," "Music and Nature," "Sociable Songs," "Music Tells Tall Tales," "Moods of the Seasons," "Storms in Music," "Our Animal Friends," and so forth. Such units distract from genuine learnings about the art of music; they also trivialize music. None gets to the heart (or soul) of music—its essence as sounds organized to be expressive. A curriculum planned to get to the heart of the matter must focus, in a systematic, ongoing, developmental way, on how music works as an art—its elements, its processes, its styles, its creative procedures, its human functions, its aesthetic nature, how it relates to the other arts, how it is unique as an art, how people can share it in all possible ways. These are the sources of a valid music curriculum, and while we do not know—and there may not exist—the single, best way to sequence such topics with all the related activities and involvements they entail, nothing less than a thoughtful, professionally guided series of such learnings within each year and across the years will do. No subject with self-respect would settle for less.

INADEQUATE BASES FOR SEQUENCE

The second serious error in the systematized phase of the curriculum, in addition to the use of invalid sources for sequence decisions, is to base the sequence of learnings on a limited set of musical behaviors. For example, a sequenced program focused entirely on developing aural skill in the narrow sense of dictation-interval recognition-sight singing-chord identification can be very effective in and of itself and very easy to accomplish because it consists of pure training and training is always easier to arrange in steps than education. Because of the ease by which such skills can be inculcated using rote-drill-modeling methodologies, and because results can be quick and dramatic, and because it makes so few demands on the musicianship and pedagogical skills and general understandings of teachers, it is seductive in the extreme to build a general music program entirely or primarily on such a base. Such a program, in which these skills become the end rather than a useful means, is a travesty of music education.

Another example of a program base too narrow to sustain a viable curriculum was the Manhattanville Music Curriculum Program of the late 1960s and 1970s. While it introduced creativity in composing as a healthy balance to performance-dominated programs, its single-mindedness in depending on composing as the dominant source for musical learning, and the necessity to use modern, improvisatory types of composition to avoid the technical hazards of more traditional composing, led to its early demise. The excellence of what it added to traditional modes of learning was not conceived as another important way to study the art of music but as *the* way to study it. It toppled on its narrowness, as it had to.

The same comments apply to the methodologies of Carl Orff and Zoltan Kodály when they are used as the sole program of study, as some music teachers improperly use them. Each adds an excellent dimension to musical learning, but each in and of itself is inadequate to constitute a curriculum. In and of themselves they are methods of training, because (1) they are not founded on a genuine philosophy of music education but on a limited set of assertions and beliefs and idiosyncratic interests, (2) they are not conceptualized to embrace all valid areas impinging on a total curriculum but limit themselves to only those program choices manageable within the confines of their interests, and (3) they focus on limited aspects of skill training as the primary or sole basis for sequence decisions. These are the three conditions that identify training: narrow rationale, limited concept, sequence by skill. As in the example of ear-training-as-music-education, the seductiveness of methodologies such as these is that they produce results very easily and quickly and demonstrably, and they make few demands on teachers to be broadly educated rather than narrowly trained in the restricted methodology they employ. The success such programs achieve is precisely of the scope they attempt, which, while superficially impressive, is actually deleterious to the image of music as a subject capable of being a curriculum. We tell the community of education professionals by such programs, when they constitute the total curriculum, that music education equals skill development, that music education has no viable philosophy, that music education is a delimited field unlike the subjects deserving to be considered basic for all children. In giving such messages these programs have indeed been successful. If they were carefully used components *within* a comprehensive curriculum they would give a far different message.

We have not yet succeeded in delivering the message of comprehensivity, partly because we have been diverted from formulating it by these partial solutions. But we have taken significant steps toward the level of systematization worthy of a curriculum, as most clearly exemplified in the excellent textbook series of the 1970s and 1980s, each of which embodies a curriculum concept and a developmental sequence of learnings that is, in many ways, as solid and valid as can be found in curricula in the traditional basics. Each of these general music curricula has its weaknesses, of course, but all demonstrate the directions curriculum development needs to take to continue to improve. Their sequencing by the study of significant musical characteristics, including listening, singing, playing, moving, composing, improvising, conceptualizing, analyzing, evaluating, as the means to experience more fully the particular characteristic being focused upon as it relates to music as a whole, is the most effective system available for progressive learning. We have much to do to optimize this concept of sequence within a comprehensive music curriculum, and we should devote our energies to it seriously if we hope to convince people that general music is not a training program but is an authentic school subject.

THE INTERPRETED PHASE OF THE CURRICULUM

The first three phases of the curriculum establish its theoretical foundation. The second three phases operationalize it. The interface between theory and practice is the interpreted phase—the place where curriculum ideas meet programmatic actions.

Suppose there existed a philosophy of music education so complete, so valid, so clearly articulated, as to approach perfection (a nice dream). Suppose the philosophy was actuated in a concept of the general music curriculum encompassing all possible fields impinging on music education, each of which perfectly implemented the philosophy (an even nicer dream).

And suppose a systematic arrangement of learnings was then created so that all children were able to handle all the challenges with optimal success and all the learnings were perfectly relevant to music and to the developmental mastery of it. (The dream has become a complete fantasy.) Now we give this perfect theoretical plan to ten general music teachers and say "Go forth and put this curriculum into action." Six months later we visit each of them in their schools. What do we find?

No doubt ten different curricula. Here we are confronted with bedrock reality, which tells us that when theory meets practice, prediction goes out the window. Even when theory is encompassed in explicit learning materials created by the theory makers specifically to avoid any possible misinterpretations and misapplications (as when curriculum developers in the 1960s and early 1970s tried to create "teacher-botchproof" programs), the influence of individual interpretations and the resultant decisions and applications will alter the plans significantly. There is simply no way to fill in the theory-practice gap completely. Individuals are so diverse in their belief systems, their orientations to their subject and to learners, their knowledge and understandings, their motivations, that no two people are likely to interpret something as complicated as a curriculum plan identically. Further, each individual exists in a social-institutional milieu in which others have their hand in what can be attempted and what can be accomplished. The curriculum and the teacher of it do not exist in an educational vacuum, and each outside influence changes the curriculum and the teacher.

What can we do about this situation? Probably learn to live with it. There is, after all, a certain wisdom inherent in the loss of complete predictability we might otherwise wish for. In a society like ours, uniformity is not the highest virtue. What we need is intelligent, informed, expert applications of a solid curriculum, and we must be open enough to accept the fact that there is likely to be a good deal of variation in how a good curriculum gets interpreted. What should not be accepted is a curriculum interpretation by a teacher not acquainted with a philosophy of music education, not knowledgeable about all the fields relevant to a concept of the curriculum, not sophisticated about valid and invalid bases for systematizing the curriculum. The interpretation such a teacher is likely to give, even of a curriculum excellent in and of itself, cannot be trusted to be valid. The best theoretical foundation will crumble in the hands of an unknowledgeable teacher.

How do we ensure that our teachers will be competent to make interpretations that are professionally sound even if individual? That question raises the entire issue of preservice and in-service teacher education. Obviously such an issue cannot be dealt with here, but a single implication would seem relevant in the context of this chapter. That is, both teachers in training and teachers in service need to be steeped in (1) a valid philosophy of music education and new developments in philosophy, (2) an understanding of the relevance of related fields to the music curriculum including new developments in those fields, and (3) knowledge of valid bases for sequence decisions and changes in that knowledge as they occur. These are basic matters that should be included in college teacher education curricula in addition to musical and general studies and methods of teaching, and they are basic matters that should be addressed in graduate degree programs and in all the in-service activities of our profession. That they are so neglected in the education and reeducation of our teachers in favor of technologies of teaching (necessary as those are) accounts in large part for the weakness of curriculum decisions teachers are prone to make and their adoption of invalid and/or inadequate music programs. Our professional infrastructure, if it is to support excellent school curricula, must itself be excellent. That means a more sophisticated balance between necessary theoretical foundations and equally necessary practical applications. These are essential teacher-quality issues for any subject aspiring to be regarded as basic in American education. The United States has achieved a level of music teacher education and graduate education and professional in-service education unparalleled in the world. That it is not optimally effective as yet may be inferred from the not yet optimal general music curriculum in the schools.

THE OPERATIONAL PHASE OF THE CURRICULUM

Here, finally, teachers and students interact. All the previous curriculum phases aim toward the quality of this interaction. Critics of education, unacquainted with the complexity of the enterprise, focus their attention on this phase in the simplistic assumption that it constitutes all of schooling: "You have teachers and you have kids, so what else is the problem?" As we have seen, the problem of imperfect education can stem from an imperfection in any phase of the curriculum and in the ensuing interactions of that imperfection with all the other curriculum aspects with which it is intertwined. Given the inevitability of imperfections in a system that is as complex as anything humans attempt, it is amazing that teachers actually do manage to be as effective as they are at this "payoff" level of the curriculum. Anyone acquainted with the fiendishly complicated beast a curriculum is should not be surprised that it is seldom if ever faultless: the surprise is that it works at all!

But the operations of teachers as they go about their work are, in and of themselves, extremely intricate. For at this level all the professional aspects of teaching embodied in the previous curriculum phases get funnelled through the personality, values, beliefs, human potentials, and human limitations of that person who is a teacher. The teacher's craftsmanship—the thousands of "knowing hows" called upon hour by hour—is here given its full challenge and its full expression. The teacher's sensitivity, both to people and to music, guides each operational decision in order to optimize the experience of the former with the latter. Imagination, as brought to bear by a teacher, is the exhilaration with which he or she suffuses the interactions of music and students, so that learning opportunities are fresh and vivid. And the teacher's authenticity ensures that both students and music are being treated with the genuineness and respect each deserves. No curriculum, however exemplary, can overshadow the influence of the professionalism and personhood of the individual teacher, so powerful it is in what actually gets experienced by students. So when we think of teachers who combine a high degree of professional expertise in all that they must know before actually teaching, with a high degree of all that a human being must manifest personally for the teaching act itself to be effective, we are thinking of individuals as admirable as people can be. If anyone should be held in highest esteem, it should be the excellent teacher.

Ironically, that teachers are not so esteemed in our culture stems in large part from the misperception that their work is limited to the operational level of the curriculum. That is, in ignorance of all that a teacher must know to be a professional, and in seeing only the tip of the iceberg at the operational level (equally ignorant about its complexity), it is easy to view the teacher as a technician or as an elevated type of child care worker. When the perception is accurate, as it sometimes is for teachers who *are* primarily technicians rather than educators, the lack of respect may be excusable. However, when any teacher, emphatically including the teacher of an art, is operating as the bearer and transmitter of a genuine curriculum, the respect due should be limitless. Our education of the public as to what schooling as a whole actually entails has not yet been accomplished sufficiently. Our education of the public as to what general music education actually requires of teachers has hardly begun to be accomplished.

The status of general music as a basic school subject and the support it is given as such will depend, in large part, on how fully we can realize our potential to be a curriculum rather than a set of activities, and how well we articulate to the larger community that we are capable of fulfilling all the requirements a genuine curriculum imposes. That will not be possible if our teachers are limited to operational skills, necessary as those are. Our own fixation on this phase serves us poorly when we see it as the only important aspect of music teaching. Until we develop a broader concept of the general music curriculum, we should not fault those who regard it as limited and devalue it accordingly. The limited respect for general music in the schools does not stem from lack of recognition of the high level of many music teachers' operational skills: these are widely regarded as being among the very best among all teachers. It is, instead, because teaching skills at the operational level is seen as the be-all and end-all of the music program that the subject is not regarded as worthy of inclusion among the basics. So we must continue to strive for operational excellence while embedding it in a foundational curriculum setting.

THE EXPERIENCED PHASE OF THE CURRICULUM

Suppose, once more, that we have a perfect philosophy, a perfect conceptualization of the ways a curriculum will carry it out, and a perfect systematization of all the desired learnings. In addition we have a teacher who interprets the curriculum with deep, accurate insight and who is a master of every possible teaching operation. So we have achieved perfection in all the component parts of the curriculum to this point. Now the teacher goes forth and presents all this perfection to students. Obviously they will each learn perfectly! Right?

Wrong. Here we encounter another of life's little tricks, which is that the best laid curriculum plan can become a shambles when kids get hold of it. Each of those human beings brings along to school a set of capacities, experiences, interests, beliefs, and dispositions not exactly like anyone else's, so that everything the curriculum presents and everything the teacher does is processed somewhat differently by every learner. That is an ultimate truth in education.

So what can one do about that? What every attempt to educate must do—the best it can for every person. Knowing that learnings in any subject will fall on a normal curve, the curriculum must accomplish two essential tasks: (1) it must be relevant for the experience of the largest number of pupils who fall in the middle of the curve, and (2) it must provide for the needs of the smaller number of pupils who fall at each end of the curve. Effective instruction attempts to maximize the learning experience of every pupil by providing necessary group learnings and "fine-tuning" by individual attention. But given the awesome complexity of this task, in that each learner is different not only in respect to every other learner but also in his or her own internal capacities for learning various aspects of every subject, the best we can hope for is to reach most of the students most of the time. The most perfect curriculum and the most perfect teacher cannot, by the facts of the nature of learners, achieve perfect learning.

So much is obvious. What does it imply? That an effective school program, such as in general music, must be "good enough." And here we enter the arena of relativity, as real in education as in physics. What constitutes enough success that a curriculum can be considered excellent? What deficiencies mark a program as moderately successful or minimally successful (or "disasterville")? Questions such as these are faced by every subject in school and must be faced squarely by general music. Much depends on the breadth and depth of the answer, for without a convincing set of criteria upon which to establish reasonable standards for demonstrable success, the program cannot be considered to be practicable for schooling. It is not acceptable to claim, as music educators often do, that music is so unlike anything else the schools include that criteria for success cannot be articulated and evidence of success cannot be offered. On the other hand, any criteria and evidence must be authentically musical or the point of a *music* curriculum is lost. We face a moment of truth in this matter. Can we conform to the expectation in education that evidence be given that learnings are taking place and that they are taking place sufficiently that the program can be regarded as successful? And can we present such evidence about learnings that are genuine to the nature of the art of music, undistorted by the demands of overt evidence?

The answers are "Yes." Not perfectly, perhaps, but equally as well as any other subject in school. Genuinely musical learnings can be identified, and evidence that they are being attained successfully can be offered. To do so is to deal with the question of objectives. But before explaining them the seventh phase of the curriculum must be mentioned.

THE EXPECTATIONAL PHASE OF THE CURRICULUM

Everyone involved with education, directly or indirectly, has expectations of it. Students, teachers, administrators, school boards, parents, citizens, politicians—everyone has a finger in the educational pie. So influential are all these expectations on what gets taught in schools that they constitute a phase of the curriculum itself, determining to a large extent what occurs in all the other phases.

The finger of expectations tends to be deeper into the pie for music than for the traditional academics because music is more of a shared communal phenomenon, allowing everyone to feel that he or she has a right to an opinion. Further, since music is perceived to be one of the specials rather than the basics, it can be more easily assumed that one need not be an expert for one's opinion to be taken seriously. So general music teachers, while in the same position as all teachers in having to straddle the fence between internal professional standards and external community expectations, have to do so more skillfully.

The skill consists in balancing one's devotion to aesthetic education with expectations that may not always be consonant with it. Philosophically, one must be secure enough about the values issues that one can bend reasonably without surrendering one's veracity. The skillful teacher can deal with a variety of expectations about the goals and purposes of general music and transform them into philosophically valid guidelines that satisfy most people yet also satisfy the requirement that music be honored as art. Music teachers are constantly being confronted with demands on their program that are only tangential to aesthetic education or are hostile to it. Sometimes dramatic opposition to such demands is called for: "That is not in the best interests of students or of music and it is not possible for me to comply." But that occurs rarely. Most often it is a question of sensitive management—listening in goodwill, seeing other points of view as having some measure of value, adapting the philosophy here and there while not altering its underlying foundations. It is not possible to do this successfully if those foundations are not securely in place; that is when general music programs get sidetracked into nonmusical dead ends. To the extent a philosophy is valid and securely held it can withstand expectational pressures by bending without cracking.

The same applies to the conceptualized and systematized phases. If they are solidly grounded, occasional digressions to satisfy nonaesthetic expectations can be handled with grace. When they are faulty to begin with, they can easily fall apart when outside pressure is exerted. The teacher's ability to maintain conceptual and sequential veracity, through a dedication to a valid interpretation of what is most important to teach and the operational skills to get it taught effectively, are the keys to the maintenance of an internally solid general music program in the face of inevitable outside expectations.

But those expectations themselves are amenable to change. It is often said that teachers must teach far beyond the classroom: the truth of that saying is nowhere more striking than in general music. It is necessary to demonstrate to students but also to their parents, other teachers, administrators, school board members, and so on, that general music is a genuine subject based on valid curriculum principles, because to the extent that demonstration is made to them they will begin to regard the program as important. Nothing will change people's views about general music so much as proof that it follows the same guidelines as all other basic subjects. General music teachers must exemplify in why, what, when, and how they teach that they are the bearers of a legitimate curriculum. That exemplification must first of all be through what actually takes place in the classroom, but it must also spread beyond by vigorous advocacy and demonstration efforts, supported by the music education profession as a whole. It may be unfortunate that the case for general music as a curriculum must be made to the larger community, but it is true and we must live with it, including the sad fact that we ourselves are largely to blame for the common but too-true perception that we are not a curriculum. Until we achieve a program of studies in general music worthy of aesthetic education as our philosophy and worthy of the teacher education and graduate education systems we have built, we will remain in our present secondary position. Young people, music, and we deserve better.

OBJECTIVES OF THE GENERAL MUSIC PROGRAM

Without an overall, philosophically grounded goal or aim for general music, programs cannot be directional. This book has attempted to provide a philosophy that gives the general music program (and the performance program) a valid goal toward which to work. But just as a philosophy requires a curriculum to give it flesh and bones, the goal suggested by the philosophy requires explicit objectives to give it specificity.

It is not possible for a book such as this to deal with learning objectives at the class session level (the students will use dynamics appropriately in a new song) or even at the unit or year-long levels (the students will distinguish among pieces exemplary of several historical style periods). The objectives to be discussed here are at the level of organizers for the total program. They are halfway between the goal or aim and the specific learnings that take place in the course of instruction. That halfway point is crucial. Without it there is too big a gap between the goal and the specific learning objectives, so that the multiplicity of the latter overwhelms the former and the specifics begin to scatter wildly, with not enough structure to hold them together and give them consistency. And without consistency—well-managed clusters of learnings related to the essential structure of music—the detailed learnings have no point and no accumulative effect. Many teachers are haunted by the feeling that, while they are teaching lots and lots of stuff, it doesn't seem to add up—it doesn't seem to get anywhere that matters. They are probably correct. All the particular learnings must relate to objectives at a higher, more important level, those objectives themselves being directly related to the philosophical goal of the program. When the teacher sees these connections, *and when the students see them also,* specifics are not meaningless bits; they are the lifeblood of tangible experience leading in understandable ways toward greater aesthetic sensitivity.

There are seven basic modes (or "behaviors" in the broad sense) through which people interact with music or any art. The objective of the general music program is to improve these interactions. (The improvement of these interactions through the performance program will be explained in the next chapter.) The seven musical behaviors are as follows:[6]

Ends Behaviors:		Perceiving	Reacting	
Means Behaviors:	Creating	Conceptualizing	Analyzing	Evaluating
Outcome Behavior:		Valuing		

---

[6]The original conceptualization of the seven basic ways that people relate to music was my "Aesthetic Behaviors in Music," in Bennett Reimer, ed., *Towards an Aesthetic Education* (Washington, D.C.: Music Educators National Conference, 1971.)

The end or goal or point of interacting with music is to experience it, as explained in Chapter Six. Instruction in music must help that experience be as powerful and satisfying as possible. The general music program must, if nothing else, help students perceive music more deeply so that their reactions to it can be concomitantly deep. That is the "bottom-line" objective.

In music, perceiving and reacting (aesthetically experiencing) occurs through listening. One need not compose in order to experience music. One need not perform in order to experience music. But one cannot experience it without listening. Further, no matter how well one might compose or perform, one's ability to experience a vast diversity of music of any level of complexity through listening will always far outstrip that tiny bit which one can compose or perform oneself. All people, including those very few who engage in composing or performing in any serious way, interact with, experience, and enjoy music through its essential behavior—listening.

It should go without saying that the primary objective of general music should be to improve every student's capacity for musical listening, that is, their capacity to perceive all the ways sounds become expressive, in contexts that encourage feelingful reactions to what is being perceived. It should also go without saying that many traditional general music programs, and Kodaly and Orff programs, treat listening as a minor activity in favor of a massive concentration on performing, primarily through singing and the technical-notational skills associated with singing. (Orff programs also concentrate on movement and performing on instruments.) There are historical reasons for this, of course, in that performing, primarily singing, was the only practicable way music could be available to people until the invention of recordings made all musics of all periods and all cultures available to all people no matter their skills or interests in performing. That general music continues to rely so heavily on performing, especially singing, not as an absolutely necessary means, which it is, but as the sole or major mode of experiencing music, testifies to the heavy weight with which history burdens us.

It also testifies to the relative lack of operational skills teachers have developed for presenting exciting, active listening lessons and the relatively higher levels of musicianship required to do so successfully. To teach listening skills directly and to do so effectively requires a broad acquaintance with music literature, with musical structure at smaller and larger levels of form, with music history, with a great diversity of stylistic characteristics. But these competencies, after all, are what our undergraduate and graduate music training are supposed to provide, along with the operational teaching skills to make them functional in schools. And the creation in recent years of simple devices that focus perceptual attention on the important expressive events in pieces as they are being heard through time (such as the variety of "Call Charts" in instructional materials) adds immeasurably to teachers' available tools for good listening lessons. So there are few excuses for not devoting a reasonable amount of time in general music programs to the direct teaching of listening—the one behavior essential to the experience of music. Of course the teaching of listening can be overemphasized. In overall terms, however, listening, because of its centrality for the art of music, needs more attention in future general music programs than it has been given in the past.

There are four basic means for achieving heightened aesthetic experiences of music in addition to listening to it. The first, creating, gives direct access to musical experience because it requires that artistic decisions be made about sounds—new sounds being imagined as in composing, or sounds being actualized as in performing and conducting, or both simultaneously as in improvising. Listening is inextricably a part of creating. So the combination of intensive listening while creating the very sounds one is hearing (along with others who are also doing so as in group performance) is as powerful a musical experience as people can have. Musical listening is also inherently creative, as explained in Chapter Seven, and makes all music available for creative experiencing, which is why it is the universal behavior. But the use of composing and performing, both as a means for developing perceptual skills and as a means for developing skills of artistic decision making, is essential for all learners.

In the performance program, as Chapter Nine will discuss, creating is *the* major means for musical experience. In the general music program it is *a* major means. The most common abuse of performing (and to a much lesser extent composing) occurs as the result of overwhelming focus on the technical aspects of performance. So much time is spent by so many teachers on the mechanical dimensions of performing, including all the intricacies of notation, that musical experience—the involvement of both mind and feelings with expressive sound events—is often not enhanced by performing but is instead diminished. Of course technical details must be paid attention to, especially in the performance program, which is why the technique-expression dilemma is so central there, but they must be paid attention to as the means by which more expressive sounds are created and therefore experienced, not as ends in and of themselves. The major error in general music programs and the major reason for their ineffectuality is their overemphasis on the technical-mechanical aspects of performing. Until a better balance is achieved between technique as a means for achieving expressive performance and technique as an end, general music will not have reached the maturity as a subject it must reach if it is to fulfill its potential. There is a simple, foolproof way to ensure that musical performance will have the powerful effects on musical experience it should have. It will be given at the end of this discussion on means behaviors.

The second means for enhancing the quality of musical experience is conceptualizing, as explained in several previous chapters. Since the middle

1960s, when concepts about music began to be used in a systematic way as organizers for the general music program, an unfortunate confusion has existed about their role in musical learning. Many people mistakenly assumed that the end of instruction was the development of musical concepts. As this book has tried to explain, concepts are only a *means*. We do not teach concepts for the sake of teaching concepts; we *use* concepts as a way to organize teaching-learning episodes so that deeper perceptual structuring—improved perception and reaction—can be fostered. Concepts *about* music give us a logical, developmental, artistically focused medium by which to build progressively more challenging experiences *of* music. So they are the best tools we have for creating manageable curricula. But they are *only* tools, and it is important that we understand that, so we do not misguide our activities as we teach. There is a simple principle to ensure that conceptualization will serve as the powerful means it is rather than as an overemphasized end. It will be given at the end of this discussion.

Analysis is a mode of conceptualizing which focuses on the internal conditions that make sounds expressive. The word comes from the Greek "to loosen up." Analysis combats confusion (things "fused together"). When things are fused together we can't see how they work—what they are made of, how parts interact, what makes a thing tick. So the confused thing bewilders us. When we "loosen it up"—analyze it—we begin to see the parts and their relations into wholes. The thing begins to make sense. Good analysis is an indispensable tool in the process of enhancing musical understanding, the clear discernment of the artistic interrelations of "sounds organized to be expressive" (see the definition of art in Chapter Five). But misused analysis goes beyond loosening up confusions. It picks a thing apart and leaves the parts in disarray. That is an abuse of music and an abuse of analysis. How do we ensure that analysis will vivify musical experience rather than deaden it? A simple principle will answer that question.

Evaluation—the making of judgments about the quality of pieces of music and their performance—can be used prematurely, as discussed in Chapter Six, and thereby get in the way of openness to musical experience. But when used appropriately, this mode of conceptualizing, focused on the effectiveness by which sounds become expressive, is a necessary means for illuminating the inner workings of music and exploring its affective power. General music teachers must be skillful in providing opportunities for their students to make judgments about aspects of music they are learning about. Students must learn that there are basic criteria for judgments (review the discussion in Chapter Seven) and that their application requires thoughtfulness and knowledge and experience, all of which they are capable of demonstrating to some degree. The point of evaluating is not just to be critical but to be more discerning. As with the other means behaviors, evaluating is a major way to encourage deeper, more refined musical experience. How can we see to it that it does so?

The answer to the question raised in the previous paragraphs—the simple guideline for ensuring that the four means behaviors will be effective in enhancing musical experience—is to keep them in reasonable balance (1) among themselves and (2) with listening. Performing and composing begin to be unproductive when they go on for long periods of time with few opportunities to listen to the piece as a whole, little conceptualization about what is going on, little analysis of what is happening musically, and no judgments being made about the quality of the decisions. Creating then becomes dumb soundmaking. Conceptualizing, when it goes on without sufficient listening to music exemplifying what is being discussed, without sufficient performance to keep the learning musically creative, without appropriate probing of inner musical conditions through analysis, and without musical assessments, becomes academic in the worst sense. Analysis, when unbalanced with all the other musical interactions, deteriorates into puzzle solving and rule applying, which turns music into meaningless fragments unconnected to affective experience. And evaluating, separated from all the other behaviors which give it its point, becomes empty criticizing or equally empty admiring. When all four means behaviors are constantly reinforcing each other in contexts in which listening is ever present, the interactions ensure vivid, meaningful, active involvements with the vital forces of music. And the music class atmosphere is likely to be vivid, meaningful, active, and musical.

The objectives of general music education are to improve musical perception; to encourage musical reaction; to enhance musical creativity through more expert and sensitive performing, composing, and improvising; to increase the depth and breadth of concepts about the art of music and how it works; to develop analytical abilities; and to promote more refined evaluations of music. To the extent these foundational objectives are being met successfully, students are likely to achieve a desired outcome—they will value music intrinsically. Teachers cannot require that their students value music as a whole, or this or that kind or type or style of music, or this or that musical activity. What people choose to value is their own business. Our obligation as music educators is not to require or even expect that everyone will value music, or value the music we value, or value the kinds of involvements with music we think they should value. Our obligation is to teach music comprehensively and effectively, which is to say that we must attempt to meet the objectives of a valid curriculum. Then we can safely entrust the outcome of our instruction to the power of the art of music to be valued in a variety of ways and at a variety of levels by the great variety of people. We are not directly responsible for peoples' valuing of music. We *are* directly responsible for representing music authentically and teaching it systematically, which means fulfilling our objectives of developing the musical behaviors enumerated earlier.

How can we present evidence that we are doing so satisfactorily? Each of the musical behaviors with the exception of reacting is amenable to evaluation and, if we choose, to measurement. Musical reaction—the inner feeling caused by the expressiveness of perceived sounds—is not compatible with evaluation, as explained throughout this book. But every other behavior emphatically is, including the levels of value people attach to music as a whole or to particular types of music or to particular involvements with music. We can very easily measure values, which are essentially "attitudes toward." We can also assess perceptual abilities with high accuracy. We are expert in evaluating performance and composition. And it is quite straightforward to assess skills and growth in conceptualizing, in analyzing, and in evaluating.

The profession needs much more experience in gathering and presenting evidence about the growth of essential musical behaviors, and we need, as well, good tests to help us gather and present this evidence. Such tests will have to reflect the revolution in thinking about testing now under way, as behavioristic assumptions and their applications to piecemeal, atomistic, stimulus-response testing modes are being recognized as incompatible with new insights from cognitive psychology. Tests in the future will be more holistic, more oriented to real-world problem solving and processing of musical information and the making of musical judgments and decisions; that is, to the measurement of musical intelligence in a variety of manifestations. Such tests and other modes of professional evaluation will add to our status as a bona fide curriculum and add to our professional expertise. Tests can be abusive, as we know all too well, but they can also be powerful aids in effective education. There is no reason why general music should not be at least as expert in using evaluation and measurement as any other basic subject in the schools.

MUSIC LITERACY AND MUSIC READING

Since the beginnings of music education in the United States, dating back to the original colonies, notation skills have been given a major portion of instructional time in general music classes. There are several reasons for this. First, when music can be available only by performing it oneself, as was largely the case until this century, one would be limited to rote performance if one could not use music notation functionally, that is, to have sufficient sign decoding skills to translate notation into musical sounds so the sounds can be experienced. So it was important to try to help students develop "functional literacy" with notation.

Immediately a problem arose. An ideal notation system is one so perfectly matched to the musical demands made on it that it imposes no technical-mechanical problems beyond those required for encoding the sounds being notated so that they can be performed by others. If a system of notation is more complex than it needs to be, it requires facility to be developed that will remain unused, so a great deal of wasted effort must go into it. If the notation system is too simple for the musical uses to which it is being put, it limits the creativity of those employing it as they compose and therefore imposes limitations on that which performers are able to experience by using it. So a notation system can be too complex, but it can also be too simple.

Staff notation such as is used in Western music (and now in most of the world) is sufficiently complex to have served the needs of the greatest composers in the culture for over four centuries, and it continues to be sufficient for most contemporary musical demands: new notations for contemporary pieces are by far the exception rather than the rule. So we are presented with a dilemma. Staff notation is very complex even when limited to one stave. If we want all school children in general music classes to develop functionality with it, even if only for the rather simple music that students in such classes will sing and play, we must spend inordinate amounts of time teaching notation skills. In fact we have done exactly that for around two centuries with humiliatingly poor results. Only a tiny percentage of learners ever develop more than primitive functional abilities with notation, and most if not all who do are those who choose to become involved with performance in some committed way such as joining a school performing group. Even among those, the number who develop beyond low levels of functionality is small, primarily being the few who choose to go into music as a career or who continue performing actively as amateurs, and even those few will spend their lives struggling with notation difficulties as an ongoing aspect of their musical involvements.

So only a tiny percentage of all the students who have been taught notation will ever use it in any way related to their ongoing enjoyment of music. Those who do not choose to be involved as performers in any persistent way find themselves with a largely useless skill, insufficient for real functionality, overdeveloped for the few performance demands they will ever make on it, and unrelated to the way they enjoy music as part of their lives—as consumers of music. Notation gets consigned to their dust bins of limited and irrelevant skills. For the great majority of people, the few skills of notation they managed to acquire, even in general music classes which drilled them in it mercilessly and in performing groups where they managed to hang on by the skin of their teeth, get dumped into those bins unceremoniously and with relief.

Recognizing that there is a painful gap between the complexities of staff notation and the likelihood that the majority studying it will ever master it functionally, many attempts were made to invent simpler alternative notations for school children, usually with only modest success because staff notation has such great prestige for those who have managed to gain a fair measure of skill with it, such as music teachers. Staff notation is not only perceived as the "one true way" to record sounds but it becomes deified—it comes to be regarded as equivalent to that which it symbolizes, which is an artistic counterpart of idolatry. To learn staff notation, for many people, is to learn music. To learn notation is to become musical. Notation becomes the end or at least the major means of musical learning. Simple yet effective notation systems much more suitable for the kinds of music that students in classes are likely to perform, that are easily learned and applied, don't stand much chance because they are considered inherently inferior to "true" notation. This is the case, unfortunately, far outside the borders of the United States. In mainland China, for example, a simple number system of notation has been used in schools for many years, giving the students an extremely effective tool for singing, playing, and composing. Now, in the cause of "modernization," this excellent system is being dropped in favor of staff notation because that is, somehow, the more "up-to-date" way to do things. The high levels of functionality the masses of Chinese youngsters were able to develop easily with the simpler notation, allowing them to perform and compose with excellent facility, will be abandoned for endless, frustrating attempts to learn staff notation, which few will ever succeed in doing or will ever need to do. Welcome, China, to the American experience.[7]

But there is another reason, beyond issues of functionality, why notation is emphasized so heavily in typical general music classes. This is the widely held idea that the ability to read music from notation and write it in notation is equivalent to music literacy. Since the word literacy is generally taken to mean the ability to read and write, the seemingly logical conclusion is drawn that music literacy consists of being able to read and write music notation.

But this notion ignores several important differences between language and art. It also ignores crucial distinctions among various definitions of literacy.

What would it mean for a person to be literate in an art that has no notation, say, painting? Painting possesses no notational equivalent for its works. Does that mean it is not possible to be "literate" about painting? Surely a person would be considered literate about painting who understood a great deal about the art of painting—its history, its techniques, its many styles, its major practitioners, where to go to see good examples of it, how to make discerning judgments about it, how to respond to it appropriately and sensitively. Such a person would be considered literate in the fullest sense of that word—educated, perceptive, knowledgeable about painting. It would no doubt add to his literacy if he could paint to some de-

[7]My comments about Chinese music education stem from a three-month study undertaken in spring 1986 of that country's music education system in schools, colleges, and conservatories, sponsored by the Chinese government and the Rockefeller Brothers Fund, coordinated by Harvard Project Zero and the Center for U.S.–China Arts Exchange at Columbia University.

gree (although a great many serious painting lovers and even professional curators, dealers, etc., do not actually paint). So literacy in this instance means well educated—able to share richly in that which painting exists to provide—and notation plays no role whatsoever.

What about an art at the opposite end of the spectrum from painting—an art such as literature in which the basic material is language itself? We are likely to call a person unable to read the words of a novel illiterate. But suppose a person could decipher each of the words in a novel by performing the sign decoding skills involved in reading words. Going from word to word, the person is able to pronounce each word and tell what it means. In that sense the person is "literate," at least at the basic level. But if that person was unaware of the larger forces which make that novel a work of literary art—its inner structure of dynamic events and ideas that make it more than a long string of words each of which has a meaning—that person could not be called literate in the full sense of "well educated about literature." A person who is literate in that sense would have attained literacy of a *different sort* from sign decoding skill. She would be a person who understood a great deal about the art of literature—its history, its techniques, its many styles, its major practitioners, where and how to find good examples of it, how to make discerning judgments about it, how to respond to it appropriately and sensitively.

In the case of literature, unlike painting, it would be difficult (although not impossible) to be literate in the larger sense without being literate in the limited sense of functional sign decoding skills, because there is only limited access to literature if the words on paper cannot be read. (A great deal of literature is now available on recordings, allowing blind people especially to develop high levels of literary sophistication without depending on direct reading or even Braille.) So in literature, basic literacy at the level of encoding and decoding words is an important skill, but meaningful literacy goes so far beyond it as to be different not just in degree but in kind.

The experience of all art comes from direct perceptual structuring of expressive events. Therefore, Walter Pater's comment about music (page 120) could in a real sense be altered to say, "All art constantly aspires towards the condition of *painting*," because painting requires no intermediary signs—we get its experience directly from itself. Literacy in painting is developed directly with no need for a functional sign-decoding type of literacy to be coped with as a means. That is true as well of sculpture. Architecture, theater, film, and dance all use some form of encoding system, but we seldom need to get involved with them. We certainly do not need to study architectural renderings, or film and theater scripts, or various dance notations to be educated about those arts. We can and do become knowledgeable about them from direct experiences of them. Would that knowledge be assisted by including some acquaintance with the special systems they employ notationally? Probably, which is why a comprehensive curriculum in each of those arts would include, as a helpful way to explore their nature, some attention to the notations they use. But it would be absurd to equate a knowledge of their notations with being literate about them.

Musical experience comes directly from sounds organized to be expressive. Listening to music—perceptually structuring music—has nothing to do with notation. The composer's musical experience does not come from notation—it comes from expressive sounds he or she is imagining. Those sounds will disappear if not notated, but the notation is not the music, and if recorded directly (electronically), notation can be bypassed entirely. The performer's musical experience does not come from notation; it comes from expressive sounds he or she is producing. Those sounds have been notated, but the notation is not the music, and if the performance is by memory, the notation is no longer relevant; it has served its function as "signs of sounds" and can then be ignored. Even when notation is present to remind the performer of what sounds to make, the sign decoding skill being employed is not what makes the performer an artist—a musician. Making expressive sounds is what a performing musician does. Notation is helpful as a reminder of the sounds to be made.

Functional literacy in music can be defined as the ability to apply sign encoding and decoding skills at high enough levels that composing and performing can be aided significantly by those skills. As discussed, few people attain truly functional literacy with staff notation. But what about music literacy at the level of being well educated about music? Surely a person would be considered literate about music who understood a great deal about the art of music—its history, its techniques, its many styles, its major practitioners, where to go to find good examples of it, how to make discerning judgments about it, how to respond to it appropriately and sensitively. Such a person would be considered musically literate in the full sense of that word—educated, perceptive, knowledgeable about music. It would no doubt add to his literacy if he could compose or perform to some degree and had the notational skills to help him do so. But literacy in the broad sense means well educated—able to share richly in that which music exists to provide—and that is an attainment of a *different sort* from sign recognition skill even in an art that uses notation as a way to encode expressive events.

What kind of literacy should the general music curriculum aim for? Clearly, notation skills in and of themselves do not constitute literacy except in the narrowest sense. Our goal must take us far beyond this limited concept of literacy, and we must not regard notation skills as the only route to that goal because if we do, we will never achieve very much for the vast majority of children. We must be clever enough to attain levels of educated responsiveness through listening, composing, performing, improvising, conceptualizing, analyzing, and evaluating that are far in advance of skills of notation. Notation, used wisely, can be an excellent aid in that process, so we must use it but not be used by it. And we must continue to learn how to use newly available technologies that allow us to deal with music directly and artistically without depending on notation. Each of the objectives for the general music program just enumerated can benefit from judicious use of staff notation and graphic notations and other notations, but each must go beyond what notation is capable of doing.

Notation skill is one of many devices a good general music program will employ as it strives to develop musically literate people in the significant sense of "well educated about the art of music." That is what literacy will have to mean if general music is to hope to be a basic subject. When literacy is equated with mastery of notation—reading and writing in the literal sense—the irrelevance of such literacy for all but a few students (let alone the lack of success that is inevitable) will ensure that the program devoted to it will be considered esoteric. Rightly so.

GENERAL MUSIC IN THE HIGH SCHOOL: OUR BIGGEST CHALLENGE

Whatever the need to improve the general music program in grades K–8, making it a genuine curriculum worthy of status as a basic subject, the profession has at least paid attention to it. Textbooks for it have been available for over a century, specialist teachers of it are prepared in hundreds of colleges and universities, and some time is given to it in most schools even if less than the desired standard and even if most of it is taught by classroom teachers (in grades K–6) rather than specialists. It can be criticized for its shortcomings and it can be praised for its successes. At any rate, the thing exists.

And the performance program in elementary schools, middle schools, junior high schools, and high schools (to be discussed in the next chapter) exists at levels unmatched in all the world.

What has not existed in school music is the opportunity for high school students not in performing groups to study music. Less than 2 percent of high school students are enrolled in any nonperformance music course, and the great majority of the tiny percentage enrolled are likely to be those also involved in performing groups.[8] Because only 12 to 15 percent of high school students participate in any performing group, school music education for the overwhelming majority of American youngsters ceases after grade 8.

So the high school general music program is, by far, the most neglected, most embarrassingly deficient aspect of music education in

---

[8]*A Trend Study of High School Offerings and Enrollments* (Washington, D.C.: National Center for Educational Statistics, 1984).

American schools. The reasons for this are too obvious and too painful to enumerate. So let us be grateful that the profession is finally beginning to show signs of wanting to do something about it.

What would a course or courses in music look like to be worthy of being considered basic in the high school program, that is, to be worthy of being required for all students? It would take far more space than can be given here to answer such a question adequately. But a few guidelines can be suggested.

1. The general course, by whatever name, will have to build on but go farther than the learnings achieved in grades K–8. So it will be related to the antecedent general music program but must present challenges appropriate to the more mature capacities and expectations and learning styles of high school students. The most common error in this regard is to underestimate what these youngsters can handle. Performance directors have the tendency to condescend to students not performing in their groups, feeling that (1) they probably have little interest in music, and (2) they are untalented and unknowledgeable. This accounts, in part, for the disinterest many high school music teachers display about such courses.

But these attitudes miss the reality that many if not most high school students are deeply interested in and involved with music in a variety of ways not necessarily related to bands, orchestras, and choruses. Their knowledge and sophistication about music are often at high levels, especially in regard to styles the music teacher may know little about. Often, then, the challenge of a good general course in music will be at least as great for the teacher as for the students. Rather than seeing this as a threat, it will need to be seen as an opportunity for teachers to grow and learn and adapt, while offering their students the breadth and depth that a professional music teacher can provide.

2. The objectives of the K–8 general music program—to improve the aesthetic behaviors relevant to the art of music—remain the same at the high school level but the balance among them shifts somewhat:

a. Perceiving and reacting through direct development of listening skills becomes even more pertinent. A wide variety of guided listening aids designed to provide challenging, active, focused experiences of music as it moves from beginnings to ends of pieces will need to be employed, including call charts, response charts, mapping devices, and so on.

b. Creating (composing, performing, improvising) will continue to be a useful means to enhance perception but must be used very carefully because for all high school students, even including those who are involved in performing groups, the ability to perceive a great variety of types and complexities of music has far outstripped their ability to perform or compose. Too heavy a reliance on those activities will be both repressive of learning and embarrassing to these self-conscious youngsters. But performing and composing activities should not be abandoned: when used intelligently they can be very powerful in aiding perception of musical processes, and they can also be greatly enjoyed for their own sake. The teacher's sensitivity and imagination (and sense of humor) will be crucial in keeping the right balance in this matter.

c. Broad-ranging conceptualizations about music—its nature, its values in society, its qualitative criteria, its varieties both in this country and around the world, its relation to art in general, its relevance to the full life, and so on—will need to be integrated with the immediate experiences of music being provided. The key to success here will be to include these conceptual learnings without making the course pedantic. Musical *experience* is the essential content. Ideas about music should enhance and broaden that content.

d. Musical analyses will be able to be more sophisticated and at higher musical levels than before. Invented graphic representations of the overall form of pieces and many of their significant details within the larger form will be especially useful. Students should be encouraged to create their own analytical maps or charts or diagrams (including standard notation when helpful) of a variety of pieces they choose and are assigned, and share them with the class in lessons they present.

e. Skills of evaluation—of pieces and of performances—become more emphasized. Criticism for the sake of being critical must be avoided and is a real risk at these ages. Thoughtful application of criteria for judgment, such as craftsmanship, sensitivity, imagination, and authenticity, as suggested in this book, should guide all the evaluations being made.

3. A wide diversity of musical styles from all over the world and from every historical period, including whatever styles are popular among these students, should be included. The impression must be avoided that the covert objective is to wean them away from what they like to what we like—an often justified suspicion among high schoolers. It is dangerous, therefore, to "start with what they like"—a common way to organize such courses. Starting with *their* stuff and showing how it relates to *our* stuff perpetuates the "yours-mine" dichotomy and can come across as condescending and manipulative. It is likely to be more effective to explore essential musical qualities—melody, rhythm, tone color, and so on—as they exist in many styles, including plenty of popular examples along with other examples but in random order or in "more obvious to more subtle" order, which will not always be *from* popular *to* other styles but can in many cases be the reverse. The idea is to explore all musics freely and openly and with a nonprejudiced attitude (this applies particularly to the *teacher*), seeking for musical understanding and enjoyment wherever it can be found. This is not to say that popular styles can never be the springboard for wider exploration, only that we must be cautious not to make this the only strategy.

4. The core content of a solidly built general course will be the core material of the art of music—its expressive elements, the many styles in

which the basic elements are actuated, the many ways people interact with music personally and societally, the relation of music to the larger domain of the arts. There is probably no single best or right way to organize this content sequentially. As in all effective learning of music at any level, the most useful principle guiding sequence is "from the more obvious to the more subtle." Whatever skills are being developed (listening, performing, composing) or understandings are being fostered (conceptually, analytically, judgmentally), the movement is from more easily handled tasks to those more challenging. As a variety of content arrangements are experimented with, we are likely to become more sophisticated about which are more productive and which more problematical. But we must not delay action on these courses in the belief that we can't get going until we figure out the "right" course outline. That may simply not exist.

5. While the core content is the basis of the course, there are a great variety of related matters from which individual students or small groups should be able to choose for special explorations—invented instruments, invented notations, group composition, music theory, playing guitar or keyboards or whatever, electronic/computer opportunities, special study of particular styles (jazz, rock, new wave, various ethnic musics, gamelan, etc.), acoustics, music of the film, and on and on. All such topics can be treated as auxiliary units from which students can choose, depending on the length of the course and the time available, or they can become follow-up electives as single-focus courses or several-module courses. As with course sequences, experience is likely to teach us how to combine core learnings with special opportunities in the most effective configurations.

High school performance directors willing to tackle the challenge of a course open to the 85 percent or so of students not in their groups, and those who are performing also, are likely to benefit in a variety of ways. Their credibility and visibility in the entire school will encourage more students to want to perform. They will have the satisfaction of influencing the musical enjoyment of large numbers of youngsters. They will also find themselves learning about music and about students in ways stretching them beyond what can occur in their ensembles. No, such courses are not all peaches and cream. They do require time and effort and a certain degree of risk for those inexperienced with them. But the payoff, professionally and personally, can be very great.

The high school general music offering provides us with a great opportunity to reach an unconscionably neglected population. Filling in that gap is among our most pressing needs. In addition, our recent interest in expanding both downward, to the preschool population, and upward, to the postcollege and later adult populations, is a sign of growing professional maturity. We have too few societal structures available as yet for us to make the contributions to out-of-school music education we are capable of making, and we are as yet so wedded to the K–12 program and its supporting college and graduate degrees that it is difficult for us to conceptualize how best to reach the nonschool ages beyond the excellent guidelines that are beginning to emerge. We can all look forward to continuing growth in this new challenge of music education beyond the school, which can allow us to make a broader contribution and also to become more securely a part of our total culture.

The general music program is our way to heighten every person's experience of the art of music. At every point in the program and in every activity we must constantly aim toward the immediacy and enjoyment of music as experienced. Music itself, and the power it exerts on our subjectivity, is the be-all and end-all of our teaching, and we must never get so involved in the details of what we are teaching that we leave the actuality of musical enjoyment behind or delay it for some future time. Aesthetic significance always is the product of actual, immediate aesthetic involvement. The general music program is our means of providing musical depth to the experience of people at every point in their development. It would be difficult to imagine a more humanizing contribution to the quality of every person's life. When we succeed in making that contribution through a curriculum that is as comprehensive, as systematic, as aesthetically and pedagogically valid as the art of music deserves and all students need, general music will have reached the maturity that can qualify it for full membership among the community of basic subjects in the school. It can also be a strong partner in a larger endeavor that can lead music education to a brighter future. Chapter Ten will explore that possibility.

The philosophy in action: The performance program

9

In all the world there is little if anything to compare with what the United States has achieved in offering practically all young people the opportunity to perform in groups supported by the schools, usually during school time. That some 15 percent or so of our secondary school students choose to participate in such a time-consuming, expensive, high-energy, and high-demand activity testifies to the attractiveness of our performance offerings. No other country achieves this overall level of commitment. And it is practically unheard of, except in the United States, for college teacher education programs at both undergraduate and graduate levels to prepare specialists to offer school performance experiences. While particular performing groups in particular schools in particular countries reach high levels of excellence, the breadth and quality of American school groups sets the world's standard for what can be achieved musically in an open education system. With the supporting structure of contests and festivals and all-states and professional associations and journals and research activities and on and on, we have every reason to regard our performance program as one of the education wonders of the world.

Yet for all our success we continue to be nagged by doubts about what we are doing, why we are doing it, how we go about doing it. Rationales for the performance program are too often embarrassing in their super-ficiality. The literature performed is often excellent but sometimes com-mercial and insipid. The concert-after-concert steamroller buries us under the pressure to produce rather than teach. While the great majority of youngsters in our groups are not unusually talented and have no intention to go into music professionally (we wouldn't know what to do with them if they did), we often use them to bolster the training of the few who will go on in music. The effect of our performance programs on the broader musi-cal literacy of the majority who participate seems to be minimal. The focus on technical proficiency, necessary when public performance is perceived as the be-all and end-all of the endeavor, throws the delicate balance be-tween technique and understanding way out of kilter, leaving many if not most students with skills unusable after high school and meager musical sensitivity to the nature of the art in which they have been engaged so mechanically. Even the tiny percentage of students who do go on to college to major in music find themselves competent in performance technique but undernourished in general understandings of the art of music. On and on goes the litany of complaints about which we are all so uncomfortable.

Is our cup half full or half empty? The answer would seem to be "both." It would be a great mistake to be so troubled by the part that is empty—by all the very real problems and issues as yet not satisfactorily ad-dressed—that we do not honor the part that is full—our incomparable level of success. What we must do is to try to overcome our weaknesses while preserving and building on our strengths, in a spirit of doing better what all professional educators are obligated to do better—offering significant learnings to all who choose to involve themselves with us.

THE IN-SCHOOL OR OUT-OF-SCHOOL DILEMMA

How can we best do this? First, within the schools. This is no longer too ob-vious to deserve mention. The threat, and in some cases the reality, of losing school support in favor of private/community sponsorship is a fact of life we must become increasingly adept to deal with. Many people have begun to argue that, since the schools cannot be expected to do everything, especially having become so heavily overburdened with new social-ethical-health expectations that put enormous strains on the school as an institu-tion, we must begin to look carefully at many of its traditional activities that might be just as well carried on outside. Performing groups are vul-nerable targets for such arguments. After all, they serve only some stu-dents, they appear to be an extracurricular activity rather than a subject: those who choose to participate could do so in evenings and weekends and could pay their own way rather than using up precious tax monies.

We must be courageous enough to acknowledge that we bear much of the burden of blame for such perceptions. Many performance programs are, in fact, primarily training grounds for the talented, with little if any genuine concern for the musical learnings of the majority of participating students. The issue here is not whether we have an obligation to discover and cultivate musically talented youngsters—we most assuredly do have that obligation and must fulfill it. It is how we do so that gives people the message that it is either our only concern or, more reasonably, one legitimate concern among others. Many people would say it seems to be our only reason for existence, and too often they would be correct. To the extent they are correct we are vulnerable to loss of school support.

The "extracurricular activity" perception is filled with complexities and ironies. Most communities expect our performing groups to provide all sorts of extracurricular services that are primarily functional rather than dominantly artistic. And there is, after all, good reason for people to feel that a publicly supported program should contribute to the communal life which naturally requires music as a contributing component. The most obvious and most visible example is the marching band, without which one of the most important socialization activities in our culture—community building through football identification—would be unthinkable. That we are needed in this important aspect of our culture and that we serve that need so excellently should make us proud of our contribution and our competence. This applies also to all the other social services we provide so well.

The irony, of course, is that all these activities are only tangentially related to the basic role of the school as an education institution, and the same community expecting us to contribute to them also regards us, therefore, as contributory rather than foundational. This leaves us between a rock and a hard place. Extracurricular services are valid, important, even necessary given the role music always plays in the collective life of any society, and we should provide those services with expertness and with grace. Yet to the extent we do so, we open ourselves to the criticism that we have no unique, essential role in and of ourselves as do all the basic school subjects.

Can the performance program exist just as effectively if it is taken out of school? The answer is "yes," if (1) it is conceived entirely as special training for the musically talented or (2) it exists entirely to fulfill extracurricular functions. Of course, if it becomes dissociated with schools, most youngsters will never have access to it because of finances and competing activities and remoteness from the one institution that involves all young people and a host of other reasons. But that would be of little concern because those youngsters fortunate enough to have parents able and willing to recognize and support their interest would benefit from the training their parents provided. No doubt there would be enough such young people to keep the need for musicians sufficiently filled. Of course we would lose many who are very talented, but it would be a loss we'd have to accept. And as for the social needs, communities that wanted music services would see to it that they got as much as they wanted and were willing to support—surely an efficient way to take care of supply and demand.

So what is left of the argument that musical performance should be an essential component of schooling, publicly supported and equally available to all? Not much, except if a different argument is made. This book has attempted to offer such an argument: that music is one of our basic modes of cognition, that music educates our subjective nature as nothing but art is capable of doing, that musical intelligence exists to some degree in all young people and is capable of development for all and must be developed if all are to be as fully intelligent as they can be. If that argument has merit, all students should have equal opportunity to (1) be engaged in the development of broad musical literacy through a systematic, required general music program from grades 1–12, and (2) elect performance experiences that extend general learnings in ways unique to musical performance. But if the second goal is to be achieved, the performance program will have to be more than only talent training or social activity. It can include both of those (in fact it *must* include both of those), but it must also be what any other subject worthy of inclusion in schools must be—a valid curriculum offering learnings not available through the study of something else.

PERFORMANCE AS CURRICULUM

The major task facing the performance program is to become a genuine curriculum of musical studies through the medium of performance. This is not in any way to suggest that it become general music. In fact, if it did, the two programs would be redundant, and one of them would have to be dropped. In Chapter Eight it was suggested that the goal or aim of the general music program is to develop, to the fullest extent possible, every student's capacity to experience and create intrinsically expressive qualities of sounds or, to put it another way, to develop every student's aesthetic sensitivity to the art of music (page 153). The goal of the performance program is precisely the same. What is different, and what defines the special character of each of the two programs, is the point of and balance between "experience and create." In the general music curriculum, the point is to experience the great diversity of musics in the only way possible for all people when music is required—through the direct development of each student's capacity to structure perceptually and respond feelingfully to all kinds and types of music; that is, through listening as the fundamental behavior. Performing, in the general music program, is an essential but contributory mode of interaction with music. It is a powerful means, among others, for enhancing musical understanding and experience. But the balance between listening and performing will favor listening (although the age of the students will be a factor in precisely what the balance can be in particular grades and on particular days). The balance stems from the very nature of general music as having the entire world of music as its essential study material. General music is *extensive* and *comprehensive* in its approach to the art of music.

In the performance curriculum the point is to experience a particular genre of music (choral, orchestral, band, chamber, etc.) through the actual creation of it at the performance stage of its being brought to full realization. To do this, a very small sample of music must be chosen from one particular genre—those pieces capable of being performed by such and such particular instrument or voice or group. Performing continues to be a means to experience the music and the creation of it, but it is not a contributory means as in the general music program—it is the primary means. The difference in balance from the general music program stems from the nature of performance as having only a tiny percentage of the world of music as its essential study material but with each piece being experienced exhaustively. Performance is *intensive* and *selective* in its approach to the art of music.

The intensive nature of the performance program is its special reason for existence. How can it be what it authentically is and still fulfill the demands of being a curriculum? The seven phases of the curriculum explained in the previous chapter will guide our explanation.

THE VALUES PHASE OF THE PERFORMANCE CURRICULUM

The one thing the performance program needs above all else is to get its values straight. Until it does, it will go on and on not knowing what it wants to accomplish. The hundreds of trivial, nonartistic claims made for the value of performing continue to keep our programs from being perceived as anything more than trivial and nonartistic. Unable to claim a value that is unique to performance and essential for all to experience—a value that can order our priorities and give them direction—we go on churning out claim after claim as if we were selling snake oil rather than offering experiences with one of the great arts. The literature of salesmanship for musical performance is among our profession's sorriest productions.

Recognizing, if only unconsciously, that the salesman's scam demeans what we are offering, we then sometimes leap to the other extreme, making claims so overblown that playing an instrument or singing begin to sound like the one true route to the establishment of God's kingdom on earth. Performing will give truth to life, will nurture love, will give life ultimate meaning and goodness, and will make our youngsters paragons of every human virtue. How come we as musicians do not quite live up to these achievements? Um, well, let's get on to the rehearsal.

The array of claims—actually pretexts—we make for performance, from the petty at one extreme to the excessive at the other, leaves us with a great big hole in the middle. It is high time we finally plug that hole with a philosophically justifiable reason for existence—one that is faithful to the art we serve and that is valid for this particular aspect of that art.

What value of performance ties it directly to music, is unique in its musical function, is essential for people to experience to gain this value? Simply, the value of being involved in the act of musical creation at the performance phase. The special nature of this act requires that craftsmanship, sensitivity, imagination, and authenticity be brought to bear on the inherent expressive needs of a piece awaiting actualization. Those involved in the actualization process both subsume their own needs to that of the piece, and funnel the needs of the piece through their own musical personalities. It is that double obligation—serving the music yet bringing it to life with individuality—that characterizes all artistic performance. It is that experience, combining the expressive needs of something larger than oneself with one's own, inner nurturance of those needs, that so touches and can so transform the subjectivities of those undergoing it. People who are performers serve their art uniquely. Art serves such people uniquely.

The performance program exists to provide focused, refined opportunities for musical creation—far beyond the capacity of the general music program which provides it in a broad, exploratory context. All activities in the performance program must be guided by the value of artistic creation. This is obviously the point of concert groups, but it also underlies the functionality of all the community service groups, which can be artistic, musical, and creative in addition to serving other needs. When a solid offering of concert-type groups exists as the core of the program, supplemented by as broad an array of additional service groups as is reasonable for particular communities, both being musically authentic according to their functions, the performance program will have achieved an artistic integrity commanding respect from all associated with it and an educational integrity worthy of building a curriculum upon. We can achieve this artistic and educational strength by honoring our art as it deserves to be honored, honoring performance for its unique, essential role in our art, and honoring all the students who choose to engage themselves in our program by offering them the experience of being musical performing artists. Our curriculum can then be built as a systematic program of studies devoted to carrying out in practice the essential value of musical performance.

With this basic value in place as the guide for all that occurs in the curriculum we can also reap a great many secondary benefits directly related to the primary one, with no fear that these will splinter the program. We can use advocacy arguments tailored to people's nonartistic concerns so long as we also stress that secondary benefits arise because we offer a program devoted to the primary benefit—artistic creativity. Can youngsters experience discipline through artistic creativity? Of course: the special kind required by such creativity. Can they enrich their social lives through artistic creativity? Of course: through the community of shared feeling that artistic creativity forms. Can they experience responsibility this way? Of course: the requirement that one assume responsibility for authentic, sensitive, craftsmanly, imaginative expression of music. Is it "healthy" for young people to be involved in artistic creation? Of course: psychological, emotional "health" is promoted by experiences of clarified, unified, deepened, refined, extended, organized inner feelings, which is what the experience of creating art produces. On and on it goes. When a value is dependent on genuine artistic creativity as primary and natural-ly arises as a result of devotion to it, it can be claimed honestly and valid-ly. If a value can*not* be tied to the primary one it should be dismissed as irrelevant. Musical creativity cannot do everything. What it *can* do is so powerful in and of itself and in related values that we need not ever cheapen our claims by going beyond valid ones. And we can build our per-formance curriculum to produce the values only art can offer, focusing on the special function within art of creating it as performers.

THE CONCEPTUALIZED PHASE
OF THE PERFORMANCE CURRICULUM

In the previous chapter this phase of the total curriculum was explained as it pertains to the general music program. The same issues relate to the performance program but in a distinctive way.

All the subject matter fields impinging on curriculum development are just as relevant for a performance program as for any other. For ex-ample, psychology, as explained previously, has shifted ground dramati-cally in recent years away from Behaviorism toward Cognitive Psychology. The implications for a performance curriculum are enormous. Under a be-havioristic model it was possible to think at the level of isolated, tiny per-formance behaviors such as were capable of being stated in terms of "behavioral objectives." An accumulation of a great many of these (num-bering in the thousands if not more) constituted a program. Reinforcement techniques could be applied to step-by-step learning, and evaluation of learning could be conceived at the level of measuring individual steps and strings of steps. Rehearsals and practice sessions could be structured ac-cording to all the techniques used to produce correct behaviors, a good strategy entailing the isolation of specific tasks and stamping them in until well conditioned, using reward (and, when necessary, punishment) as rein-forcers of desired behaviors. The influence of all this was very great on how performance directors actually went about their business, specifically for those who had studied Behaviorism and its applications and, more general-ly, as an underlying approach for those who had not.

Now all this has gone by the boards. Of course, some useful remnants remain and can continue to be helpful in the specifics of performance to which they apply: mostly at the technique-skill-automaticity level. But the overall approach to teaching and learning has moved on to a radically different set of assumptions and strategies, and these *also* have enormous implications for how a performance curriculum must be conceptualized. The focus now on higher-order behaviors requires that learning episodes—rehearsals, individual practice, coaching, and so on—be structured to engage thinking, problem-solving, perceptual, expressive, synthesizing characteristics of mind. Isolated bits of behavior are meaningful only when they are embedded as parts of larger, unified patterns of thinking and doing, so the bits and pieces must be learned within larger contexts or at least immediately used within the larger context to which they contribute. A good rehearsal or practice session will have to demonstrate skillful, insightful applications of what psychology is now suggesting we need to attend to in order to produce meaningful learning.

This chapter is not intended to be a methods text for the performance program: the point of the example from psychology is that a valid performance curriculum must be as influenced by current thinking from psychology as all basic subjects in the school must be. If we exempt ourselves from knowing what is going on in the larger field of education, or having to apply new knowledge to what we do, we must also exempt ourselves from being considered a subject worthy of school support and respect. To the extent we are as aware of new developments as anyone else, and capable of using them judiciously and relevantly, we can claim to be bona fide members of an educational staff offering an educational program of studies such as schools are supposed to provide.

The same applies to all the other areas directly involved in teaching and learning—human development as it applies to the development of skills and cognitions necessary for performance, research as it suggests efficient ways to influence performers positively, the history of education and of music education as it clarifies past values and approaches and their continuing influence on us today, music history and theory as they help us deal with music authentically, developments in conducting as an area of study so that advances in understanding of the conductor's role can be applied, new schooling patterns of organization that can be taken advantage of to strengthen our program, and so forth. All these must be taken into account as we form a concept of what a good performance program must consist of.

This is not in any way an academic exercise or a way to prove to others that we are just as smart as they. It is a necessary condition if we intend to be regarded as full partners in the education enterprise and if we intend for music performance to be regarded as an endeavor deserving a home in the school as an education institution. We cannot retreat to the esoteric position that music is so different that knowledge about good teaching and learning does not apply. Yes, music *is* different, which is why it must be part of schooling if its values are to be shared. But we are music *educators* and can learn from and use educational principles as validly as anyone else, adapting them to our subject and to our goal. This is a big responsibility, but it is one every other teacher in the school accepts or should accept. It is a responsibility in consonance with the extensive undergraduate and graduate training our performance directors receive—training, as mentioned previously, incomparable in the world. To offer such training, as we do, and then to settle for school performance programs limited to skill development and skill display (as we too often do) is overkill in training and underestimation of what young people are capable of learning about music and what performance of music entails. The opportunities for learning through performance are far too great to be fulfilled through skill development as an end rather than as a necessary means. To fulfill all its opportunities for rich, creative musical experience and for the growth of musical intelligence, every performance program should be broad enough to warrant the term "curriculum."

CONCEPTUALIZED GUIDELINES

At this period in history a performance program constituting a genuine curriculum will have to display several characteristics.

1. Beginning performers, no matter what their age, will have to be engaged quickly in musical decision-making responsibilities. The very first lessons, whether individual or group, will have to include opportunities to use, in imaginative musical ways, whatever sounds the performers can make at that point. It will have to be clear to them, *from the very start of instruction,* that they are engaged in studying *music* and that their instrument (which includes the voice) is their means of learning about music by *producing it creatively.* Their program of study— their curriculum from that point on—will be a systematic, developmental study of *music* through the vantage point of its performance.

2. Beginning experiences with performance, at the level of the very first lessons, will have to make clear that technique—the ability to produce sounds skillfully—is a means to musical ends. The curriculum is based not on skill development but on musical learnings. Skill development will be a necessary component of the program because, in performance, musical learnings can be more challenging as growing skills allow music of more challenge to be explored. But the curriculum is *not* a sequenced set of steps developing technique. It is a sequenced set of experiences with music through performing it. That is the foundational understanding to be introduced in the first lessons— a learning that will grow in meaning over the course of many years of instruction.

3. To begin the curriculum of study at the beginning, musical learnings relevant to artistic decision making will have to be included in the

very first lessons. For example, when as few as three tones can be made (some would say that two are sufficient), the first musical learnings should be introduced. How loud or soft can these three tones be produced? How do you go about making tones louder or softer? And, most important, how can you use louds and softs to create something musically interesting with these three tones? In your practice for the next lesson or class use louds and softs as you produce those three tones, deciding, according to *how it feels musically,* which combinations seem to be expressive. In the next lesson or class we'll be dealing with your solutions, and other solutions, and we'll also spend plenty of time on how you are producing those three tones (and maybe we'll add a fourth tone) because there are many skills you need to gain in order to have better control of those tones so you can be more musical with them. And we'll be making other musical decisions with the tones you're learning. What makes them sound more musical in their tone color? What practice will be needed to get the sounds closer to a beautiful musical tone? How will body position and breathing, and so on, help you produce good sounds, both loud and soft, so you can be more expressive as you explore musical possibilities? Can we add longer and shorter tones to the louds and softs? In addition to the sequences of tones (the melodies) I'm teaching you, can you create some of your own? In addition to the longs and shorts (the rhythms) I'm teaching you, can you create some of your own?

On and on go the musically creative tasks. Learnings about music, creative exploration of music, guidance toward more sensitive solutions to creating expressive sounds, skill development as an ongoing component, all blend into a creative, musically focused, sequential series of learnings through performing.

4. At all stages of the curriculum, including the very first lessons but upward to advanced instruction, skills, understandings, and creative decision making will be kept in optimal balance, none of them dominating so much that the other two seem to disappear. Of course there will be times when one or another needs more focus for good progress to be made. But these times are exceptional. Usually all three will be present and will be mutually reinforcing. The major, most serious, most debilitating errors in performance instruction are (1) to separate skills from their musical uses; (2) to so overemphasize skills, especially at the beginning stages, that they become the end rather than the means; and (3) to conceptualize a program of study as step-by-step skill training. Music education through performance is not just skill training; if that is all it is we can and should kiss it goodbye in the schools. It is a curriculum of study including skill training as an ongoing aspect. Until we learn this, and apply it from the beginning to the end of our program, and demonstrate to our students and everyone else that we are teachers of music and its performance rather than skill drillers, we will not have a curriculum and we will not be serving our stu-

dents or music as they deserve. If a beginning instructional methodology is so skill bound that little if any musical expressive exploration is taking place, little if any individualized problem solving of a creative nature is taking place, little if any diversity of stylistic possibilities is being experienced, little if any leeway is provided for using technique imaginatively rather than in endless, repetitive, convergent drill on exercises that are devoid of musicality, then that methodology is engaged in training in the narrowest, most restrictive sense of that word. Such a methodology produces automatons rather than musicians, dependence rather than independence, a view of music as regimented technique rather than as creative expression. The values of such a regimen are antithetical to aesthetic education in performance, which is devoted to *music making* through skillful performing. *Music making* is the point, and the point must be made from the very start if musical values are to be internalized as being primary rather than as being secondary to technique or even nonexistent.

5. To be successful teachers of music through performance, we must use as the core study material a rich array of pieces of music at graded levels of difficulty and in a wide variety of styles within the particular performance medium with which we are dealing. That literature is what we teach, including the expressive experience each piece offers, general musical learnings each piece fosters, skills of performance each piece helps develop, and understandings about performance itself as an essential artistic role that arise from creating each piece.

6. In addition to the core literature ranging from the beginning to the most advanced levels, practice material will be needed to bolster the skills required for acceptable performance of the pieces. This practice material should not be separated from the literature to such an extent that it is seen as a separate, unrelated literature of its own, as so often happens. It needs to be closely related to pieces of music being performed, so that the transfer of skill to musical expression occurs constantly and consciously. To choose pieces that are sufficiently challenging musically and technically to keep progress going while providing success at every step, and to supplement this literature with practice material related to it, fruitful in building skills called for by the literature yet also progressive so that skill development is occurring consistently and logically, is among the most complex teaching challenges in the entire field of education. Performance directors who are successful in keeping the balance between literature as central and skill study as complementary, the two constantly reinforcing performance ability and musical understanding, should be regarded as the very pinnacle of professional mastery in the field of education. That we do have many such teachers should make all of us proud to be music educators, and more dedicated to helping all music teachers achieve more of that excellence.

7. Included in a concept of a performance curriculum, in addition to the graded literature and the practice material related to it, will be general

learnings about music, about creativity in the arts, about the role of the performing arts in culture, about art as it relates to the quality of human life. These learnings enrich the curriculum, adding a dimension of thoughtfulness to the intensity of the ongoing devotion to the creative act. This is not to imply a series of lectures as a dominant part of the program (although occasional "let's think about what we're doing" sessions can have powerful effects). It is that some time must be taken along the busy way to stop at appropriate moments to raise issues arising from the activity, to ponder the values being pursued, to ask questions causing young minds to reflect about what all this hard work adds to their lives and to the lives of others pursuing performance and to those enjoying the performances they present. This implies that performance directors must be fairly sophisticated about such matters; that is, they should have a well-developed philosophy of music education that can be articulated clearly enough that they can share it with their students, so their students can build their own philosophy of music as part of their education and of their lives. The education of performance directors, at both undergraduate and graduate levels, should include such study so that it can be translated into an ongoing component of school performance curricula.

8. Underlying the concept of a performance curriculum, including all the musical learnings it should develop and all the uses the curriculum will make of knowledge from related fields impinging on education as a process, must be an understanding that performance is a creative act and that the performance curriculum exists to involve students in that act. In Chapter Four, on *Creating Art*, it was argued that youngsters involved in performing must be involved in making decisions themselves and in understanding why and how their teacher-director is shaping and molding their performance through his or her creative decision making. When they are sharing in the making of musical decisions, by their teacher's guidance as they make their own and by a clear sense of why the teacher is making his or her own, they will be producing music creatively, that is, as artists. A curriculum claiming to be artistic, or musical, or creative must be a developmental series of learnings about how to get better at being artistic, musical, creative. Creativity cannot be conceptualized as being the sole prerogative of the teacher-director, the students being artisans who only carry out his or her artistic wishes. The students must share in the creativity, under the insightful, unifying governance of the teacher. It will be difficult for many performance directors to give up complete ownership of creativity to become nurturers of it. But when they do, they become music educators, offering the gift of musical creativity to their students' experience and sharing that gift as they shape the unified creative act. The gain for both students and teachers is very great. The gain for performance in the schools is that it can then be an ongoing, progressive, planned, unified study of musical creativity through the actual experiencing of it; that is, a valid performance curriculum.

THE SYSTEMATIZED PHASE
OF THE PERFORMANCE CURRICULUM

As explained in the previous chapter, sequence decisions should be based on two essential factors: (1) the nature of the subject being taught and (2) the nature of learners as they develop. In the performance program this implies that a planned series of learnings should be based on (1) creative musical tasks of growing scope and complexity and subtlety and (2) adaptation of these tasks to the physical and musically cognitive capacities of those being taught, using research as an essential guide.

INVALID, INADEQUATE BASES FOR SEQUENCE

The invalidity and inadequacy of several approaches to systematizing or sequencing learnings in the general music program, discussed in Chapter Eight, have counterparts in the performance program. The most obvious one has already been explained abundantly—the mistake of conceiving a curriculum sequence as being the step-by-step training of skills. Performance is caught in the training-versus-education dilemma severely, because the reliance on skill development is far greater than in the general music program. So the tendency is even greater to build a skill development system rather than a curriculum. The dangers of doing so, however, are equally great, because such a system demonstrates clearly that musical performance is not a cognitive domain requiring the development of a particular kind of intelligence but instead is an activity of muscles and positions and breath control and counting beats and translating notational codes. All these and hundreds of other externals of musical performance, when they determine what is being learned and when the learning will occur, are then correctly perceived as being what the learning is all about. That is a false message and a self-defeating one because it reverses the values of performance.

The second major error in sequencing learnings in the performance program is to use a series of performances as the basic way to arrange for progression through the years. In that approach to sequence, as soon as students are able to join a group that can perform publicly, the public performances determine every aspect of what they will be learning and in what order, skill development paralleling and supporting the performances. Curriculum planning becomes a matter of choosing pieces for the next public appearance and curriculum progress consists of getting those pieces ready to perform. What is demonstrated by this notion of curriculum, of course, is precisely what most people including many performance directors have come to understand performance in the schools to be—a sequence of public appearances rather than a school subject with its own, internal structure of learnings that must determine sequence.

   What would give the performance program a basis for sequential learnings broader and more solid than skill development or public performances,
yet continue to integrate them as essential elements? New answers to this
question have begun to appear in recent years as thoughtful performance
specialists have grappled with the issues raised by the need to forge a wider
notion of sequence. These answers center on the use of musical concepts as
organizers of learning, just as comprehensive curricula in the general music
program have been doing. The concepts chosen are those central to music as
an art and to performance as artistically creative. They include, for example,
a focus on melody as an organizer for a set of learnings connected to a planned
concert. All, or some (or even one), of the pieces programmed for the concert
are chosen specifically because they demonstrate particular aspects of melodic
expressiveness. Learning these pieces requires attention to a host of factors
in addition to melody, of course, but their melodic content gives a unifying
focus to all those learnings. Skill development related to the pieces must also
incorporate many factors beyond melodic control, but, again, melodic expressiveness gives related skills a musical direction. The program can then include an explanation (in program notes or as part of a preconcert or
postconcert demonstration or as remarks during the concert) of what has been
attempted by this program (or by a selected piece or pieces in the program).
The program itself becomes a vehicle for all that a curriculum of studies in
performance must include—progressive skill development related to pieces
of music, understandings of how music is "material (sounds) organized to be
expressive," creative decision making as a requirement for bringing music to
life through performing, specific understandings of particular pieces through
an intensive study of their expressive contents, and the sharing with an
audience of the expressive power of the pieces learned (which is, after all, the
function of performers). The program also educates both the performers and
the community to the fact that the performance program in the school is
guided by a planned series of musical learnings that can be shared publicly.
   The focus on melody in the preceding example can then switch to
another concept for the next planned set of learnings leading to a public
performance (formal concert or informal program or demonstration or
workshop or open rehearsal or whatever). Concepts can relate to musical
elements (tone color, rhythm, form, texture, dynamics, etc.), to musical
styles (the romantic impulse, the classic impulse, a particular modern
style, etc.), to particular composers, to particular musical types (marches,
chorales, overtures, suites, etc.), to musical functions of particular groups
(the chorus in community celebrations, the chorus in entertainment, the
chorus as an aspect of worship, the chorus in a variety of cultures, the
chorus in a particular period of history, etc.), to aesthetic issues (what is a
"good" performance, artistic decisions and how they are made, performer
and conductor, large-group/small-group challenges in performance, the
role of craftsmanship in performance, balance and blend in performance,

incorporating history into performance, etc.), to whatever other concepts an imaginative director can think of to help youngsters learn about the art of music through creating it.

With concepts such as these as a guide to sequence, a director can think in terms of one-year and multiple-year curriculum objectives. What would be a rich array of learnings, including some specific topics (harmony and counterpoint) and some more general topics (historical styles) and some all-inclusive topics (how artistic decisions are judged), that students might be involved in during their four years in the high school concert band (or chorus or jazz band or chamber orchestra or marching band or swing choir or whatever)? What will they learn about music as an art, about musical creation as an artistic function, about craftsmanship and its role in creativity? What will they then be able to take with them throughout life whether or not they choose to continue as performers after they graduate? How can these planned, sequenced learnings be made evident to the students and other faculty and administrators and parents and community so that all understand that *music education* is taking place in the performance program—that the performance director is guided by a curriculum of studies aimed toward developmental growth of music literacy as well as skills?

These are the kinds of questions begging for answers by the music education performance community and by our entire profession. This is where our energies need to be directed, rather than toward endlessly proliferating public appearances which demonstrate a kind of mindless display rather than a thoughtful sharing of musical learnings. We cannot go on blaming others—administrators, communities, "those other directors at those other schools"—for the treadmill we find ourselves on. That only perpetuates the problem.

Can we get off that treadmill onto a curriculum which includes but transcends public performances as the be-all and end-all of our programs? This question leads directly to the next phase of the total curriculum in performance.

THE INTERPRETED PHASE
OF THE PERFORMANCE CURRICULUM

In the discussion of the interpreted phase of the general music curriculum, a point was made that applies equally to the performance program—that even the most perfect theoretical foundation for a curriculum, in the values phase, the conceptualized phase, and the systematized phase, will be interpreted differently by different teachers when they start to put the curriculum into practice, and that this is probably a good thing. We don't need a lock-stepped, rigid program slavishly carried out "by the numbers." We need informed, skillful professionals who, while moving in the same general direction toward aesthetic education, do so in ways that are imaginative and sensitive to the needs of the particular situation with which they are dealing. This implies teachers well grounded in theory—philosophy to guide value choices, a broad grasp of education-related fields to guide the overall concept of the curriculum, a firm sense of how to sequence learnings fruitfully. Then an individual's interpretation of how to put the curriculum foundations into effective practice can be made with confidence that it will be sound educationally and valid artistically.

Where do performance directors gain a solid curriculum foundation? Four influential sources of education and experience contribute to the curriculum concept held by music educators in this specialization: (1) the school experience they underwent as students, (2) their overall college teacher education program, (3) the performance aspect of their college training and, (4) the activities of their performance community peers including professional in-service efforts. Each of these exerts significant influences on what performance directors envision as a proper curriculum. And all, unfortunately, tend to reinforce a narrow sense of such a curriculum.

Given the emphasis in school programs on performance as product, and the fact that the best student performers in those programs are the ones most likely to go on to college as music education majors, we start the teacher education process with people whose image of success is largely one of performance excellence as the primary or only goal. The rewards, the encouragement, the ego gratification, the musical enjoyment these students have received have come from their talent as players and singers. So it is perfectly natural that their values reflect their experience. And it is also perfectly healthy for this to happen. We do, indeed, want the best, most talented youngsters to be the ones who go into the music education profession. The unfortunate aspect is that they tend to regard their own experience as the norm to which all students should aspire, so that school performance groups exist primarily to fulfill the aspirations of students such as themselves. From the very start the balance between musical expertise and musical understanding becomes heavily skewed toward the former rather than toward a mutually reinforcing parity between the two.

So the talented performers go to college as music education majors or, as is common, as performance majors who only after a year or two begin to realize that a performance career is pie in the sky, so settle for music education as a compromise. Yet their performance prowess and performance orientation continue to exert the major influence, reinforced by practically everything happening to them as music majors. The core of their program is regarded to be (1) their private lessons with heavy practice demands and (2) their performance organizations with heavy concert schedules. Theory and history tend to be seen as unreasonable intrusions, having little to do with performing and being frustrating and anxiety producing because the students are so ill-prepared to deal with music in contexts wider than through playing or singing. So they are suffered as necessary evils rather than as ways to liberate musicianship from too-narrow confines.

In lessons and performing groups a massive concentration on technical learnings tends to occur, the goal being to produce the best possible performing musicians. Studio teachers, after all, are driven to turn out fine performers; that is how their success is judged. Performers directors are driven to present fine concerts; that is how *their* success is judged. Who has time, or interest, or devotion, in such a situation, to the presentation of a model of what a balanced music education process should consist of? Even in colleges in which all or the great majority of music majors are music education majors, the model in lessons and performing groups continues to be that of training for professional performers. And in colleges which have large numbers of students in professional performance programs that orientation clearly dominates. So the images of competence internalized by prospective teachers through their training are largely images of themselves as teachers of talented students, as directors of fine-sounding groups, as identifiers of people like themselves who can be sent off to major in music, perpetuating the cycle.

All these reinforcers of performance-for-the-sake-of-fine-performance are then further intensified in the community of school music teachers, whose values, shaped by all the forces described, center strongly on producing the best possible players, singers, and groups. The "best possible" means, clearly, the "finest-sounding." So the elaborate system of professional activities created by the school performance community is one almost entirely devoted to the showcasing and rewarding of "fine-sounding" individuals and groups. It is just about impossible for a teacher to avoid getting sucked into this professional whirlpool and playing by its rules, if he or she is interested in being considered successful.

The irony of all this—the complexity of this whole issue—is that, in a real sense, it needs to occur and should occur. None of it is negative in and of itself, in the values of fine musicianship-as-performance it inculcates. We *want* excellent performance because fine performance *is* a value we cherish. So what is it about all of this that makes us squirm?

Simply, what it leaves out. And that is the essential fact that school music educators are not professional performers and they are not professional conductors. They are also not college teachers of lessons to music majors or college directors of organizations made up of music majors. They are, instead, educators responsible for teaching music and the performance of music to youngsters who with very few exceptions will not pursue performance in any committed way after high school. And while the special needs of the few who will go on as performers must be met expertly (by additional opportunities outside the school as well as within it), those needs cannot be the sole or even major determinant of the performance curriculum. Yet it is precisely those special needs that too strongly determine the curriculum, because of all the factors discussed already that center on performance expertise as the sole driving value.

How can a better balance be struck so we can secure for all in our groups the values of musical education through excellent performance and for some the values of training potential professional musicians who are also musically educated?

Two extremes must be avoided. The first is to abandon performance quality as an essential component of the curriculum. To perform well is to shape inner experience by shaping musical sounds artistically—the central reason to involve young people in performance. So we cannot say, "Well, we don't have to care how it sounds because we're aesthetic educators." *That's sheer nonsense.* "How it sounds" is the public display of the inner, artistic shaping of feeling. So the product itself—the performance of this particular piece with craftsmanship and sensitivity and imagination and authenticity—is not separable from the processes of learning to perform it. *How it sounds* as a performance is the absolutely necessary determinant of all the processes of learning that are going on.

But the other extreme ignores the performers' needs to understand and be involved in the processes, in favor of securing the product as the only result that matters. Product then so dominates that education disappears.

All this boils down to the requirement that performance music teachers be equally expert in three domains: (1) broad musicianship so that teaching can go beyond technicalities, (2) refined musical sensitivity and skill so that artistic insight can guide the learnings toward excellent performances, and (3) educational understanding that makes each episode—lesson, class, rehearsal, public performance—valid in itself as a learning experience and that makes all episodes part of a larger plan that qualifies for the term "curriculum."

Few if any tasks in education are so complex. There is no hope of being successful at it if the training of performance directors does not balance all three, if the community of performance directors does not equally value and reward all three, if school performance programs are not suffused with the values of all three. When performance directors, as a matter of course, interpret an excellent program to be one which includes all three in consonance we will have arrived at the professional maturity we seek.

There is a good deal of evidence that we are, indeed, moving toward such maturity, but there is also a good deal of evidence that we have plenty of work cut out for us. School programs continue to perpetuate the performance treadmill, college teacher education programs continue to emphasize performance skill as the major value, the model of private lessons and performing organizations in college continues to be that of professional training rather than of musical education, and the community of school performance teachers continues to worship performance prowess. So how can more progress be made toward the balance that so many music educators are calling for? Where do we concentrate our efforts? The answer can only be "everywhere." There is no one, magical point from which progress can be made. We must be aware of opportunities for change wherever such opportunities exist and be courageous enough to take those opportunities in the face of inertia and the fear of change. But certainly one essential factor must guide whatever we do—the belief that musical sensitivity is the ultimate educational value we pursue, and that all our teaching, including the teaching of performance, is a means to cultivate it.

THE OPERATIONAL PHASE
OF THE PERFORMANCE CURRICULUM

In the discussion of the general music curriculum, it was suggested that the actual teaching operations involved in the music classroom are extremely intricate, requiring high levels of professional craftsmanship, of sensitivity both to music and learners, of imagination so the atmosphere is charged with vitality, and of authenticity to the nature of music and to the nature of young people. All these requirements for effective operation as a teacher apply with particular force to the performance director, whose challenges are among the most complicated in all of education. The vast amounts of technical know-how involved, of instruments, the voice, conducting, complicated scores, performance practice; the musical demands of bringing pieces to imaginative artistic life; the psychological finesse needed to deal with a variety of small and large groups as teacher, guide, artist, ultimate authority; the energy called for to keep youngsters focused and excited and challenged while also rewarded; all these are the daily realities of the performance director. In addition are the requirements that the operations of the program be guided by a sound philosophy, a deep and broad curriculum concept, a valid, insightful sequencing of learnings, a penetrating interpretation of what a good performance curriculum must achieve. But further, the performance director must have organizational skills and political skills and social management skills and public relations skills and sheerly business skills that few other teachers ever have to develop. In short, no one who has not been a performance director is likely to be able to appreciate sufficiently all that it takes to be a good one.

That is precisely why performance directors are seldom given as much credit as they deserve. Seeing only the surface of their work, in public performances that seem to be so smoothly handled and untroubled with any problems (as good performances *should* be seen), it all seems so easy, so delightful, so effortless. "How lucky the performance director is, to make a living at such an enjoyable, pleasant activity while all the other teachers have to work so hard!"

Among the ironies in this situation is that this perception does have a bit of truth in it: performance teachers, over and above all the unseen, little understood complexities of their work, do benefit personally from the public display of their skills required by their position. Few other teachers enjoy the admiration of both students and community won by successful directors, and few other teachers provide both students and community with the pleasures that performance directors offer regularly. It *is* a lucky position to be in, after all, not because it is easy, which it decidedly is not, but because bringing music to youngsters in a way that is sharable with audiences is among the most satisfying roles in all of education.

The problem, of course, is that the pleasantness of it all overshadows the fact that, underneath, serious education is going on. Performers are not just "playing"; they are engaged in one of the most complex challenges to mind, body, and feelings that humans can undertake. They are exploring and learning to understand some of the most complicated products of human mentality, pieces of music. To do so, they are mastering skills—of instruments and the voice, of notation, of precise hearing, of exquisitely coordinated group interactions—that few if any other activities can match in their intricacy. They are doing all this while exercising creative artistic judgments, sometimes alone or in small-group contexts, sometimes as part of the unified creativity of a large group, and these judgments call for the exercise of intelligence of the highest order. And through all these learnings they are becoming more sophisticated, by actual experience, about how the art of music works and how it is dependent on the contribution of performers. All this is taking place through a rationalized, carefully planned sequence of developmental learnings based on a philosophically valid belief system and a broadly conceived curriculum structure.

When a good performance curriculum exists—a curriculum embodying all the foregoing conditions—education is given a model of what it can be when it achieves its highest potential. Yes, it is enjoyable, but as all of education *should* be enjoyed, as the joy of becoming more fully human by developing the unique capacities with which humans are endowed.

The daily operations of a good performance program can be the moment-by-moment manifestations of excellent education when they are carrying out a valid curriculum. Our profession has yet to achieve sufficient success at creating such curricula as the norm rather than the exception. And we have yet to convince the public that a good performance curriculum can be understood as a model for all that education should be. Our unfinished tasks, if we are to become a member in good standing of the school community of subjects, are to build solid performance curricula and to educate the public that we are far more than what they see at the surface. It is to those tasks that leaders in the performance aspect of music education should be addressing themselves, because unless we achieve more success at them in the future than we have in the past, we will continue to skid along at the edges of education rather than being accepted, as we should be, as contributing an essential component to its core.

THE EXPERIENCED PHASE
OF THE PERFORMANCE CURRICULUM

What should the youngsters in our performance programs experience as a result of their involvement? And how can we give evidence, to ourselves and others, that they are improving in the experience we claim they should be having? These questions are asked, properly, of every subject in schools, including general music. They must be asked of the performance program as well. They are the questions of our objectives.

As explained at the beginning of this chapter, the objectives of the performance program are precisely the same as those for the general music program; what differs is the degree of importance of producing music as a means. The end remains what it is for general music—the enhancement of musical experience itself.

In the general music program the musical experience is gained primarily through perceptive, feelingful listening to the broadest array of pieces. In the performance program the pieces experienced are primarily those being performed (with related listenings to recordings as one way to broaden understandings of the musical expressiveness of a piece being learned). The listening experience in performance is far more limited to very few pieces, but far more intense with each piece.

Therefore, the expectations of what can be achieved in detailed musical perception can be commensurate with the detailed study performance requires. Within the narrower range of literature experienced, a deeper probing of perceptual complexities and nuances can be expected. We need to develop ways to glean evidence that such perceptions are, in fact, being cultivated, both of the pieces being performed and related pieces. Part of the evidence comes from the performance itself, of course, in that the control of musical details in performing implies that those details are in awareness. We know, however, that much of the awareness is in the mind of the teacher rather than in the mind of the student(s) performing. So we also need measurement devices separated from the actual performance ("test charts" of the pieces being played or sung, for example) as a way to (1) get some valid feedback as to whether our teaching is producing the heightened awareness we expect, (2) clarify to the performers the perceptual learnings they are pursuing, and (3) demonstrate to the education community that we are capable of both pursuing tangible learning objectives and giving evidence that they are being met. The performance community needs to develop more sophisticated measurement devices for perceptual learnings than now exist, as a necessary curriculum component. Doing so will yield several benefits. It will give more control and focus to rehearsals, helping ensure that perceptual learnings will accompany technical improvements. It will make clear to students that their musical learnings are relevant beyond their performance (an important understanding given that most will be involved in performance for only a short period of their lives). It will show other professionals that we are pursuing goals broader than technical ones. It can also help us organize learning sequences based on desired perceptual improvements rather than only on skill development or concert programming. Most important of all, the inclusion of a reasonable amount of attention to the specifics of musical perception will have a positive influence on the quality of musical experience of our performing students.

How can we gain and give evidence that the objective of musical reaction is being enhanced by what we do?

As pointed out throughout this book, the feelings music causes are incapable of being translated into other terms: they are, despite their great specificity and particularity and concreteness, ineffable. So we cannot measure them in any usual sense of that word because we cannot pinpoint them internally and we cannot give reliable external signs of them. They are of a nature incompatible with measurement as that term is used in education.

However, performance gives us a powerful way to surmise what is being felt. Sounds shaped expressively are the embodiment of the feeling undergone. Music (as all art) gives objective tangibility to subjective experience. So when we listen to a student shape a musical phrase expressively we are getting as close a counterpart to the inner feeling of that phrase as it is possible to get: the feeling and the sounds embodying it are essentially the same. That is why when we help the student refine the sounds of the phrase by changing this or that expressive detail we are directly influencing the internal feeling captured in those sounds. That is one major way that aesthetic education is "the education of feeling."

Performance teachers work directly with the outer manifestations of inner feeling. When teachers guide an exploration of alternative ways to perform a phrase musically they are helping their students explore alternative inner feelings. And when a particular phrasing is discovered that is musically appropriate and sensitive, the inner experience is a discovery of an appropriate, sensitive feeling. As the phrase is further refined by the guidance of the teacher the inner feeling is further refined. That is why it is so important that teaching focus on sounds used expressively rather than only on the technical control going into the sound making. The former is the creating of art and therefore the creating of inner feeling. The latter, by itself, is the making of sounds separated from their artistic use. (Of course the latter must also be attended to; in itself, however, it is preartistic.) When we hear a performance by a student, we are being given as direct evidence as is available as to the aesthetic feeling being experienced. When we hear a performance by a group, we lose some of the specificity (some of the performers can be largely or totally uninvolved), but we are also being given evidence of the shared aesthetic expressiveness being experienced. This may not be "measurement" in the strict sense, but it is surely an important way to evaluate the quality of the aesthetic sensitivity being manifested.

Performance gives us an excellent opportunity to evaluate the growth of aesthetic reaction, and we must be far more clever about doing this. We need to judge not only the products of teaching, as when a student performs a piece prepared through study in private lessons or a group performs a conducted piece, but also pieces prepared entirely by students without instruction. These can give us excellent insights about how expressive decisions were made—a powerful way to judge the student's status artistically as it is being fostered by his or her performance teacher. Small-group performances prepared by the students entirely would also give similar insights. Contests, festivals, auditions, all need to include opportunities for performers to demonstrate their aesthetic sensitivity by the way they have embodied it in music they have prepared themselves. This and other ways to give evidence that our objective of enhancing musical reaction is being attained should be high on our agenda for action.

The four means behaviors for achieving the ends of heightened musical perception and reaction—heightened musical experiences—are the same for the performance program as for the general music program. But here performance is the dominant behavior with conceptualization, analyzation, and evaluation being tied to and realized through performing. All four means are capable of evaluation in a great variety of ways including, when helpful, measurement.

We are already expert at assessing performance skills and must continue to refine this expertise. Especially important will be improvements in regard to giving our students a variety of specific musical performance problems to solve, involving technique, notation, stylistic interpretation, ensemble, and so forth. Our present product orientation leads us to overemphasize evaluations of the finished product. We also need to evaluate how performers engage themselves intelligently in dealing with problems of *process*—how they structure a performing problem they are faced with, what imaginative ways they employ to solve it, how they use their musical understanding as an aid, the steps they go through, their critical judgments about their solutions. We must continue to evaluate the growth of skills, but we must pay far more attention to assessing the growth of musical intelligence and musical independence as demonstrated by problem solving as relevant to performance. This will be a major new direction in performance (and in general music as well) as cognitive psychology develops, giving us better insights about evaluation at higher levels of human functioning than we were able to get from a behavioristic orientation. The opportunities for assessing performance as a manifestation of intelligence will be very great.

Similarly for gathering evidence about growth in abilities to conceptualize, analyze, and evaluate (make musical judgments about pieces and performances). As our performance curriculum becomes more broadly conceived, we will have to demonstrate that relevant conceptual learnings are taking place, that skills of analysis (which means abilities to understand and explain how musical expressiveness has been accomplished) are growing, that competence in judging music sensitively and knowledgeably is deepening. Performing gives a rich opportunity for all these learnings to occur, but they have largely been ignored in our programs. That reflects the unfortunate narrowness of their objectives. As we expand our sense of the performance program as a curriculum these learnings will assume their rightful place. And we will be able to approach the evaluation of them in the creative, problem-setting-and-solving mode we are now recognizing as being more valid because more true to life than more traditional testing approaches.

As in the general music program, the key to ensuring that the ends of better musical perception and reaction are being fostered is to keep a reasonable balance among the four means. That is not at all to suggest that they be given roughly equal time, as is more the case in general music. In the performance program, performing rightfully dominates and channels the concepts and analyses and judgments being dealt with, giving them the immediacy of application and specificity of detail that is the special province of creating sounds in performance. But the balance has to be there, so that playing and singing are musically intelligent, that is, informed by the understandings given by relevant concepts, analyses, and evaluations. There is no strict rule for how to achieve the optimal balance. Experienced directors will be guided both by their musical intuition and their professional know-how to achieve an effective balance at every step along the way. Those steps emphatically include the very first ones a young performer takes: the balance is needed as much or more then as when skills are highly developed. No matter how far along the process goes, no matter when a youngster decides not to continue performing seriously, the balance will ensure that he or she has gotten from performing the richness of musical education it is capable of giving.

When the objectives of a performance curriculum are being met with reasonable success, the outcome for the participants is likely to be that they will place a high value on their involvement. They many not and need not "like" every piece they study. That is never the point, for if they did like every piece it would be a good sign that they were not being challenged sufficiently. But they should feel that the efforts they are making are paying off in valuable ways, in their sense of growth both musically and technically, in their experiences of the pieces they are learning, in their enjoyment of performing for audiences, in their growing understanding of music and of the creative act as an essential component of music, in their sense that no matter whether they continue to perform in the future, their experience will have allowed them to cherish music in their lives with particular keenness and sophistication. Their performance experience will have given them all a good curriculum can be expected to offer.

THE EXPECTATIONAL PHASE
OF THE PERFORMANCE CURRICULUM

Because of the public nature of performance, it is far more influenced by community expectations than the more concealed activities going on inside classrooms. So this chapter has already included many comments about the effects of peoples' expectations on what the performance program can be. We know that we will have to satisfy a great many demands beyond our central commitment to aesthetic education. We know that those demands can so undermine our primary reason for being that little is left of it. We know also, however, that we can protect our musical and educational integrity while at the same time adapting it to a variety of involvements beyond the concert hall, each of which can be made into an opportunity for musical growth if we insist that genuine musicianship remain the core of what is occurring. And we must insist that those musical involvements with the highest potential for musical learning be the ones that dominate the program. When those are in place and are the foundation of our curriculum, we can surely include—and enjoy—as many others as can be handled reasonably. Here too it is a question of a productive balance.

We are the people most responsible to strike that balance. We have to be committed to it first of all. If we are not we will surely be eaten up by the peripherals because there will be no center to hold things together. So the first thing we have to do is be sure our own values are straight. No one else can do that for us.

Then we have to be politician-educators. If we are only politicians, we will not have the solidity of a foundational value system to back us up, and we will come across as empty wheeler-dealers. Our persuasiveness depends on our being perceived as having something extremely valuable to offer that requires us to protect and enhance it.

That's where the educator part comes in. Here the word refers both to the value we are insisting must be served primarily and also to the effectiveness by which we inform people about that central value. We cannot change public expectations by salesmanship because that leaves the public uninformed about why they should change. And we cannot continue to so underestimate the public's intelligence—to so condescend to everyone outside the community of music educators—that we give up on educating them because we assume they are all beyond hope. That's just too easy. And we too often do it, perhaps because we ourselves are not up to the task of education so we let ourselves off the hook by saying it's useless. Well, sometimes it may indeed be useless, so we either capitulate or look for a new job. But that is not the case in the great majority of situations, in which school leaders and parents do, after all, want what is best for their kids. We must be good enough as educators to convince them that what is best for their kids is growth in musical sensitivity through performance, and that when we have a program solidly based on that value—a program that is capable of *giving evidence* that it is based on that value—we can also be a great many additional things. In most communities music educators can provide leadership and can move things in positive directions and can build programs they can be proud of as aesthetic educators, including community services that are valid musically as well as socially. But we can do none of those things if we do not understand what aesthetic education is and how a performance curriculum exemplifies it. Those understandings are ours to gain and then ours to share through effective education both of our students and of the communities of which they are a part.

THE COMPOSITION PROGRAM:
A MAJOR NEW OPPORTUNITY

For a variety of complex sociological reasons, our culture tends to value products over processes. We are among the most product-oriented societies in history and in the modern world.

One manifestation of our fixation on products is our high regard for public performances, in music, sports, politics, religion, movies, TV, and so on. Famous performers in all these fields are products of a celebrity-making system that thrives on the glamour of the display of special people doing special things. Even nonperformance fields, such as business, medicine, education, and literature, produce famous public personages who are then rewarded for their fame by being paid relative fortunes. No wonder so many ordinary people have Walter Mitty fantasies: our society is a breeding ground for the notion that success is the product of being publicly recognized for our achievements.

The shadow side of all this is the inevitable tendency to value the outward appearance of achievement rather than the nonvisible processes inherent in reaching the achievement, best symbolized by celebrities who are famous only for being famous. There's little glamour in the sweat and drudgery it takes in the process of getting very good at something. Yes, we've got to pay our dues, but the reward is not inherent in that process—

it comes from the shining public product at the end of the rainbow. Those who never reach that pot of gold, but instead spend their lives involved in the ongoing processes, have somehow not "made it," because the process is not seen as the value. It is only a means.

In music, those who do not present public performances—the products of work accomplished—are generally not regarded as highly as those who do. For example, the teacher of a successful performer is not likely to be rewarded, in fame or fortune, as his or her pupil will be. The general music teacher is never likely to be regarded with quite the adulation awarded to performance directors. In fact, performance directors, building on the reward system they have come to expect as a natural payoff of what they do, have created a complex edifice of self-congratulatory activities—medals, awards, honors, halls-of-fame, celebratory events, all paying public homage for public achievements. Nothing like this exists or is likely to exist in general music.

Of all people involved in the art of music, the most crucial to the endeavor are composers, without whom performers and listeners could not exist. Yet composers for the most part are invisible, laboring in solitude and not present when their works are performed (except in special circumstances). Being out of sight, they are generally out of mind. It is the performer (including the conductor) we applaud at a concert, and it is successful performers and conductors who become wealthy. To be sure, some composers other than the old masters manage to become household names, either through sheer longevity and the popularity of their music (Aaron Copland) or because they are highly visible as performers as well (Leonard Bernstein). But for the most part composers are unknown outside the professional music community. Music, we claim constantly, is a *performer's* art. To learn music, therefore, one must learn to *perform* music. The royal road to involvement with music—for some, the only road—is to *perform* it. We are, in short, a musical culture almost totally dominated by performance.

This has kept school music focused dominantly on performance, not only in the performance program but also in the general music program. As has been pointed out, many approaches to the teaching of general music emphasize performance almost to the exclusion of everything else, under the assumption that performing music is the only really musical thing to do.

Adding to the performance orientation of school music programs as it reflects our cultural value system is the difficulty of involving students actively in the processes of listening and composing.

On the listening side the need for far more attention to be paid in music education to the cultivation of creative listening involvements has been mentioned many times throughout this book. Our backwardness about the teaching of listening has historical roots. When the phonograph was invented the face of music was changed forever. For the first time in history all music, past and present, became accessible to all people. Musical literacy was no longer limited to acquaintance with pieces one could perform oneself or hear others perform live, with the concomitant needs for skills of note reading to allow the performances to take place. Now literacy was able to mean the scope and depth of a person's acquaintance with the limitless realm of music as experienced directly, without the limitations of one's own performance ability or one's immediate community's capacities to offer performances. Music education has yet to understand fully the implications of that revolution and to adapt itself to its reality. We cling to an older concept of musical experience no longer viable, exacerbated by the "performance-as-product" mentality now current. Listening gets caught in the squeeze.

A similar revolution is now occurring on the composing side, with burgeoning technologies as potent for allowing all people to compose as the phonograph was for allowing all people direct access to all music through listening. This time we must not be caught napping, and we must not try to ignore this massive change we are now witnessing at its early stages. If we do, as we did and continue to do to an unfortunate extent with listening, we shall risk becoming even more irrelevant to the larger musical culture in which we exist than many feel we now are. We must not trail behind the changes in the ways musical experiences are becoming available, and we must not cling to old patterns because of the security we feel with them. We must be at the forefront of this inevitable new opportunity, showing the way by keeping up with the technologies as they develop and applying them richly in the teaching and learning experiences we offer our students at all levels of schooling.

This means that we must add a new program to the two now operative: a third curriculum focusing on composing as the major means for musical experience. In the general music curriculum composing will continue to be one means among many others, as performing is, but the major means will continue to be listening, within the comprehensive, extensive format that distinguishes general music. And composing can add a useful dimension to the performance program, as listening does, while performing remains the major means to achieve the selectivity and intensity it requires. Within the composition program, listening and performing will be contributing means, but its special nature will come from composing as its major means, through which all others will be funneled. So while there are fruitful overlaps among the three programs, each will have its special reason for being, its special balance of musical behaviors, its particular opportunities for musical involvement, general music forming the required base, and performance and composition as electives for those drawn to the characteristic activities of each.

General music and performance have long histories as noncurricula which must be overcome to transform them into curricula. That is the burden of the past, and there is no going back to change what was. The composition program can *start* by being a curriculum, learning from and avoiding the inadequacies in the history of the other two. How can composition be a genuine curriculum from the start? By building a program based on all the phases required for any subject aspiring to full curriculum status.

In the values phase, a philosophical foundation for the benefits of original musical creativity will need to be articulated. There is already a considerable literature in this area, of course, including material about creativity in the nonperforming arts which is useful because of overlaps with composing. That musical experiences of great immediacy and richness and challenge are now available through composing is obvious, because we can engage children in creativity with sounds at levels of musical intricacy and in breadth of stylistic diversity and in depth of expressive sophistication so far outstripping anything heretofore possible as to constitute a whole new ballgame. We will need to explore the philosophical ramifications for education of this unprecedented new opportunity, explaining both for the profession and the larger community why composing is as musically valid as performing, so that all young people should have the opportunity to choose to involve themselves in it in a committed way, as we have argued for years they should have the opportunity to do in performance. We should witness a burgeoning of thought on this issue in the music education profession in the near future, as people share their ideas from a variety of perspectives. We can only gain as a profession from this, in self-understanding, in philosophical sophistication, in relevance to young people and to education.

In the conceptualized phase we will have much to learn. At what developmental stage would it be reasonable to begin special opportunities in composition beyond the exploratory ones offered in general music? We begin performance instruction systematically in the middle grades: Will that work well for composing instruction? Some children start performance much earlier: Could ways be devised to do the same with composition? What will research teach us about musical aptitude for composing, about methodologies that can optimize learnings, about transfer from other musical learnings to composing and from composing to other musical learnings, about which technologies produce which competencies, about musical intelligence as manifested in original creativity, and about style differences children develop as related to their cultural preferences or intrinsic subjective modalities or teacher influence or other factors? An explosion of research opportunities can be expected, as can a healthy reliance on research for guidance if the research community is up to the task and approaches it in an organized fashion rather than in the chaotic way it characteristically carries on its work at present.

And how will school programs be implemented at the elementary, middle school/junior high school, senior high school levels? How can we avoid the splitting off from general music of those electing special work in composition? We know how deleterious it is for those choosing performance to lose the comprehensiveness general music provides: we must avoid that error as we plan. How can we provide for the integration of the composition program with the general music core, enriching general music by having the special learnings in composition feed back into it? How can we integrate composition with the performance program, each benefiting from the presence of the other and from the natural interdependence of the two? Public performances of student compositions would be an ideal wedding, as would classroom study of students' works. In fact, student compositions could be "commissioned" by general music classes as exemplars of various processes being studied and by performance groups to enhance experiences with particular expressive/technical problems being addressed. A fruitful integration of the three programs, within levels and across levels, could occur if we use this new opportunity as a catalyst.

In the systematized phase of the curriculum we are starting almost from scratch. In many traditional approaches to the teaching of composition the student is expected to retrace music's history, learning what was done centuries ago under the assumption that "you can't get here except from there." Does that assumption hold water given what contemporary music has become and what contemporary technology allows? What, exactly, *is* the relevance of Baroque harmonic practice for youngsters manipulating a computer? Some will insist that a sequence of learning retain a historical progression. Others will argue as vociferously that one can start with what exists now. Still others will opt for a combination of older and newer stylistic practices. We will have to observe carefully, describing what seems to occur in the development of composing competencies from a variety of sequential bases.

Who will be the professionals competent to put a composition curriculum into practice? At the interpreted phase, where theory becomes actuated, we will need teachers with a broad base of musical understanding, specific skills in composing, and mastery of the technologies available for involving students in creative musical decision making. This requires teacher education programs to prepare such people. Our present Bachelors degrees in music education allow (or *should* allow) specializations in general music, instrumental music, choral music. Clearly, we will also have to develop a specialization program for teachers of composition. Of course there will be overlaps among the programs, as there are now, but to ignore the special needs of each is to underestimate the professional complexity of each. We have long since gotten past the stage in which one could be a "music teacher" in the generic sense. Especially if a genuine curriculum for each program exists, rather than an unorganized set of activities, specialists for each are required. We have our work cut out for us to devise an undergraduate composition specialty as solid as we know how to make it, and then Masters and Doctoral programs that support and expand it as now exist in the traditional specializations.

A competent teacher of composition at the operational phase will exemplify the same characteristics as teachers of general music and performance—high levels of craftsmanship, sensitivity, imaginativeness, and authenticity. Surely the challenges here are as great as in other two programs, but just as surely an effective teacher will have to meet them. In one sense it will be harder for those who will be the pioneers starting this new specialization, in that the specifics of their teaching craftsmanship, their sensitivity to compositional learnings and to the cultivation of them, their imagination in inventing new methodologies, their authentic treatment of music as it exists and as it newly comes into existence, are all awaiting discovery with little accumulated expertise to fall back on. But in another sense it will be easier to achieve operational effectiveness precisely because there is not the burden of old, well-established assumptions and expectations. Standards and procedures and outcomes and patterns of programming will all be newly developed, allowing those providing the leadership to share in the joys of discovery and achievement. It will take real courage on the part of music educators to get this ball rolling in schools and colleges, but the rewards are likely to be very great for those willing to be operational explorers.

What will youngsters who choose to become involved in composition experience musically, and how can we assess their growth in musical experience? Clearly, the same objectives apply here as to general music and performance, the special nature of this program coming from its use of composing as the major means of musical involvement. The ends remain the enhancement of musical perception and reaction—musical experience itself in its richness of subjective knowing. The means, in addition to composing as the essential interface with "sounds organized to be expressive," will include listening to a great variety of music as fodder for creative decisions, performing as it concretizes sounds to sharpen responsiveness to their potentials for development, conceptualization as necessary to understand and apply creative principles and procedures, analyzation of one's own music and others' to see deeply into their expressive form, evaluation as it is called on moment by moment in the making of musical decisions and as it is applied to assessing the effectiveness of whole pieces, particular compositional processes, and stylistic potentialities.

The outcome of all this is a way to value music from as deeply inside it as one is likely to get. We can only imagine, at this point, the effects on students' identification with and understanding of music from their serious, long-term, developmentally structured experience of creating it at its primary phase. It is possible that we will witness the birth of a class of people whose musical sophistication will have major influences on the level of our total musical culture, and in turn have major influences on what school music programs will need to be to serve that culture well.

But none of this will occur unless the expectation system of the music education profession adapts to a new set of realities. If we cling to what we now have out of inertia or timidity, we are likely to see ourselves left in the dust. Young people *will* involve themselves in the new composing technologies because they will grow up with them as an accepted part of their world. The question is, will they be given the opportunity to benefit from professional guidance as part of their schooling, or will they do it as a hobby unconnected to education? In the former case, composition can become a strong third pillar of school music and therefore benefit far more youngsters with a genuine curriculum of study, taking them light-years beyond what they are likely to pick up on their own as a strictly recreational activity. And music education as a profession can become more secure from offering, in a serious way, a program devoted to this necessary role in the art of music. It would be totally anomalous for us to continue to insist that schools should support the performance program as fully as they now do but not give the same level of support to an equally relevant, equally important, equally available musical involvement. But we are not used to such a position, and we are likely to have the impulse to fight it off because of the threat of change and the fear that it might weaken what we presently have. We will have to rise above that natural defensiveness, recognizing that we as a profession, and those we exist to serve, and the musical culture we are devoted to, can all profit from this historic new opportunity to engage people in musical creativity at its primal level.

The challenges this presents, forcing us to reassess ourselves at every level from the most theoretical to the most practical, can also profit us by giving us a renewed sense of professional mission, not only in creating this new curriculum but in reassessing our present programs in light of what we learn from this task. We have the capacity, finally, to represent the music of Western culture in its three essential aspects: listening, performing, and composing. For the first time in history, all three can be given the richness of educational opportunity they deserve. For the first time in history, therefore, music education can become complete.

Toward
the transformation
of
music education

10

CAN WE HOPE FOR A BETTER FUTURE?

The philosophy articulated in Chapters One through Seven of this book is intended to offer the field of music education a foundation of self-understanding on which it can rest securely. And the applications of the philosophy to a curriculum embodying it, as outlined in Chapters Eight and Nine, give, it is hoped, a broad picture of how we can put our ideals into practice.

Every field in education is obligated to explain its values to itself and to others and to have a plan for how those values can be gained through schooling. But there is a special character to the need for the field of music education to do so, because of its status, throughout the world, on the fringe of the education enterprise. That status causes us to try harder. We are, as a professional field, extraordinarily devoted to improving ourselves, no doubt because our tenuous position in the schools makes us feel sufficiently insecure to keep us scrambling. So we expend enormous amounts of energy on self-justification and self-help.

To persist, as we do, to strive mightily for improvement in the face of our position outside the privileged circle of educational basics, takes courage. That word—courage—is not often applied to music education but its aptness seems evident. It is courageous of us to battle incessantly for our place in the education sun. It is courageous to continue to believe in ourselves—in that which we represent and in that which we do—despite the fact that our ardor does not seem to rub off on a great many people outside our own professional community. We do have the courage born of hope: hope that our value for music will some day be shared by others to the degree we have always held it. Then we will take our rightful place at the core of education, our hope will be vindicated, and our security will finally have been won.

Is our courage foolhardy? Is our hope vain? Are we whistling in the dark, making ourselves feel better but largely wasting our breath? What, exactly, can we hope for in the future, and what exactly, can we do now to conform ourselves responsibly to what our future might be?

Of course there is no crystal ball that can give reliable answers to such questions. We can project a reasonable answer, however, by reflecting on the past and present status of music in American schools and then surmising some likely future on the basis of what we discover. This exercise is far more than empty or idle speculation. We all have the obligation, as individuals trying to make sense of our personal lives and as professionals trying to make sense of our working lives, to take stock of ourselves now and then and to bring ourselves into whatever equilibrium our wisdom allows us to achieve. We can come away from such episodes of self-searching better in tune with ourselves, with renewed hope if that seems warranted or with a sense of realistic acceptance of what is and what will remain if that seems to be the wiser course. It is in this spirit of pragmatic speculation that the following reflections are shared. The conclusions will be, no doubt, both surprising and provocative—surprising because they will present what might seem like an insoluble paradox, and provocative because they will suggest the possibility that the paradox might be resolved in our favor if we have the courage to do what would be required of us.

OUR STATUS PARALLEL TO BUT BELOW THE CENTER OF EDUCATION

A key to understanding the past and present position of music education in the United States within the larger education field, and to projecting a possible future, is the cyclical nature of the fortunes of education as a whole. Education has good times and it has bad times, the good and the bad being functions of the public's regard of education, the financial and political support it receives, the amount of energy put into examining it and improving it and nurturing it. The cycles are most usefully envisioned as a rising and falling curve. As one examines the relative degree of health of education over time it becomes apparent that the curve rises to counterbalance a fallow period, then inevitably turns downward after a period of good health, only to head upward again after the low period has spent itself. Depending on how one plots this rising and falling movement the cycles seem to take some fifteen to twenty years to change course and move in the opposite direction.

This cyclical phenomenon seems to be a given in education as it is in so many other aspects of human life and human culture.[1] If there is anything we can depend on from the perspective history gives us it is that things are not likely to be wonderful always nor are they likely to be dreadful always. We all live through rises and falls in every aspect of our lives. Our continually changing fortunes, in larger and smaller things, is the inevitable consequence of our being live creatures, aware of ourselves and of our story. Our cultural institutions, education emphatically included, embody our nature as cyclical beings only writ large. As if they were alive they move with the ups and downs, the stresses and the resolutions, that are indigenous to our conscious natures. We should not be surprised that human institutions are pervaded with qualities of the human condition.

If we represent the changing fortunes of education as a rising and falling curve, where does music education fit into that representation? The proposition can be well argued that the fortunes of music education are precisely parallel with the curve of education as a whole but at an interval of an inch or two below it. When things are good for education—a period at the top of the curve—things are then relatively good for music education also. When education goes into a slump, swinging downward to a low period, music education suffers a parallel slump. But no matter where education happens to be in its ongoing cyclical movement, music education remains not at the core and center of the enterprise, and certainly not above the center in the degree to which it is valued, but always moving along *parallel to and below* the central line. That is why music educators always and correctly feel beleaguered. When times are good, we can relax and enjoy ourselves and we feel relatively secure, but only relatively. We know that we are still not home free so our security is always a little nervous. There's always that looking back over our shoulder to see if any axes are about to fall. And when education is going through difficult times—when money is scarce, criticism is severe, psychological and material support is hard to come by—music education feels positively desolate. The great danger to our field during such times is that we might lose our perspective, forgetting in our pain that our suffering is only relative. It is, indeed, greater than that of education as a whole because of that inevitable gap between us and the center, but it is not more than that constant gap. When conditions improve for education, as they always do when things hit bot-

---

[1] An excellent explanation of the cyclical nature of history as it applies to our own country is given in Arthur M. Schlesinger, Jr., *The Cycles of American History* (New York: Houghton Mifflin, 1986), in which he traces many alternating cycles of from twelve to twenty years.

tom, they will improve for us and the cycle will continue. The question at that point becomes, how badly have we hurt ourselves by our thrashings during the low period? Have we suffered with dignity and with insight and with perseverance, preserving ourselves and our strengths for the better times that will surely come? Or have we, in our fear, abandoned our best sense of ourselves, betrayed that which we most value, acted out of panic because of our loss of perspective?

Answers to these questions are conveniently at hand because during the past thirty or so years education in America has experienced both an extraordinary high and an extraordinary low swing in its curve, music education having followed the curve exactly. It will repay us to take a brief look at this remarkable, dichotomous period, so that we can face future changes with a better grasp of how to adapt to them and take advantage of them.

In the early years of our century, from around 1915 to around 1935, American education was heavily influenced by what was called the Progressive Education movement, fueled by the thinking of the great philosopher and psychologist John Dewey. This was an innovative, productive time for education and also for music education, which was ideally suited for the activity-oriented, child-centered values then dominant. The progressive education movement dwindled by the mid-1930s and for a period of some twenty years education displayed little in the way of intellectual excitement or excellence. This sluggish period came to an abrupt and dramatic end with an event that shook American culture and politics and education to the quick—the launching of *Sputnik* by the U.S.S.R. in 1957. Dismayed at having been beaten at our own technological game, the country went into a state of shock soon followed by a frantic attempt to find something to blame for our embarrassment. The finger was pointed in many directions, finally stopping when it located education.

The history of those times has been told often, so it need not be given again here.[2] But a few points need to be highlighted; those having to do with what happened to music education when education in general fought off the initial assault and began a period of self-examination and innovation and revival unparalleled in American history before or since.

[2]For histories and descriptions of education reform and particular curriculum projects, see John I. Goodlad, *School Curriculum Reform in the United States* (New York: The Fund for the Advancement of Education, 477 Madison Avenue, 1964) and the many publications of the Association for Supervision and Curriculum Development, NEA Building, 1201 Sixteenth Street, N.W., Washington, D.C. 20036. Applications of specific curriculum reform principles to music education have been made by the author in "The Curriculum Reform Explosion and the Problem of Secondary General Music," *Music Educators Journal*, LII, no. 3 (January 1966), and "Curriculum Reform and the Junior High General Music Class," *Music Educators Journal*, LIII, no. 2 (October 1966). For a description of several curriculum reform projects in music education, see the author's "New Curriculum Developments in Music Education," in Gladys G. Unruh and Robert R. Leeper, eds., *Influences in Curriculum Change* (Washington, D.C., Association for Supervision and Curriculum Development, 1968).

First, the initial accusations about the ineptitude of education were not leveled at music education at all and the calls for reform were also devoid of interest in reforming music education. No one said, "My God, the Russians are beating us—we've got to improve music education or we'll be in real trouble." Would that that were the case! But as soon as the shock waves diminished a genuine search for solutions—a concentrated effort to achieve excellence—began, and while, very naturally, it was focused on the sciences and social studies, the upswing soon caught us up in it, and we, along with education as a whole, enjoyed a period of growth that changed us forever.

We can learn from this that when education is in a period of struggling upward from a low point it is likely to get its impetus from societal disaffection and therefore societal criticism. This will not be directed specifically at music education, and we must not allow ourselves to become paranoid that attention is being paid, not to us, but to the traditional core subjects. Or course that is what is at issue because that is what our society conceives as being most important. It is fatuous of us to take it as a slight that people are not exercised about the fortunes of music in the schools as the major and most pressing concern in reforming the schools. Attention must inevitably and correctly go to the core and not to those subjects like music occupying a place an inch or two below the core. But as the curve of improvement rises because of improvements in the core, we shall also benefit and improve and rise in fortune to parallel the upward movement. We must be patient, supporting education reform in all helpful ways, keeping the spotlight on the need for improvements, and cleverly shining that spotlight on ourselves at every possible opportunity to show that we too are concerned to become as effective as all education needs to be; that we too are regretful of past sins and are anxious to mend our ways as we search for higher standards. We must, in short, be intelligent enough not to fight the realities of education reform but to co-opt them.

In the education reform movement of the post-*Sputnik* era—a period of some fifteen years—music education fought off its dismay at not being the focus of initial attention and joined the growing and ever-widening concerns for excellence in all of education. As education flourished music education began to flourish. Government money became available for research projects—certainly nowhere near the levels spent on the "new math" and "new social studies" and "new science" projects but at levels an inch or two below those, and certainly at levels we never before had achieved.

As the core subjects were examined for strengths and weaknesses, attempts to improve began, typically, by focusing on mechanical and procedural matters—how many minutes per day were being devoted to this or that subject, what equipment was available, how to reestablish "discipline" in the schools (an absolutely predictable rallying cry in every reform movement), how to raise the standard of teachers and of teacher preparation (equally predictable), and so forth. But then a remarkable change began to occur. In addition to all the external factors being debated, major qualitative issues began to be raised. What is the core of concepts and operations that define a particular subject? How can education impart to all students—not just to the gifted—a sense of each discipline's basic nature? How can courses of study be developed that focus on the most important ideas and skills in a subject, transmitting them and refining them in a growing spiral of complexity and sophistication? How can the best knowledge of experts in a particular subject be translated into educational strategies that retain the subject's integrity yet are learnable by even very young children? Such questions radically transcend the usual tinkerings that constitute education "repair," and they raised that particular movement of the 1960s and early 1970s to the level of what might be genuinely characterized as "reform."

The concerns of music education followed those of the larger education community. After the inevitable superficialities had been addressed, a new phase began in which the hard questions, the deep questions, the questions requiring answers at the level of self-definition, were both asked and answered with unprecedented seriousness. This process had begun for music education in the United States in the late 1950s, with the books *Basic Concepts in Music Education*[3] and *Foundations and Principles of Music Education.*[4] These were the first scholarly attempts to forge a justification and an identity for music education beyond the dimensions of the recreational and the extramusical. Those early efforts reached a new height of sophistication under the impetus of the reform movement of the 1960s—a level that may well serve as the ideal for our profession for many years to come. It was then that we began to understand ourselves to be primarily a vehicle for aesthetic education—the education of aesthetic sensitivity to the art of music. We began to shift our perspective on our dominant activity—performance—by recognizing that it had to be aesthetically educative in addition to being technically proficient. And we also began to realize that performance in and of itself was inadequate as a mode for general education in music; inadequate in that it involved only a fraction of the school population and inadequate as the sole musical experience of even the small percentage of students who chose to perform. New attention was focused on general music. The emerging principles of curriculum reform guiding the transformation of the basic subjects began to be applied to a new approach to curriculum organization for general music, based on foundational concepts of music. Musical activities became ways of broaden-

---

[3]Nelson B. Henry, ed., *Basic Concepts in Music Education* (Chicago: University of Chicago Press, 1958).

[4]Charles Leonhard and Robert W. House, *Foundations and Principles of Music Education* (New York: McGraw Hill, 1959).

ing and enriching the experience youngsters had of music as an art rather than ends in and of themselves as had previously been the tendency.

All these developments plus others that contributed added up to a major qualitative change. We had attained a high degree of professional maturity—probably the highest in our entire history of over 150 years as a recognized subject in the schools of America.

Those heady days came to an end with the inevitable downswing of the curve in the middle 1970s, when a conservative backlash swept American politics, culture, and education. Now after a low period of some dozen years we are beginning to see new stirrings that may signal the beginning of the predictable upward swing. Unfortunately, the current debate about the inadequacies of education, while absolutely necessary as a way of focusing attention on the need for improvement, has settled in at the level of the mechanical to the almost total exclusion of the substantive. Education in the United States is inundated with criticisms and suggested remedies. All deal with administrative and procedural and technical details—salaries, number of minutes of instruction, testing, class size, teacher incentives, internship schemes, and on and on. All are valid concerns but none address the deeper issues of teaching and learning.

Music education, as usual following the trend, responded at the procedural level. The MENC "Goals for 1990," for example, stipulated that (1) all students should have access to music instruction, (2) high schools should require at least one Carnegie unit in the arts for graduation, and (3) colleges should require one unit in the arts for admission. But what, exactly, would constitute high-quality instruction in the various aspects of the music program? What would the content of understandings and skills be for a viable, effective course worth a Carnegie unit of credit? How do we build and evaluate a "balanced, comprehensive and sequential program of music instruction" as the "Goals" urge us to provide if we do not attend to the underlying issues of what constitutes a good balance of musical studies, and what is required if musical study is to be "comprehensive," and how arrange for sequence if we have not determined what the essential musical learnings ought to be? All of these questions, of course, raise issues of philosophy and curriculum rather than political policy, and the present climate of debate does not begin to allow for such issues to be acknowledged let alone explored.

This brief history of the most recent upswing, then downswing, and now hints of an impending new upswing in the fortunes of education in the United States leads to the present condition of music education which was referred to in the introductory paragraphs of this chapter as being paradoxical. Music education, we discover, is swept along by the same forces that move education as a whole upward and downward through time. However, these forces are brought to bear on music education not by society, which single-mindedly focuses on what it considers to be the basics, but by music educators themselves, who are infinitely sensitive to the prevailing winds and infinitely susceptible to being caught up in them. When those winds are updrafts, lifting all of education to new heights, we are capable of steering along with the flow and achieving new levels of self understanding and maturity. Yet when the winds turn downward we are equally capable of the self-defeating, self-demeaning posture we have assumed during the past tough ten years, arguing again the old nonissue of whether our value in education stems from the art of music or from whatever nonmusical value happens to be hot at that moment. Good times bring out the best in us, and we are heartened to be reminded of how good that can be. Then bad times come and, rather than strengthening us in our integrity, they tear us apart and reveal our opportunism and superficiality. We are confronted by such events with the poignancy of our divided nature—capable of so much that is admirable and also of so much that is not.

The paradox in all this is that we swing so widely from one side to the other not because of societal pressure, which is practically nonexistent, but because we feel compelled to act as if we were at the heart and core of the education debate raging around us. We would be perfectly safe simply to weather the storms and continue growing in all the ways we need to, because our position a couple of inches below the center provides excellent shelter from the storms. But of course we won't settle for that. Our tendency toward inflation impels us to take ourselves far more seriously than anyone else does and to thrash ourselves around accordingly. We have not achieved the wisdom that would allow us to acknowledge, with honesty and with forbearance, our position in education vis-à-vis the basics, and to do what we must do in regard to that position, which is (1) to try to understand it, (2) to ponder how to change it, and (3) to use it to our advantage whenever we can rather than beating ourselves to death with it.

We might just as well do these things, because, paradoxically again, none of our attempts to improve our situation by linking ourselves to current education hotspots, whether reading, writing, and arithmetic, or discipline in the classroom, or special education, or computer literacy, or whatever else happens to have the searchlight on it, will ever change our status in the larger education picture. That is not to say that we should ignore what is going on around us. Or course we must involve ourselves in current realities. Of course we must continually search for ways to improve ourselves, internally as a discipline and externally through astute political action whenever opportunities arise. But we must not deceive ourselves into thinking that action at those levels, absolutely necessary as they are, will by themselves change our uncomfortable position on the periphery of the education enterprise.

So now we come to the larger questions. Why are we not among the basic subjects? What, if anything, can we do to improve our status essentially rather than superficially?

Those questions need to be addressed at three different yet related levels—one dealing with the long-term dimensions of the issues, another with the short-term dimensions, and a third at an intermediate level having the most profound implications for our foreseeable future. The long-term level gives a broad perspective within which we can view the other two levels in a realistic context. So the broad picture will be sketched before getting to the specifics of more tangible problems.

CLOSING THE GAP: THE LONG TERM

Around four hundred years ago, during the sixteenth century, the Western world went through one of the major global shifts in mentality that have occurred periodically since recorded history began. The shift was fundamental, changing forever our notions of what truth is, how it is generated, how we know what we know, what our essential nature is as living creatures. That shift was from the medieval world view to that of the Renaissance, which embodied a way of learning about the world using an entirely new method of investigation—a method we now call modern science.

The newly established view has now existed for about four centuries. During these years the values of the intellect—the rational capacities of human beings—have grown in breadth and influence, transforming every parameter of human life from the philosophical-religious dimension of the meaning and purpose of life to the technical-practical dimension of the way we interact with people and things in our daily activities. Human values, in these four centuries, have been pervaded so deeply and so thoroughly by the myth of rational thought that it is difficult—almost impossible—to conceive ourselves and our world without the presumptions with which our modern myth cloaks our minds. We think and feel and respond as we must—in the mode provided by our belief system.

The word "myth" is used here not in its common meaning as something that is not true but is widely believed to be true nevertheless, but as a symbol for the particular set of grounding beliefs and values that determines for a culture what truth can possibly consist of for that culture. Because our underlying myths are so pervasive in our minds and beings, we take them to be ultimate truths, forgetting, quite naturally, that they are human constructs serving human needs in peculiarly human ways.

When a historical, global change in the myth occurs, as it did with the Renaissance, a period of great upheaval accompanies it, lasting for many years (over a century in that case). Then the myth develops and grows until it has fulfilled its potential and begins to wane. Another crisis will then occur: a period of turmoil during which the old belief system will have been dealt several body blows by new discoveries undermining the very foundations of the myth. The ramifications of the crumbling of the foundations will be felt throughout the culture, as beliefs begin to adapt to new realities, as values begin to adapt to new beliefs, as actions begin to adapt to new values. A new myth will be born with new potentials for growth affecting every nook and cranny of the human mind and the human condition.

A tremendous weight of accumulating evidence points to the certainty that we are living now in such a period of myth transformation.

In the physical and biological and psychological sciences, irreparable damages have been inflicted on the contributions of Copernicus, Galileo, Newton, Bacon, Descartes, Locke, and others on whose discoveries the myth of modern science was built. Contemporary scientists, beginning with Lamarck and Darwin and ranging from Einstein to Bohr to Freud and his followers to the more recent work of Polanyi and Pribram and Chomsky and Goodman and a host of others, led by myth-shattering discoveries in micro- and macrophysics, have so battered the older views of truth and the ways that truth can be discovered as to constitute nothing less than a scientific revolution. Inevitably this has led to a reexamination of the other major dimensions of the myth, with concomitant groundswells of movement in our understandings of religion, politics, cultural institutions, and the physical environment that supports us. We are becoming aware, painfully but inevitably, that new paradigms of human social organization on this planet, based on new belief systems and value orientations, are not only desirable but may in fact be necessary if we are to survive the dangers to which the older myth has led us. Painful as it may be to be alive in a time of myth change, the need for change and the traumas of change are our best hope for a better future: with the realities of present technology perhaps for any future at all.[5]

In the value system established during the Renaissance and lasting until the present the arts have played a major yet supporting role. They have indeed been a necessary and important part of culture, but they have occupied a place an inch or so below the central values of culture. This largely accounts for the gap between the basic subjects and the arts in education, exacerbated in this case by our belief system attributing far less utility for survival and success to the arts than to the fields more closely connected to our central societal values. We must recognize, therefore, that our present status is an accurate reflection of forces far larger than any of our own parochial issues and personal enthusiasms and professional loyalties. Music education as we know it today throughout the world is not going to be able simply to pull itself up to the core by its own internal, bootstrap efforts, and we cannot go on pretending that it can because all we will accomplish by that self-deception is our continuing frustration.

[5]A helpful history and explanation of the concept of cyclical social processes and of the present as a period of massive change is Fritjof Capra's *The Turning Point* (New York: Simon & Schuster, 1982).

In the longer run, however, all indications point to a major elevation of the arts among societal values as paradigms of human meaning begin to be rebuilt. In every dimension of change now under way, in science, politics, economics, theology, psychology, the peculiarly human nature of our beliefs and values is becoming more widely recognized. In that significant sense our world view is becoming "humanized" in a new way. In that view the human condition is seen to be the product of what we must do for ourselves to build a culture in which our human potentials for health and growth and satisfaction and meaning are the highest values. In that view the arts will, of necessity, be at the core of our value system.

That core has an ethical-moral dimension deeper than the one mentioned in Chapter Seven. At a conference of the International Transpersonal Association, in Kyoto, Japan, in April 1985, speaker after speaker from all over the world focused on the many ways our view of human nature is changing and must change if we are not to be strangled by the limitations of the present ethos. One of the ideas raised, by a Japanese Jungian psychoanalyst named Kazuhiko Higuchi, was so stunning as to be awesome in the power of its implications. It is that in a future, more humane system of human interaction, the guiding principles for behavior will no longer be good and evil, these having been the underlying cause of over twenty centuries of human violence, cruelty, and factionalization. Instead, the basic guidelines for humane living will be beauty and ugliness. The standard of judgment for behavior will become an *aesthetic* standard rather than a moralistic one. All of us have shared the intuition that the arts embody a dimension of human meaning which is somehow "moral" yet beyond the level of morality as being "good and bad." The most salient statement of that intuition was made (appropriately) by a poet, John Keats (1795–1821), who said

> Beauty is truth, truth beauty—that is all
> Ye know on earth, and all ye need to know.
> (Ode On a Grecian Urn)

Think, for a moment, of what that claim might mean for human life if it became the foundational value of human culture. Think, for a moment, of what that might mean for the role of the arts in education: "all ye need to know" as taught by those whose entire purpose for being is to share beauty—aesthetic educators. It will take many years of struggle with the awesomeness of what this idea suggests for us to be able to assimilate its implications, both for the future of the human species and the future of aesthetic education. But that such a future would change our status profoundly seems clear.

Given the perspective suggested by these long-range, global considerations, are there some things we can do now and in the foreseeable future to advance our cause in education within the general framework established by the broader dimensions of human history? Or would it be wisest to settle for our present reality, to be grateful that we have done as well as we have done, to pull in our horns and try to make peace with the situation as it currently exists?

It is extremely appealing to answer the latter question with a "yes." Perhaps we should, after all, settle for what we are now and allow the larger historical forces to carry us upward if that is where they take us. But two circumstances prevent us from doing so. The first is that we can improve our status, even if not radically, by actions we are capable of taking in the short term. The second is that there is, in fact, a way to change our status more significantly if we choose to do so.

CLOSING THE GAP: THE SHORT TERM

Every music educator can make a long list of "items for improvement." To compile an inclusive list could easily double or triple the length of this book. That is not a criticism of music education—every field has its endless agenda for self-improvement. But it is not enough to just "try to improve." What music education needs most to optimize both its specific activities and its general status is a clearer sense of direction. It is improvement *toward an ideal* that makes for progress. In our zeal to improve everything we have not paid enough attention to the something we want to become.

That something can only be a value so powerful as to unify our myriad activities, a value unique to our art and essential for all people. This book has made an attempt to explain what that value might be—the education of feeling.

Our short-term tasks, then, are as follows:

1. To continue to try to refine our understanding of this philosophical claim and to generate complementary and alternative claims to strengthen and expand and improve our philosophy.

2. To teach our undergraduate music education majors that their chosen field has a philosophical basis on which they must build their self-concept as professionals.

3. To do the same for our teachers in-service through coherent, directional, professional activities.

4. To translate our philosophy into general music and performance and composition curricula that exemplify, in every detail, the value underlying them.

5. To honor those individuals, those school programs, those undergraduate and graduate programs that best represent a solid philosophical position that is carried out in effective action.

All these tasks point up a single principle: we must, above all else, identify ourselves as the bearers of an important value if we are to be regarded as important and valuable. That is our essential short-term agenda, underlying and shaping whatever specific items we choose to improve. Without the guidance of a shared ideal we can only continue to fly off in a million directions, dissipating our energies and our impact. We cannot go on that way and expect our position in the schools to change for the better during our lifetime.

But we must also recognize that even if we do what we must, and improve our status as a result, there are inherent limitations on what we can become given the societal value system still operative and given what the field of music education is. Can our profession become something more than it has ever been or can be so long as it retains the shape and form in which it presently exists? Can music education be transformed rather than only prolonged?

FORGING A NEW VISION

It is feasible for music education to strengthen itself, both for the short and long terms, by doing something far more significant than continuing to improve what it is now, essential as that remains. But there are several limitations on what it is possible for music education to become and what it is desirable for music education to become. It would be disastrous in every way for us to change simply for the sake of change if doing so were to threaten or diminish our historic mission and our professional integrity. These limitations—which are also our most hallowed obligations—are that we continue to serve the two causes embodied in our name: music and education.

First, we are now and must always continue to be determined in our nature by the nature of the art of music—music as it has existed throughout history, music as it exists now, and music as it might change and develop in the future. Always our mission must remain to understand the art of music as deeply as we are capable and to adapt our practices to best reflect music's artistic essence. It is the power of music that provides our essential energy. We must never betray the art we exist to nurture.

Second, we are now and must always continue to be bounded by the nature of education. We must not forget that teaching and learning are our primary functions, so that we must conform to the best that is known about how to teach effectively and how to provide the most fruitful possible environment for learning to occur. In every instance when we have weakened our bond to education we have weakened our strength as a profession, as, for example, when the entertainment function has superseded the teaching-learning function or when our scholarship has become detached from educational issues. The art of music provides our reason for existence; the process of education determines how we function. Anything we become must preserve those two verities.

What, then, is the alternative between not changing significantly on the one hand or abandoning our inner nature on the other? Only one answer to that question seems possible. That is, that we become an integral part of a field that depends on our essential, authentic character yet is larger than, more important than, more influential than we can ever be by ourselves.

That field is arts education. By allying ourselves with our sister arts, in common cause to establish the arts as a basic subject in the school curriculum, we will be able to achieve a movement upward toward the core of education achievable by no other means within the existing culture.

Why is this so? Why would we be better off as part of an inclusive field of arts education than we can ever be by continuing to go our own way? Several compelling reasons can be offered.

First, we can benefit philosophically. Any claim we can make for the value of music in education can be made equally validly by every other art. Every claim we make for the uniqueness of music as an art can be made as well for the uniqueness of each art. And if it is essential for music to be offered to all students in public education it is just as essential for every other art to be offered. Of course each art has distinctive characteristics, but who would argue that any one of them is more or less suitable for schools than any other? And who would argue that young people should not have equal access to every art, to find pleasure from all and perhaps a special affinity for one or a few? There is simply no philosophical leg to stand on to justify any one art as being essentially more valuable than any other or essentially more appropriate for education than any other. And if we were to be inclusive in our valuing of the arts we would be able to build a philosophical foundation for them that is far more solid than can be built for any one of them alone. Such a philosophy, extending the arguments in this book to cover all the arts, would be an unassailable foundation for claiming a rightful place for the arts in schools, including but exceeding music.

Second, we can benefit politically. Alone, fighting our solitary battles as if we had no allies, we are perceived by people as what we truly are—a special interest group among hundreds of other special interest groups, each scrambling to establish a better toe-hold for itself. Caring only for ourselves, as if the broader artistic welfare of young people were less important than our own security, we come across as self-serving, of limited breadth, preoccupied with our special nature to the exclusion of those as special as we. But the arts as a unified field rise above the special interest category. Despite their position below the central core, they are nevertheless too important as a field to be neglected when perceived as a whole. If they were presented as a field of study, with the combined strength of all the separate arts fields working together for the good of their larger cause, their impact would be considerable. The total political clout of the arts as a coalition would be dramatically greater than the sum of its separate parts.

Third, we can benefit psychologically. Our history has been one of almost total isolation from our natural family, and we have suffered in our personality from the selfishness this isolation has caused. We tend, because of our separateness, to be inward looking, defensive, suspicious of whatever might impinge on our own needs. This does not make us generous, even to our students let alone our professional family. If we were openly and willingly devoted to a cause larger and more important than our narrow self-interest, we would participate in the expansiveness it would allow us to feel. Our image of ourselves, as individuals and as a field, would both deepen and broaden when we understood ourselves to be linked to forces including us but transcending us.

Fourth, we can benefit practically. We will never win for ourselves the amount of time we want to have in the schools because our demands are perceived as being unreasonable and selfish. For example, we have as our standard that around 20–25 minutes a day of music instruction should be offered in each elementary and junior high grade. Why can this standard not apply as well to visual art education? Fine. So now we have 50 minutes a day accounted for. Well, doesn't dance have an equal claim? It would be very difficult not to agree that it does. Good. So now we've used up 75 minutes a day. Now let's add equal time for theater, and for poetry and literature, and for film, all of which have just as good grounds as we for claiming their share of the pie. So far we have scheduled 2 1/2 hours a day, and a few other arts constituencies have yet to get their fingers into the pie.

That way lies madness. And it points up, in bold relief, the narcissism of music education, which blithely claims its share in complete obliviousness to the fact that others have an equal right to the same share. No wonder that we have not gotten anything like what we want. No wonder that, by ourselves, we never will. We must learn the hard lesson that our needs must be met in the context of our family's needs. That reality will not only force use to be more generous to our family, but will, ironically, yield us more minutes per week than we have ever managed or will ever manage to cajole on our own. We have nothing practical to lose by cooperation with the arts and a great deal to gain.

Finally, we can benefit professionally. Most important, our contribution to the quality of young people's lives can be magnified immensely when our goal becomes to introduce all the students to the richness of all the arts. That is a professional stance truly worthy of us. Further, we can learn so much, about the arts and about education, from our colleagues in the other art education fields. Believe it or not those people are often very smart. Some of them are superlative teachers. Some of them are profound thinkers. Some of them do excellent research, and some are incredibly astute politically, and some have deep insights into children's creative abilities, and some are enormously effective administrators, and a few of them, scattered here and there, are awfully nice human beings. We should know some of these people. And they should know us because we have all those things to offer also. It is a shame that we hardly know our family. It is about time that we all make each other's acquaintance and begin to work together because we all have so much to gain by aiming for the greater good or our larger profession.

HOW CAN THE ARTS COOPERATE?

Starting in the middle 1960s and continuing for a decade or so, there were many attempts to develop combined approaches to the arts in the schools. Then when all of education went into decline, there was a parallel decline in arts education activities as the conservative climate put a halt to innovation and forced a retrenchment to the tried and true. Now there are signs of life in many aspects of education including a revival of interest in arts programs of a variety of sorts. So we have an opportunity to make progress in this direction in a way that can avoid many of the weaknesses of the earlier attempts.

Before reviewing some of these weaknesses and offering suggestions for how we can avoid them, a few basic principles about the arts and their interrelations need to be stated. The major one is that the differences among the arts are much more fundamental than are their apparent similarities. The division of the realm of art into several arts is by no means a product of modern-day compartmentalization or specialization. The distinctiveness of the various modes of art has been recognized throughout history. In fact, it is precisely because the differences among the arts are genuine and deep that the domain of art is so richly diverse, so capable of continual growth and change, so productive of new and different satisfactions. The diversity of art is a major aspect of the delight of art. To revel in that diversity, to pursue the many roads to aesthetic enjoyment, to increase one's sensitivity to the various modes of artistic expressiveness, is to take full advantage of all that the many arts have to offer.

Are the arts, then, so different that they cannot be compared? The deeper one goes into the essential nature of each art the closer one comes to the shared nature of all art. Beyond the differences among the arts is that which makes all of them "art." All art serves the same function, which is to provide a means for exploring and experiencing the nature of human feeling. All art fulfills this function in a common manner, analogous to the conditions of feeling. All art yields experiences of feeling through the same way of sharing, which is to perceive the conditions expressive of feeling and to react to their affective power.

Aesthetic education is the systematic attempt to help people experience human feeling by becoming more sensitive to (better able to perceive and react to) conditions which present forms of feeling. Such conditions are potentially present in everything but are created solely for that purpose in works of art, which is why the study of art is the major way to improve aesthetic sensitivity. In each art, education which attempts to

increase aesthetic sensitivity to that art can be called "aesthetic education." In any combination of arts, education which attempts to increase aesthetic sensitivity to each one of the arts included can be called "aesthetic
education." Whether treated separately or together the goal of teaching art
aesthetically remains the same, to make more shareable the experiences
of feeling presented by each and every art.

To realize this goal, *the distinctive ways that each art operates must become progressively clearer.* One cannot become more aesthetically sensitive
except by becoming more aesthetically sensitive to sounds, to colors, to shapes,
to movements, to verbal images, to spaces, to actions. Each of these has its
unique ways to do what all of them do. Art has unlimited potential for exploring human feeling *because* of the uniquenesses of each art mode, not *in spite
of* them. Glossing over the uniquenesses, diluting them by forced combinations, dulling them by constant equating of one with another, making them
more obscure by ignoring the peculiar, particular flavor of each, can only
weaken aesthetic sensitivity and limit the capacity to share aesthetic insights
in the wide variety of ways they are available.

What, then, can programs including more than one art accomplish
which those in each single art cannot? The value of multiart approaches is
their ability to (1) make each art clearer by showing its uniquenesses as
contrasted with the others, (2) clarify the underlying principles which
make all the arts members of the same family, and (3) give a broad view
of each art as an individual in a family and of the family of art as one among
many. These are important values. But any such program must avoid the
dangers of (1) submerging the character of each individual art by focusing
exclusively on family likenesses, (2) assuming that surface similarities
among the arts show up underlying unities when in fact they usually do
not, (3) neglecting specific perception-reaction experiences in favor of a
generalized, disembodied "appreciation of the arts," and (4) using nonartistic principles to organize the program to give an impression of unity. An
approach which emphasizes the unique flavor of each art but at the same
time demonstrates why each art is "art" should yield the advantages of a
cooperative arts program while avoiding its dangers. This general principle is an outgrowth of a point of view summarized nicely in the following
excerpt from a lecture by Susanne K. Langer:

> If we start by postulating the essential sameness of the arts we shall learn
> no more about that sameness. We shall only skip or evade every problem that
> seems, offhand, to pertain to one art but not to some other, because it cannot
> be really a problem of Art, and so we shall forcibly limit ourselves to simple
> generalities that may be safely asserted....My approach to the problem of in-
> terrelations among the arts has been the precise opposite: taking each art as
> autonomous, and asking about each in turn what it creates, what are the
> principles of creation in this art, what its scope and possible materials. Such
> a treatment shows up the differences among the several great genera of art—
> plastic, musical, balletic, poetic. Pursuing these differences, rather than

vehemently denying their importance, one finds that they go deeper than one would expect. Each genus, for instance, creates a different kind of experience altogether; each may be said to make its own peculiar primary creation....But if you trace the differences among the arts as far and as minutely as possible, there comes a point beyond which no more distinctions can be made....Where no more distinctions can be found among the several arts, there lies their unity....*All art is the creation of perceptible forms expressive of human feeling.*[6]

When the principle of "autonomy within family" is firmly in place the study of several arts comprehensively can proceed with few risks. But because so many arts approaches neglected to build their aesthetic foundation solidly a host of invalid practices occurred. It is important to review some of these so that we do not repeat old mistakes as we attempt to make progress.

One approach to "integrating" the arts (that word is among the most unfortunate one could possibly apply to arts study) was to have students produce works using materials from several arts together. The assumption is that music with words, dance with music, drama with visual elements and/or music, and so on, all illustrate how several arts can be combined to make something larger than any single art. In such an approach "allied arts" is taken quite literally—the alliance of several arts is assumed to be the best illustration of and means of entry into the realm of "art."

In fact, however, works which use materials from art domains other than their own can be successful only to the extent that the added materials become completely fused in the characteristic material of the host art. A musical setting of a poem, for example, is purely musical in a successful work because the music "swallows" the poem and transforms it into another element in the musical expressiveness. To the extent that the two—words and music—retain separate identities the work is disunified, ambiguous, incomprehensible as either music or poetry. It will be remembered from several discussions in previous chapters that nonartistic elements (conventional symbols such as a program in music, representation in painting, political statements in drama, etc.) become artistic elements when they become submerged in the expressive conditions of the work in which they are used. If a work does not succeed in assimilating the nonartistic content into its expressive form the work is incomplete and weak, the nonartistic material obscuring the work's artistic import. The same principle applies to the use of materials borrowed from other arts. When successful, music plus words equals music. Dance plus music equals dance—

[6]Susanne K. Langer, *Problems of Art* (New York: Charles Scribner's Sons, 1957), pp. 78–80. Italics are Langer's. The chapter from which this excerpt is taken is entitled "Deceptive Analogies: Specious and Real Relationships Among the Arts." This short chapter summarizes much of Langer's thought on how the various arts are and are not related. It is "must" reading for anyone connected in any way with inter-arts courses.

purely dance, *completely* dance, "unadulteratedly" dance—for the music has become assimilated by bodily movement and no longer is experienced separately as musical. It is quite possible, of course, to listen to the music separately, as on a recording of ballet music, and regard it purely as musical. When it is used in an actual dance production, however, it reverts to its status as an expressive element in the impact of dance as dance.

This "principle of assimilation" applies to any and all of the arts.[7] Whatever the material borrowed, whatever the amount of borrowing, the primary mode of expressiveness of each art continues to be the determinant of the total experience. In recent years a great deal of borrowing has taken place from art to art. Heavy borrowing always makes artistic success more chancy, but the criterion for success remains what it always is—that *everything* in a work of art must contribute to the structural excellence and expressive power of the work's unified presentation. We are learning now that old notions of "proper" materials for each art were often too narrow, in that each major art domain seems to be able to assimilate a great deal of material from other sources without necessarily being compromised or diluted. Also, several separate arts have been used in simultaneous presentations, as in "multimedia" events and "performance art." The success of such presentations is a matter for honest debate, some people finding them effective, others not.[8] As with other problematical new practices in the arts, aesthetic educators have an obligation to share new ideas freely and openly, using them as opportunities for the development of sophistication. But the ends of arts education are best served when sensitivity to *each mode of expressiveness* is the basis for teaching and learning.

Attempts to produce works using materials from more than one art are likely to be unsatisfying in education because of the extremely high levels of creative insight required to produce such works successfully. But more important is the serious hazard of indulging in invalid practices such as "combining" arts by translating a piece of music into a painting, a dance into a poem, a sculpture into a dance, and so on. These can only yield disastrous results: artistically because genuine artistic creation is impossible when conceived as a transference of expressiveness from one medium to another, educationally because of the false impression given of how the arts work and what aesthetic experience is like. Certainly the impulse to create, often called "inspiration," can come from anywhere and anything. But once begun, artistic creation depends on involvement in the developing expressive form *in the particular medium being used.* If that involve-

---

[7]For detailed explanations of this principle, with many examples from all the major arts, see Langer's *Problems of Art*, Chapter 6, and *Feeling and Form* (New York: Charles Scribner's Sons, 1953), Chapter 10, "The Principle of Assimilation."

[8]Langer's skepticism is illustrated by her famous quip "There are no happy marriages in art—only successful rape" (*Problems of Art*, p. 86).

ment is strong and expert, material from other media can be used in and fused with the primary medium. But to think that one either experiences or learns about the nature of more than one art at a time because a particular work uses more than one kind of material, or that one can experience or learn about the nature of more than one art at a time by transposing one art into another, is to misunderstand art and to subvert the process of arts education.

Several approaches taken in the past to the organization of arts programs applied particularly to the high school level in that they were conceived as courses such as high schools offer. Given the new emphasis on including an art requirement in the high school it is extremely important that we review some of these approaches so we can avoid those that are problematical.

The historical approach views the arts as a product of the conditions existing in the world at various times. It is usually organized chronologically but need not be so, some people preferring to work from the present backward or to jump from one period to another which is distant in time or to juxtapose two or more periods. Whatever the organization the emphasis of study is similar—the work of art as an object in a particular context. The assumption underlying this approach is that everything—art included—exists in context and that to understand a thing one must understand its context. To understand a work of art one must know about the social, political, religious, psychological, physical, and so on conditions existing in the world at the time the work was produced.

It is not surprising, given this assumption, that historically oriented arts courses include a great deal of nonartistic subject matter—often to the virtual exclusion of actual works of art. There is ample precedent in education for assuming that knowledge about backgrounds inevitably illustrates foregrounds. The traditional "liberal arts" or "humanities" curriculum was (and is) primarily a program of study about the historical-philosophical aspects of works of art. Performing, composing, painting, dancing, acting, analyzing, were not proper for the liberal arts course but could be safely relegated to "applied" studies. A "humanistic" education consists of knowing about influences, of studying ideas, theories, principles. The tangible, objective, explorable, unique qualities of particular objects are quite secondary to the generalized context in which the objects exist. The *background* is what the humanistically educated man knows. And the more one studies the background the more "humane," supposedly, one becomes as an individual.

The position taken in this book has been that what is humanizing about art is the *experience of* art rather than *knowledge about* art. When art is experienced aesthetically it gives, to the extent it is good art, as powerful, as effective, as tangible a sense of the human condition as is available to human beings. *This* is humanistic. *This* is what transforms experience from mundanity to meaningfulness. *This* is what adds the dimensions of significance, of insightfulness, of self-knowledge, of "wisdom" if you will, to human experience. The arts are humanistic to the extent they are *directly* known: to the extent they are aesthetically experienced. Arts education is humanistic if and when it increases the sensitivity of people to the expressive qualities of things.

Certainly background information can contribute to the aesthetic perception of and reaction to works of art. This is precisely the role of such information—a *contributory* one. When it is germane, historical, social, philosophical, political, and so on information should be used, but only to the extent that it actually does contribute to the aesthetic experience itself. Historical approaches usually are much overburdened with nonartistic information and are puny in actual experiences of particular art works. History as history is a necessary, important field of study. So are philosophy, religion, languages, and the like. But so is aesthetic education. In aesthetic education, first things should come first.

A second popular approach in interarts courses, the "topical" organization, uses as the means for allying the various arts such topics as "Man and Nature," "The Quest for Freedom," "The Idea of Democracy," and so on. The Referentialist basis of this approach is obvious. The arts are conceived primarily as statements—as attractively gotten-up arguments, as emotionalized commentary, as vehicles for nonartistic ideas, attitudes, beliefs. The meaning of art can be found in the subject matter of art. If one chooses works in different arts according to some similarity of subject matter one can show how the subject has been treated in various ways yet at the same time maintains its essential character. A landscape painting, a poem about flowers, an "outdoor" novel, a "pastoral" piece of music (you can tell it's pastoral by the oboe and flute duet), all illustrate "Nature," showing how different artists "expressed their feelings and ideas" about a common subject. The arts can help people learn about Nature, about Democracy, about a multitude of topics. Art, then, is a most useful means toward nonartistic ends.

There are so many problems with this approach that to deal with them in detail would necessitate an application of all the material in Chapters Two through Seven. At this point it should be quite clear that under any non-Referential view of art the assumptions underlying the topical approach are unacceptable. This approach reduces art from expressive form to conventional symbol, gives the impression that non-representational works are meaningless, tosses out all but the most programmatic music (which is why the music teacher in this approach usually winds up giving his own, separate little course), chooses art according to nonaesthetic criteria, equates work with work and art with art as if a similar subject negated the uniqueness of art works, focuses the attention of students away from art's aesthetic content toward its nonaesthetic content, and subjugates artistic meaning and experience to nonartistic meaning and experience. The point need not be belabored. To the degree there is merit in the position about art taken in this book, the topical approach is to that degree without merit.

Another problematical approach to arts study, primarily at the elementary level, was to conceive the arts as one aspect of the study of other subjects rather than as a subject requiring its own program. Called by a variety of names ("The Arts in General Education" was the most typical), this concept took a good idea to untenable extremes. Of course any subject can be illuminated by bringing it up in connection with any other subject. Music can be referred to when science or social studies are being studied just as science or social studies can be referred to when music is being studied. A skillful classroom teacher can make some excellent cross-references among subjects to highlight both similarities and differences among them and thereby give a sense of unity to learning. It is extraordinarily difficult to do, requiring the teacher to grasp some very subtle distinctions and then to make them obvious enough for children to understand without misrepresenting or falsifying the distinctions. But it can be done and no doubt is done by excellent teachers.

But that is far different from abandoning a logical, sequential program of studies for each of the major subjects, and in fact, the only subject for which it was suggested that an autonomous program could be waived was the arts. No one claimed that the way to study science or social studies or language or anything else was to abandon the internal curriculum structure each requires and to "infuse" them in the study of other things; that would have been patently absurd. But the arts, after all, are different. They are not, as the other subjects are, basic disciplines, each with its own special character of knowing the world. The arts are activities—pleasant to be sure but not to be taken seriously as requiring the same kind of curriculum autonomy as the subjects that count. So why not let them be attended to whenever a good opportunity arose from studying the subjects that do count? Wouldn't that ensure that at least *something* about the arts would get learned along the way?

The demeaning nature of the "infusion of the arts in general education" idea should be apparent: unfortunately it was not when it was being advocated. Now we are in the position of having to reclaim the fact that the arts deserve a regularized curriculum because they, too, are modes of intelligent human operation—disciplines of knowing—as valid and important as all the subjects requiring genuine curricula and a reasonable amount of school time to carry them out. We do the arts and ourselves no service when we capitulate to the lesser status they are presently given and become our own gravediggers. Our responsibility is to enhance the status of the arts in education as much as possible by educating people to understand that the arts are worthy of being studied as an essential mode of cognition, and that while fruitful overlaps among subjects are much to be desired they can occur only when each is being built solidly on its own base.

What would be a useful, practical, and aesthetically valid way to build a base for curriculum action in the arts as a comprehensive discipline?

A successful approach to arts study must accomplish two essential tasks of cooperative endeavors—to preserve the integrity of each art while illustrating their nature as a family. One particular way of doing this has enormous potential for the creation of effective arts programs—the so-called "common elements" approach. The underlying premise of this mode of organizing arts study is that (1) the arts as a family share many ways to do that which all of them do (to organize materials to be expressive) and (2) each shared way is manifested distinctly in each art. So "common" does not mean identical and "elements" is not limited to techniques.

This two-part premise, when conceived broadly, can serve to provide a host of learning experience that can be adapted easily to kindergarten through high school or adult levels. It provides a mechanism for planning sequenced learning episodes within each year and across the years of schooling. It emphasizes tangible, concrete involvements with the experience of the arts. It promotes creative decision making with the materials of the arts. It allows for strategic interdisciplinary episodes that highlight the existence of a common element across several arts. But it also provides for separate art study to explore the distinctiveness with which each art utilizes the common elements in order to produce its special expressive impact. It is inclusive of intra-artistic essentials from the very small, as suitable for young children ("Let's see how things repeat in music and in dance and in painting"), to the very large, as challenging for adults ("What are the qualities that make any work of art good?"). It allows for focus on specific artistic elements and techniques; on historical styles, cultural styles, geographical styles; on the creative behaviors people employ to make works of art and respond to them; on issues of the arts in culture; on criticism of the arts; on various concepts from aesthetics as to the nature of the arts; and on and on. A common elements orientation, in short, can be extremely useful for accomplishing what an active, artistic, experiential program in the arts seeks to produce—heightened aesthetic sensitivity to the widest possible array of arts.

But of course it is no panacea, because it can be abused, it can be dogmatized, it can become routinized or trivialized or made pedantic (and therefore, according to Murphy's law, it no doubt will be). Nevertheless it gives us a handle on a very complicated job. For example, we can translate the objectives of music education easily into objectives for arts education by using the common elements orientation as a guide. (Please review Chapter Eight, pages 167-172.) Our ends remain the enhancement of aesthetic perception and aesthetic reaction, but to the expressive power of each art in its genuineness and distinctiveness. Our means for accomplishing the ends remain creating, but in several arts rather than in music alone; conceptualizing, but as it applies to several arts and to the similarities and differences among the arts; analyzing, but as it is used to help us "loosen up" our perception of how specific works in several arts achieve their "emotive life"; and evaluating, but judging the success of artistic decision making (our own and others') in several arts rather than in one. And the outcome—valuing—can be an enhanced appreciation and enjoyment of the family of arts and of their distinctive manifestations and, perhaps, a personal involvement in the one (or several) that exerts special attraction for particular students.

Another powerful application of the common elements principle (again, please remember that the term is being used more broadly than it tended to be when first introduced) is to sequential planning in the arts classroom. What is needed for an effective, unified year of arts study in the elementary and middle school/junior high school grades is a set of several interdisciplinary episodes (each can take from one to three or four class meetings) which set the stage by introducing an artistic element or issue or problem as it exists in several arts. Then several weeks are devoted to the study of that element (or issue, etc.) *in each art represented.* It is a serious error to think that a comprehensive arts class must always do interdisciplinary arts activities. Those are useful organizers for a sequence of units. But four or five or six of these are entirely sufficient for a full year of study. They provide unity for each year and also a mechanism for planning year-by-year units that spiral upward in breadth and subtlety, thereby giving a unity to the entire K–8 program. But they are not sufficient in and of themselves to constitute a total program because each art requires time and focused concentration in order for skills and understandings to be fostered sufficiently to provide artistic payoffs.

This organization of the "general arts" class implies that there will be sufficient time available to accomplish both interdisciplinary and single-arts learnings. How much time is needed? Our goal in this matter must be reasonable within the total school curriculum but representative of the importance of the arts as one of the great disciplines of human intelligence. An achievable goal would be that the arts class, required for all students in grades 1–8, be allocated an hour a day (not necessarily scheduled as 60 consecutive minutes, especially in the earlier grades). Within the 5 hours per week, the division of instruction time would depend on the particular element or aspect of art introduced by the interdisciplinary lesson(s), on the number of arts being included (not every art need be or can be included in every unit), on the number of arts represented by the faculty of that particular school (discussed shortly), and on scheduling convenience and facilities availability. There are many creative, clever ways to divide the time fairly among several arts, each focusing on the same idea but each exploring that idea as it operates specifically and characteristically in that art. Music, as part of such a general arts class, would have far more time for specifically musical instruction than we achieve now in the vast majority of general music situations.

Who would teach the general arts class? Only one viable answer can be given to that question—arts specialists working cooperatively. It is not possible in any way whatsoever for a single "arts teacher" to provide the kind of instruction a solid arts curriculum must offer. It is indeed possible for one person to do a fine interdisciplinary lesson, and even classroom teachers can be trained to do so or can teach the interdisciplinary lessons given in some of the music textbook series (*Silver Burdett Music*, for example, has several such lessons for each grade, designed to be usable by classroom teachers). But a few such lessons do not by themselves constitute a program—they are organizing units within a program. The payoff of those lessons is the application of their content to the several arts individually. And to do *that* effectively requires a specialist in each art.

Ideally, each school system, grades 1–8, would employ specialists in music, visual arts, dance, theater, poetry and literature (not just English or language teachers), film, and media. Each of these teachers would hold certification as a specialist in his or her field, but each would have had a few additional courses to those presently offered in typical certification programs: a course on how to do interdisciplinary lessons and how to use them as curriculum unifiers, and a course in aesthetic education explaining the premises of the arts as a family of distinctive individuals. Those two courses would probably be sufficient to enable all the specialists to work cooperatively and sympathetically with each other so they could plan the interdisciplinary overlaps that would give the entire curriculum its coherence. If one could go beyond those two courses, in preservice teacher education or Masters-level programs for experienced specialists, it would be ideal to include introductory courses in several of the arts (other than their specialty). To be even more ideal, a course in the dynamics of school change would be included, given the innovative nature of arts programs and the need for those attempting to implement them to be able to engineer change in the conservatively oriented social structure most schools exemplify.[9] But whether teacher training included only a couple of new courses or several more, it would not at all change to any appreciable extent the special curricula as they now exist (or as they should exist with all the improvements they need). The point is that an arts program does not re-

<hr>

[9]For an example of a Masters-level course that included all these learning for inservice arts specialists and classroom teachers, see the author's "Education for Aesthetic Awareness: The Cleveland Area Project," *Music Educator's Journal*, 64, no. 6 (February 1978), pp. 66–69.

quire a new kind of teacher specialization—it requires present art specialists to be expanded sufficiently to be able to work together for a larger value that depends on the expertise of each in his or her own art. Paradoxically, this expansion of single-art specialties can benefit students and teachers and the arts profession dramatically, transforming present practices and influences rather than just adding to them. Seldom can such a large benefit be realized by such a modest change, and it would be tragic if we did not take the opportunity.

But suppose a school system could not or would not employ all those specialists (at least not until things began to change for the better). It is not necessary to have them all—desirable, of course, but not necessary. First, the same kind of program can exist if it includes just music and visual arts (presently possible in many if not most schools), or those plus dance, or whatever else can be included depending on particular circumstances. So arts programs can get going no matter how few or how many arts can be staffed presently.

Second, it is possible to include arts in addition to those represented by regular faculty members by taking advantage of expertise existing in the community. A little searching usually uncovers a great many people— parents, active amateurs, professionals—able and willing to provide instruction that can flesh out the program. What such people need is (1) instruction in the specifics of what the program as a whole is attempting and what the particular content of their lesson(s) needs to be in order to fit in to the program, (2) observation and follow-up consultation in preparation for further lessons, and (3) encouragement and appreciation. Paraprofessionals can be a very positive bonus in arts programs and can become staunch allies for advocacy efforts to build such programs. They can also provide much-needed links to the arts communities existing so richly outside the schools, encouraging youngsters to involve themselves in available community arts experiences more fully because of their growing acquaintance with them.

At the high school level, a variety of courses will be generated as we continue our attempts to reach more than the students electing performance/production classes. One effective array of courses would be a required arts core course, team taught by the available specialists plus community resource people, followed by electives in the various single arts. The core course would both build on and synthesize the arts learnings in the 1–8 program, much as the general music course would do for the specifically musical learnings in grades 1–8. The principles offered in Chapter Eight for a high school music course (pages 178-180) are entirely relevant to an arts course (with the necessary adaptations) as well as to the basic music course following an initial arts course.

Beyond the required general arts program in grades 1–8 and the required and elective courses in the high school, an effective arts curriculum will have to offer all the special out-of-class opportunities we now provide plus a host of others we have not yet managed to provide.

Choral and instrumental music (and, it is hoped, composition) will exist at least to the extent they presently do. There is no reason why a transformation to an arts curriculum would have any significant effect on our performance groups, except, perhaps, to increase enrollments as a result of heightened interest in the arts by more students and more willingness to explore arts involvements. There is nothing we would need to change about our performance program except in our continuing efforts to improve them as discussed in Chapter Nine, and, perhaps, more cooperative programming to share performance evenings with other arts groups, be a part of school arts festivals, and so on. For what should occur if an arts curriculum is developed is far more involvement by far more youngsters in far more arts opportunities than now exist. In addition to the usual music groups and visual art studio classes, we need to expand offerings in dance of various types, film (producing, directing, acting, writing, etc.), poetry and short story writing, theater in all sorts of activities beyond the "yearly play," crafts of all sorts, ethnically related arts groups, school–community arts productions, and so forth. As part of a rich, exciting array of special opportunities in the arts for those who elect them, music will continue to exert its power on large numbers of students while others find their artistic challenges in ways appropriate to their talents and interests.

This short section of one chapter cannot deal with all the controversies relating to the pros and cons of arts programs, or all the ways an arts curriculum would have to be built according to the phases of the model described in Chapters Eight and Nine, or all the political-psychological-social-economic issues a transformation to arts education would have to address. The arts professions will need to spend a major part of their energies on such matters in the years ahead if progress is to be made.

A FINAL PARADOX

Music education finds itself, at this time in its history, beset by several paradoxes. We have become more secure in the schools, more thoughtful in our scholarship, more sophisticated in research, more influenced by professional education, more expertly prepared musically, more able to justify our importance in philosophically valid ways than our founders could ever have dreamed of a century and a half ago. Yet we are deeply aware of our shortcomings in all those areas and of our continuing secondary status in education. For a field that has achieved so much, we remain disturbingly unfulfilled in what we hope and expect for ourselves.

Now we face an even larger paradox. There are a host of ways we can and must improve as a profession if we are to survive. Yet it is possible that within the broad context of our existent culture we can never be significantly more than we now are no matter how much we improve. And even in a future culture that might value the arts as basic, our present identity is not likely to be sufficient for the demands that would be imposed on us. The realization begins to dawn that we must change in a fundamental way without abandoning our fundamental devotion to music and to education, a change toward arts education.

But change is uncertain and painful. Who among us has not sometimes settled for what is, rather than face the threatening unknowns that inevitably accompany progress? It is tempting in the extreme to stick with and defend what exists, and to accept, however resignedly, our humble position in education. After all, if we do make the enormous effort that would be required, is there any guarantee that it would be successful? And in the very nature of a transformation to a broader concept of ourselves as one part of a larger arts education profession would we not find our essential integrity threatened? Would we lose our soul in favor of an uncertain advantage?

A final paradox confronts us. If it is true that music can become as basic in education as it deserves to be through transforming itself from its present isolated condition to one of a still not entirely defined unity with its sister arts, it is likely that the transformation will occur primarily or largely through the leadership of music education. We are the strongest, most well-established, most secure art in the schools of America. So, paradoxically, we are the ones who must take major initiatives toward change. We must supply much of the wisdom it will take, the energy it will use, the maturity it will call forth, the generosity of spirit it will need to guide it effectively and humanely.

Will we have the courage to undertake this metamorphosis? It is time we face this question. It is time we consider whether our future as a profession, the future of the young people and adults we serve, the future of the art of music and of every art, would all be brighter if we were to move in the direction of transcendence beyond the limitations of music education as a separate field. In that larger sphere we may finally fulfill the greatness of our potential.

Index